OLD AGE AND THE
ENGLISH POOR LAW, 1500–1700

Old Age and the English Poor Law, 1500–1700 explores the virtually unknown world of the aged poor in sixteenth- and seventeenth-century England. It asks a question of national significance – how the elderly poor managed to survive in a pre-industrial economy – but answers it at the level of the village. Through a comparison of two Suffolk villages, the many factors that make up the experience of old age (status, health, wealth and local culture) are fully recognized, acknowledged, and factored into the interpretation. Botelho argues that the key to survival for these individuals was their own efforts, over and above that of a weekly pension. In other words, even for the aged, if one did not work, one did not eat.

This study is a test case of the old poor law. Using the aged poor – a group indisputably deserving of charity, aid and relief – Botelho demonstrates that the poor law did not, nor did it intend to, provide complete support. It was not designed to be an early modern form of retirement, nor did it function as such. Instead, *Old Age and the English Poor Law* presents the complex and face-to-face world of early modern England and documents the personal agency of the poor as they fashioned their own, individualized old age arrangements that drew just as heavily upon their own efforts as they did upon charity and legislated relief.

L. A. BOTELHO is an associate professor of history at Indiana University of Pennsylvania. Her work includes *Old Age in Pre-Industrial Society* (with S. Ottawa and K. Kittredge); *Women and Ageing in Britain Since 1500* (with P. Thane); *The Churchwardens' Accounts of Cratfield, Suffolk, during the 1640s and 1650s*; and numerous articles on ageing in early modern England. Her current project is 'The Ageing Body: Popular Medicine and Old Age'.

OLD AGE AND THE ENGLISH POOR LAW, 1500–1700

L. A. Botelho

THE BOYDELL PRESS

First published 2004

Published by The Boydell Press
An imprint of Boydell & Brewer Ltd
PO Box 9, Woodbridge, Suffolk IP12 3DF, UK
and of Boydell & Brewer Inc.
PO Box 41026, Rochester, NY 14604–4126, USA
website: www.boydellandbrewer.com

ISBN 1 84383 094 9

A catalogue record for this book is available
from the British Library

Library of Congress Cataloging-in-Publication Data
Botelho, L. A. (Lynn A.)
Old age and the English poor law, 1500–1700 / L.A. Botelho.
p. cm.
Includes bibliographical references and index.
ISBN 1-84383-094-9 (hardback : alk. paper)
1. Public welfare–England–History. 2. Older people–Services for–England–History.
3. Older people–Government policy–England–History. 4. Poor–Government
policy–Great Britain–History. 5. Poor laws–Great Britain–History.
I. Title.
HV245.B715 2004
362.5'0942'09031–dc22
2004008910

Typeset by Keystroke, Jacaranda Lodge, Wolverhampton
Printed in Great Britain by
Antony Rowe Ltd., Chippenham, Wiltshire

Contents

Illustrations

Map

Figures

Tables

Note to the reader

Original spelling has been retained. Obvious abbreviations have been extended without comment. In terms of monetary notation, the abbreviation 'li' has been modernized as '£'. The abbreviations 's' for shilling and 'd' for pence have been retained. All sums of money have been recorded in Roman numbers outside of a direct quote. Direct quotes retain the original numerical notions, either Arabic or Roman. In cases where the reading of the manuscript is unclear it has been noted with a [?]. Dates are given in Old Style, except that the year is considered to begin on 1 January.

In memory of
my parents

Acknowledgements

The size and degree of debts acquired by a project of this scope and duration are immeasurable. The first acknowledgement goes to R. B. Outhwaite, my Ph.D. supervisor, who directed my first steps down the path of old age studies. His sharp eye for detail and precision left a lasting mark on the Ph.D. and on this work which flowed directly from it. Similarly, Clare Hall, Cambridge, generated the intellectual stimulation that made my time there as a post-graduate both fruitful and enjoyable. Patrick Collinson gave me both guidance and encouragement during my time at Cambridge, as well as in the years that followed. The history department at Indiana University of Pennsylvania has provided the same type of academic home, as well as the support to see this project through to completion. The archivists and staff of the Suffolk Records Office in Bury St Edmunds and Ipswich are owed a special acknowledgement for their countless hours spent retrieving documents and patiently answering a seemingly unending stream of questions.

Among the many others who have offered me advice, aid and encouragement at various stages I wish to mention, in particular, Jeremy Boulton, Patrick Carter, Joan Davies, Michelle Doehring, Michael Frearson, Gillian and Tim Harvey, Sean Hughes, Anne Kugler, Caroline Litzenberger, Judith Maltby, Susannah Ottaway, Margaret Pelling, Kate Peters, Alison Rollands, Holly Shissler, Richard M. Smith, Pat Thane, Brian Vivier, John Walter, and the members of the Tudor and Stuart Seminars at the University of Cambridge.

The entire endeavour would not have been possible without the assistance of the following funding bodies: Indiana University of Pennsylvania's University Senate Research Awards; the Pennsylvania State System of Higher Education, Faculty Professional Development Award; W. M. Keck Foundation and Mayers Fellowship at the Huntington Library, San Marino, CA; Prince Consort Studentship, Cambridge University; Michael Postan Award, LSE University of London; Cambridge Historical Society Grant; Clare Hall Bursary, Cambridge University; Ellen McArthur Grant, Cambridge University; Ellen McArthur Research Studentship, Cambridge University; Overseas Research Bursary; and the Cambridge Overseas Trust.

Parts of Chapter 4 were previously published in my 'Aged and Impotent: Parish Relief of the Aged Poor in Early Modern Suffolk' in M. Daunton, ed., *Charity, Self-Interest and Welfare in the English Past* (London, 1996), pp. 91–111, reprinted with the kind permission of UCL Press.

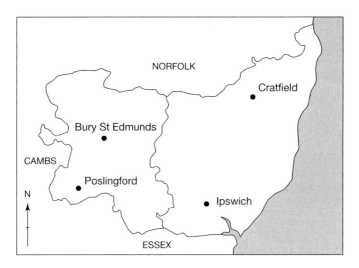

Map 1 Suffolk

Source: L. A. Botelho, 'Aged and Impotent: Parish Relief of the Aged Poor in Early Modern Suffolk' in M. Daunton, ed., *Charity, Self-Interest and Welfare* (London, 1996), p. 95.

1

Questions and contexts

Jesus' words, 'for ye have the poor always with you', must have seemed directed particularly at the inhabitants of early modern Europe.[1] In late seventeenth-century England, a rural yeoman wrote of 'The Multitude of Poore that dayly lie in every coner of the Streets notwithstanding the great Collections in every Parish'; while in Venice, the chronicler Marino Sanudo recorded the usual winter-time swarms of children crying, 'Give us bread! We're dying of hunger and cold', as well as his impressions of the intensified conditions of the 1528 famine: 'Impossible to listen to mass in peace, for at least a dozen beggars will surround you; impossible to open your purse without an immediate plea for money. They are still there late in the evening, knocking on doors and crying, "I'm dying of hunger!"'[2] Contemporaries clearly thought themselves besieged by a rising tide of poverty.

According to the best historical analysis, they were not wrong. In the European countryside, levels of poverty had reached unheard-of heights by the beginning of the sixteenth century and did not abate until the start of the seventeenth century. The number of peasants in Languedoc unable to feed their families doubled between the late fifteenth and early seventeenth centuries. Over half of the rural population of New Castile were landless labourers in the 1570s, and the English peasantry possessing only a cottage and garden rose from 11 per cent in 1560 to 40 per cent after 1640.[3] The urban poor, whose numbers were now inflated by their country counterparts, could range from 10 per cent of the population to well over 50 per cent.[4] In the Swiss cities, approximately one-fifth of the population was without 'regular nourishment'. In Memmingen, in one single year, 1521, the number of poor exploded from 31 per cent to 55 per cent. In the ten Wurttemberber villages,

---

[1] Matthew 26: 11.
[2] Undated proposal for dealing with poverty by providing more responsible vestrymen, c. 1649–1686. The Huntington Library, San Marino, CA (hereafter HL), Ellesmere Collection, EL 8572; Sanudo quoted in B. Geremek, *Poverty: A History* (Oxford, 1997), p. 132.
[3] Alison Rowlands, 'The Conditions of Life for the Masses' in E. Cameron, ed., *Early Modern Europe: An Oxford History* (Oxford, 1999), p. 53.
[4] Rowlands, 'Conditions', p. 58.

1

those who survived only through the kindness of others comprised at least 65 per cent of its 1544 population.[5]

In normal years, English cities could expect at least 5 per cent of their inhabitants to be destitute, but that proportion soared during moments of crisis, and there were many. In Worcester, for example, the 'unprovided and poor' reached 23 per cent in 1646; in Stafford, during the 1622 dearth, a full 25 per cent of the population was poor; and in Coventry, 20 per cent were considered to be in desperate straits. Elsewhere in England conditions were even worse. The plague of 1630 sent 36 per cent of Cambridge, or 2,858 individuals, tumbling on to public relief; while in Sheffield, 20 to 33 per cent of its 1616 population were begging merely to survive.[6] Given the size of the poverty problem both at home and abroad, English taxpayers may well have found themselves harder pressed to imprint upon their hearts the words which one of their number so easily printed on the title page of London's orders 'for setting roges and ydle persons to woorke and for the releife of the poore (1597)': 'Proverbes 16: He that hath pittie upon the poore, lendeth to the Lord: and looke what he layeth out, it shalbe payd hym agayne', and 'Psalme 61: Blessed is the man that provideth for the sick and needye: The Lord shall deliver hym in the tyme of trouble'.[7] This study explores the world of one group of poor, the 'aged and impotent'.

England opened the sixteenth century with a population problem without precedent in recent memory. The late medieval population was fairly stable, or in fact declining in some areas. But by the start of the sixteenth century, England's population began an exponential climb that did not abate until the early years of the seventeenth century: between 1500 and 1700 the population doubled, rising from 2.5 million to about 5 million.[8] Two factors seemed to be responsible: one, an improved, if not thriving, economy that allowed a younger age of marriage, and therefore a wider period of marital fertility that resulted in the birth of more children; and two, the decline of epidemic disease and a corresponding contraction in mortality rates. The results of increased fertility and decreased mortality quickly became problematic.[9]

---

[5] L. P. Wandel, *Always Among Us. Images of the Poor in Zwingli's Zurich* (Cambridge, 1990), p. 11. See also C. Lis and H. Soly, *Poverty and Capitalism in Early Modern Europe* (Bristol, 1982), pp. 74, 78.

[6] P. Slack, *Poverty and Policy in Tudor and Stuart England* (London, 1988), p. 72.

[7] Orders to be appointed to be executed in the Citie of London for setting roges and ydle persons to woorke and for the releife of the poore (1597), HL, Ellesmere Collection, EL 2522.

[8] Population estimates for this period are problematic due to the lack of systematic sources and inconsistencies with those sources that do exist. J. Chambers, *Population, Economy and Society in Pre-Industrial England* (Oxford, 1872), p. 19; E. A. Wrigley and R. Schofield, *The Population History of England, 1541–1871: A Reconstruction* (1981; repr. Cambridge, 1993), p. 207.

[9] K. Wrightson and D. Levine, *Poverty and Piety in an English Village: Terling, 1525–1700* (2nd edn, Oxford, 1995), p. 3.

Nowhere were the effects of more mouths to feed felt more keenly than in the cost of foodstuffs. Given the agricultural practices and knowledge of the period, the productive capacity of the land was essentially inelastic. The same amount of food was now needed to feed considerably more people. While agricultural productivity could not typically be increased, it could be decreased. The all-encompassing desire for more food led farmers across England, as well as Europe, to forgo the common practice of letting a portion of one's land lie fallow for a season in order to rebuild the nutrients in the soil. Instead, hunger compelled them to farm it anyway. The result was a short-term increase of food for a year or two, before the land began its guaranteed decline. Harvest failure, dearth and famine often resulted. England's poor harvests of 1545 and 1550 were made particularly fierce by the simultaneous appearance of the plague. Harvest failure and scarcity were also problems in 1586, 1596–1597, and 1622–1623. Harvests were again bad in 1661, 1673 and 1674, only to be followed by dearth in 1696–1697.[10] At such moments, there was even less food to feed an oversized population.

This basic situation was compounded by the English tendency towards partible inheritance among the middling and lower orders. Rather than moving the estate intact into the hands of the eldest son, most English fathers bequeathed their land and estates – in some fashion – to all their children. The result was a growing number of small landholders whose property was not adequate for self-sufficiency. They were forced to the market to purchase the difference, contributing to escalating food prices. Sadly, for the poor, the prices of the cheapest grains were the ones which rose the fastest, as many sought the traditionally cheaper grains in an effort to stretch their budgets. Instead the increased demand drove up the prices of such grains. Food prices remained relatively stable from the mid-fifteenth century until the opening years of the sixteenth, at which point they shot up even more radically than England's population: doubling by the 1540s, trebling by the 1570s, and, by the early seventeenth century, reaching heights six times that of a hundred years earlier.[11] While prices were rising real wages were declining, driven down by the hordes who were willing to work for less just to put some, if not enough, food upon their family's table. Significant numbers of those driven off the land turned to the cities and a life utterly dependent upon paid labour. The resulting

[10] Slack, *Poverty and Policy*, pp. 49–51; M. K. McIntosh, 'Local Responses to the Poor in Late Medieval and Tudor England', *Continuity and Change* 3 (1988), p. 230; A. Fletcher, *Reform in the Provinces: The Government of Stuart England* (London, 1980), pp. 187, 191; M. Todd, *Christian Humanism and the Puritan Social Order* (Cambridge, 1987), p. 174; P. Slack, *The English Poor Law, 1531–1782*, Studies in Economic and Social History (Basingstoke, 1990), pp. 11–12; P. Slack, 'Social Policy and the Constraints of Government 1547–58' in R. Tittler and J. Loach, eds., *The Mid-Tudor Polity c. 1540–1560* (Totowa, NJ, 1980), p. 98.

[11] R. B. Outhwaite, *Inflation in Tudor and Early Stuart England* (2nd edn, Basingstoke, 1982), p. 10.

drop in real wages during the sixteenth century was as much as 50 per cent.[12] Put another way, the real purchasing power of one pound in 1594 was as low as 57 per cent of what it had been in the 1560s, and only 37 per cent of that in the 1510s and 1520s.[13] Nor was this a stable economy, for England was tied directly into the financial and exchange markets of the Continent, and a slump in overseas trade, such as those in 1551, 1563, and 1568, or a foreign war, like the wars of religion, would disrupt the domestic economy and have very real consequences for the struggling labourer in England.[14] For those caught at the centre of these price/wage scissors, the cut was deep.

The process seems clear from this distance, but for those in the midst of it, the causes and mechanisms at work were far from understood. Many, in fact, cast the blame on the breakdown of England's moral fibre, the loss of traditional Christian values, and unchecked greed. Contemporaries blamed England's crises on large-scale enclosing and engrossing of arable fields in the country-side and rack-renting in the towns. In the midst of the 1550s troubles, Robert Crowley wrote of 'rent resying' that doubled, tripled and even quadrupled the price of rents in the towns, while at the same time 'gredie cormerauntes' had 'enclosed frome the pore theire due commones, leavied greater fines then heretofore have bene levied, put them from the liberties (and in a maner enheritaunce) that they held by custome, and reised their rentes'. At the end of the century, William Harrison lent his voice to the charges laid at the feet of greedy landlords: 'men of great port and countenance are so farre from sufering their farmers to have anie gaine at all, that they themselves become grasiers, butchers, tanners, sheepmasters, woodman and *denique quod non*, thereby to enrich themselves, and bring all the wealth of the countrie into their owne hands, leaving the communaltie weake.'[15] The working of the market, the mechanisms of supply and demand, were not even hinted at by the most prominent social and political commentators of the day. However, the response that such conditions prompted – more aggressive estate

[12] Slack, *English Poor Law*, p. 12; Lis and Soly, *Poverty and Capitalism*, p. 72; T. Wales, 'Coping with Poverty: The Poor and Authority in Seventeenth-Century England', unpublished paper presented at the Cambridge Group for the Study of Population and Social Structure, 1988, p. 12; A. L. Beier, *Masterless Men: The Vagrancy Problem in England, 1560–1640* (London, 1987), p. 20; McIntosh, 'Local Responses', p. 230.

[13] McIntosh, 'Local Responses', p. 230. Paul Slack, however, feels that the fall in the actual standard of living and real wages was not this steep. Slack, *Poverty and Policy*, p. 47.

[14] Lis and Soly, *Poverty and Capitalism*, p. 21; E. M. Leonard, *The Early History of English Poor Relief* (1900; repr. London, 1965), p. 15.

[15] R. Crowley, 'The Way to Wealth' in J. M. Cowper, ed., *The Select Works of Robert Crowley*, Early English Text Society (London, 1872), pp. 132–3, 142–6; W. Harrison, *The Description of England*, ed. G. Edelen (1587; 2nd edn, Ithaca, NY, 1968), pp. 238–43; also quoted in William Harrison, 'Harrison on Changes in His Day, 1577–87', *Tudor Economic Documents*, V. III (London, 1924), pp. 68–72. I would like to thank Michelle Doehring for these references.

management – was keenly noted and sharply felt. It was the breakdown of traditional paternalism and Christian charity that Harrison and Crowley blamed for the state of sixteenth-century England.

Indeed, there was an overwhelming concern with the state of Christianity within England. In what might be characterized as a reluctant reformation, England left the Church of Rome, by statute and the King's assent, initially without becoming fully Protestant, and without the revolt and revolution that characterized much of the Protestant Reformation on the Continent. These were early and tentative days for Protestantism, with much of the country still deeply embedded in the practices of the traditional church. Only East Anglia and London pursued reform with enthusiasm. The young King, Edward VI (1547–1553), and his counsellors strove to move England out of the hinterlands of reform and squarely into the Protestant camp. Time, however, was not on their side. England's Protestant movement was nipped in the bud by the accession of Mary as Queen in 1553 and England's corresponding swing back – eventually – into the embrace of Rome. While short-lived, lasting only five years, Mary's religious policy was not negligible, giving strength and support to those areas and individuals that preferred a conservative theology. Religious traditionalists would need to call upon an inner reserve of strength and perseverance under the rule of Elizabeth (1558–1603) as she strove to undo the work of Mary and her chief assistant Pole. Elizabeth is famous for her religious settlement that allowed the subjects of her by now fractured and sometimes confused country to sit upon the same pew.

By the early seventeenth century, most of England practised a Protestant liturgy, although pockets of recusants – or 'church papists' to use Alexandra Walsham's evocative phrase – flourished with the underground support of their co-religionists on the Continent.[16] Yet religious questions continued to swirl at the forefront of public debate, especially during those tumultuous years of the 1640s and 1650s. What type of Protestantism was England to practise? Especially, how Calvinistic should it be? These were vexing questions for England; indeed, as they are for its historians. Such questions were not immaterial for the poor; as we shall see, they raised yet another obstacle past which the indigent had to navigate on their way to public support. More importantly, at the most fundamental level, questions about what it meant to be a Christian also meant questions about what it meant to be poor.

Poverty held a special, if not privileged, place in Christian thought and action. Jesus, the son of God, found his place in the world as a poor man. His teachings indicated that the poor were indeed blessed by their condition, and the rich plagued by theirs. 'It is easier to get a camel through the eye of a needle than to get a rich man into heaven' is just one of many warnings directed against the lifestyle of the rich. Conversely, the place of the poor was sanctified through

---

[16] A. Walsham, *Church Papists. Catholicism, Conformity and Confessional Polemic in Early Modern England* (Woodbridge, 1994).

Christ's pronouncement that 'the meek shall inherit the earth' and with the knowledge that: 'For ye know the grace of our Lord Jesus Christ, that, though he was rich, yet for your sakes he became poor, that ye through his poverty might be rich' (II Corinthians 8: 9). Christ allied himself to the poor in two ways; as their shepherd to the Kingdom of Heaven and as their brother in a shared life. 'His spirituality was anchored in his poverty and his poverty was a metaphor for his spirituality', a position that posed a contrariety with which all Christians have grappled since.[17]

Contemporary English social commentators and economic pundits alike turned to Jesus' much repeated and well-worn refrain for comfort and solace as they struggled to understand the rising poverty that hallmarked this period. To the poor of sixteenth- and seventeenth-century England, these words may not have been so reassuring. The aged poor, the central focus of this book, would have been in greater sympathy with Psalm 71, and the sentiments it expressed: 'now also when I am old and grey-headed, O God, forsake me not.'[18] Likewise, the following lines from the same psalm summed up the fear of growing old in early modern England or anywhere that the loss of physical strength could easily mean the end of self-sufficiency:

> Cast me not off in the time of my old age;
> Forsake me not when my strength faileth.[19]

This book is about the nature of poverty in old age, about those individuals whose strength having failed and forsaken them were cast into the world of destitution, into the arms of their families, and onto the kindness of strangers.

The aged have long been awarded a privileged place in the cultural landscape of the Western world. 'Rise and honour the hoary head' has been echoed in multivalent forms, from its traditional pronouncement by Moses to its seventeenth-century equivalent, expressed in 'The Right Honorable Richard Earle of Carbery his Advice to his Sonn (1651)': 'allwaies have a respect to a gray-haired Experience and samed understanding.'[20] By the time of the French Revolution, the drafters of the 1793 constitution listed respect for the elderly as a cardinal virtue. Whatever its form, it has become 'a proverb and a by-word among all people' of Europe.[21]

Thomas Sheafe was not the first to extrapolate from aged parents to the elderly more generally, but he said it well:

---

[17] Wandel, *Always Among Us*, p. 3, including quote. See pp. 2–7 for a discussion of St Francis and Christian poverty.

[18] Psalm 71: 18.

[19] Psalm 71: 9.

[20] The Right Honorable Richard Earle of Carbery his Advice to his Sonn, Golden Grove, 30 September 1651, HL, EL 34 B 2.

[21] Quote from I Kings ix.7.

Honour belongs to the very age of an Old-Man: for it is certaine, and will not be denied, that men in yeeres, even for their yeeres, are to be ranked among the Fathers meant in the fift Commandement. Now to all Fathers is Honour there allotted, asto [sic] Fathers; and therefore even for this to Old-Men.[22]

He added a degree of incentive to the elderly themselves by reminding them that when they were both old and virtuous, the honour was even greater.[23]

Early modern England promoted the honour due to the elderly at seemingly every turn. The 1536 injunctions required the clergy to instruct the young in the Ten Commandments (as well as the Lord's Prayer and the Creed), including the cardinal requirement to honour one's father and mother. The *Book of Common Prayer* (including the 1549 edition) reprinted the Ten Command-ments, and they were also painted on the walls of every parish church. The tablets of Moses called upon all loyal Englishmen and women to honour their parents. The Earl of Carbery, writing during the politically and religiously turbulent 1650s, explained the fifth commandment this way: 'And let me tell thee if thou dost honour thy Father and Mother, thou canst neyther be Rebell or Schismatique, disloyall to the Soveraingne power, or disobedient to the Church.'[24] The author of *Dives and Pauper*, an extended commentary on the Ten Commandments, described this obligation in morally reciprocal terms: your parents raised you when helpless, now you must provide for them.[25]

English pulpits rang with preachers calling for reverence for the aged, and nowhere was this more powerfully set forth than in funeral sermons, such as that given for John Lamotte, esq, sometime Alderman of the City of London:

Old age hath been honoured by God, in choosing men of age for weighty imploy-ments, as God chose Moses and Aaron when they were stricken in years, to lead Isreal out of Aegypt, and when he would establish a standing Judicatory in Isreal

[22] T. Sheafe, *Vindiciae, or, A Plea for Old-Age: Which is Senis Cujusdam Cygnea Cantio* (London, 1639), p. 181.
[23] Sheafe, *A Plea*, p. 182.
[24] Advice to his Sonn, HL, EL 34 B 2.
[25] P. Barnum, ed., *Dives and Pauper* (Early English Texts Society, London, 1976), Vol. I, IV, C. 1, p. 304. See also S. Shahar, *Growing Old in the Middle Ages*, trans. Y. Lotan (London, 1997), pp. 88–97 for a wide-ranging discussion of the medieval obligation to honour one's parents. Englishwomen and men travelling abroad were often shocked by the explicit connection between honour due to one's parents and honour due to God, the father. Traditional Roman Catholic iconography often depicted God, the father, as an ancient, old man. 'I was very much scandalized at a large silver image of the Trinity,' wrote Lady Montague during her extensive travels, 'where the Father is represented under the figure of a decrepit old man, with a beard down to his knees, and a triple crown on his head.' While shocking to Protestant England of the eighteenth century, such images still resonated within the religious psyche. Lady M. W. Montague, *Letters of the Right Honourable L. M. W. M.: Written during her Travels in Europe, Asia and Africa*, Vol. I, IV (London, 1763), p. 26.

... nay, I acknowledge that old age is some way venerable in it self, which was the ground of that Command, Rise up before the hoary head, and honour the face of the old man.[26]

Reverence was due the elderly, according to pulpiteers and pundits alike, because they had overcome and conquered life's many temptations, such as vanity, vainglory, and especially the troubling – and trouble-making – demands of their libido. 'Old-men are the fittest for the reverence of their age, ripeness of judgement, gravity of carriage, experience in many things, and not least, for their freedome from perturbations, and quietnesses of their minds,' explained Sheafe, 'for Old-man hath overcome his carnall lusts, and triumphs over them.'[27] English children were taught these lessons young, and there was no better place to start than with the children themselves, pointing them in directions that would lead to a reverent old age: 'train up a child in the way he should go; and when he is old, he will not depart from it' (Proverbs 22: 6).[28]

Finally, this atmosphere of respect found expression in the relief of the poor, which specifically named the aged as in need of support. Traditionally, those worthy of relief were poor through no fault of their own: widows, orphans, the disabled and the old. Each, in some way, was structurally positioned so that they could not provide fully for themselves: widows struggled because of the relative worthlessness of female employment, and possibly the hindering presence of dependent children; parentless children were helpless in the face of their own needs; the handicapped were prevented from performing at levels necessary for survival; and the elderly were simply too worn to carry their own weight. These were the traditional, worthy poor towards whom Christians had for centuries targeted their alms. The rest, vagrants – vagabonds and idle rogues – were poor, at least according to common thought, because of their disinclination to work. The able-bodied were to be chased away and moved on with all possible haste, with the hope that they would become hungry enough to work and change their idle ways.

The conditions of the sixteenth century changed all that. With populations at record levels across sixteenth-century Europe, there was simply not enough food to go around, regardless of how hard one worked. Indeed, one could want to work, actively seek to work, and still be unemployed and destitute. Similarly, one could in fact be working and, thanks to declining real wages,

---

[26] F. Bellers, *Abrahams Interment: or The Good Old-Mans Buriall in a Good Old Age. Opened in a Sermon, At Bartholomews Exchenage, July 24, 1655. At the Funerall of the Worshipfull John Lamotte Esq; Sometimes Alderman of the City of London* (London, 1656), sig. D2.
[27] Sheafe, *A Plea*, p. 30.
[28] In fact, *A Spiritual Journey of a Young Man, towards the Land of Peace, to Live therein Essentially in God, who met in his Journey with Three Sorts of Disputes, Withsome Proverbs and Sentences, which the Old-Age spake to the Young Man*, translated from Dutch (London, 1659), lists this same proverb on its opening page, p. 5.

still be outright poor. England, and Europe as a whole, struggled to face the uncomfortable truth of the labouring poor and the recognition that the old ways and old ideas no longer applied. The notion of the labouring poor was actively resisted by social critics, political commentators and village worthies alike. It was not until the mid-seventeenth century that this concept found a place, albeit not always a comfortable one, within the mental world of Europe. It was also at this time that the demographic and economic conditions governing English life began to change. After mid-century the population ceased to grow and instead generally stagnated. Concomitantly, real incomes began to rise. Yet it is under this particular regime that the cost of poor relief began a marked and painfully steep climb. For the areas surrounding London, such as East Anglia, out-migration was particularly strong, as the capital drew vast numbers of labourers into its walls and suburbs, while at the same time drawing these same wage earners out of village life and economics. The absence of such family members, combined with the high cost of relief, raises intriguing issues regarding the importance of kin support in the personal economies of the poor. Throughout it all, the aged retained their pride of place across Europe as worthy of aid and alms.

The similarity of thought between Catholics and Protestants on the poor and poverty was one of many shared intellectual timbers. Among the other common intellectual and political platforms was government's tendency to consolidate affairs into a centralized government, especially in the budding nation/states of the North. No longer was it seen as advantageous to locate the seat of government in the exact location of the King himself, travelling across the country as the monarch progressed throughout his lands. Instead, capital cities emerged – London for the English, Paris for the French – which permanently housed the offices of government, making access to the courts and to state officials much easier. Similarly, there was a concerted drive to extend the King's laws evenly throughout his lands, including into those areas where local privilege flourished, such as Cornwall and the Marches of England and Languedoc and Navarre in France. This included a move to shift certain responsibilities from the church to the state. In England, the secularization of the parish, changing it from a strictly ecclesiastical division to a secular, political unit of governance, may have been the most important manifestation of this tendency. The drive for uniformity and accessibility was well under way when the poverty problem seemingly exploded.

Yet, when it came to the question of poverty, the most unifying trend in early modern Europe was an intellectual one: Christian Humanism. Drawing its inspiration and a number of fundamental tenets from the intellectual life of Renaissance Italy, Christian Humanism took a powerful hold upon the minds of many political leaders. Simply put, Christian Humanism 'stressed the responsibility of governors for the social welfare of all their subjects'.[29] This

[29] Slack, *Poverty and Policy*, p. 9.

translated into action throughout Europe, as city after city set up systems of secular poor relief that followed three shared lines: a greater role of the state; a greater degree of bureaucratization and organization; and a concern for the education of poor children, so that they need not be reliant on relief for their adult lives.[30]

Known in England as the New Learning, the works of Erasmus, More and Vives epitomized this concept there. A vital part of this thinking was that while the world and society were not right, change was possible, and that humanity had the weapons, strengths and reason to effect such a transformation.[31] According to Erasmus:

> If thou shalt loke on god thy helper, nothynge is more easy. Now therfore, conceyve thou with all thy myght and with a fervent mynde, the purpose & professyon of perfyte lyfe. And whan thou hast grounded thy selfe upon a sure purpose, set upon it, & go to it lustely: mannes mynde never purposed any thynge fervently, that he was not able to bryng to passe.[32]

Poverty and poor relief were viewed, quite naturally, as appropriate areas for such action. Significantly, the spirit of Christian Humanism, but not its theology, would reappear in the seventeenth century under the nourishment of hotter Protestants and would do much to shape the local responses to the poor in many parishes.[33]

Faced with the same material conditions – poverty, population pressure, inflation and the breakdown of traditional charity – and influenced by shared intellectual currents – Christian Humanism, centralizing governments and the secularization of community organization – governments across Europe responded in strikingly similar ways. Protestant leaders borrowed poor relief plans devised by Catholics; states adapted schemes pioneered in provincial cities. The best example was Vives' plan: it was written by a Spaniard – who had been educated in Paris – while residing in England, and at the request of the Bruges magistracy. It later became the foundation of the Ypres scheme, as well as of the English system. The Confessional Divide did not disappear; but instead, religious affinity tended to find expression in the details, but not the structural framework of relief.[34]

---

[30] R. Jutte, *Poverty and Deviance in Early Modern Europe* (Cambridge, 1994), pp. 100–15.

[31] Todd, *Christian Humanism*, p. 18; Slack, *English Poor Law*, p. 15; Erasmus, *Enchiridion Militis Christiani whiche may be called in Englysshe, the Hansome Weapon of a Christen Knyght* (London, 1534).

[32] Erasmus, *Enchiridion Militis Christiani*, sig. Dviii.

[33] Todd, *Christian Humanism*, pp. 16, 20.

[34] There were real theological differences between Protestant and Catholic schemes, centred primarily on the question of good works as Christian charity. Initially, the most Catholic countries, such as Spain, were reluctant to place limits of any kind of the giving of alms. However, by the seventeenth century, 'distinctions between different categories of poor

While sharing much of the same path, England developed in ways significantly different from on the Continent, and its road was long and arduous. In its mature form, essentially those statutes of 1598 and the minor adjustments of 1601, England established a national system of relief, funded by local rate, and organized by appointed, secular, officers of the state.[35] It addressed four areas of poverty: children; beggars and vagabonds; the poor; and parish relief administration. The programme called for the apprenticing of pauper children between the ages of 5 and 14. Rogues under age 14 were to be placed in the stocks, while those over 14 caught begging were to be gaoled until the next Sessions, and then tried for vagrancy. Beggars convicted of vagrancy, the second theme of the statute, were to be whipped, unless an 'honest' person took them into service for one year. Convicted beggars caught running away from service were to be declared vagrants. All those found guilty of vagrancy were to be whipped and an inch-wide hole burned 'through the gristle of the right Eare with a hot yron'.[36] Those convicted twice for vagrancy were to be declared felons unless service could again be found, this time for two years. A third offence was to result in felony charges and execution. For the 'aged decayed and ympotent poore People . . . forced to lyve uppon Almes', the Justices of Peace were to record their names into a 'Register Booke'. Those

were stressed no less in France and Italy (and even parts of Spain) than in England, while English preachers . . . were quick to warn their audience against allowing an overscrupulous definition of the deserving poor to limit their liberality'. As Slack notes, 'we should not exaggerate their [confessional differences] social importance or their practical consequences'. Slack, *Poverty and Policy*, all quotes p. 10.

[35] Paul Slack's *English Poor Law* and his *Poverty and Policy* remain the most succinct and lucid account of the development and administration of the Old Poor Law.

[36] (39 Eliz. I. C. 3); (39 Eliz. I. C. 4); and (43 Eliz. I. C. 2). The statute (39 Eliz. I. C. 40) is justifiably well known for its comprehensive, and long, list of persons considered vagrants. It reads: 'That all persons calling themselves Schollers going about begging, all Seafaringmen pretending losses of their shippes or Goodes on the Sea going about the Country begging, all idle persons going about in any Country eyther fayning themselves to have knowledge in Phisiognomye Palmestry or other like crafty Scyence, or pretending that they can tell Destenyes Fortunes or such other like fantasticall Ymagynacions; all persons that be or utter themselves to be proctors percurors patent gatherers or Collector for Gaoles Prisons or Hospitalles; all Fencers Bearewardes common players of Enterludes and Minstrelles wandering abroad, (other then Players of Enterludes belonging to any Baron of this Realme, or any other honorable Personage of Greater Degree to be auctoryzed to play, under the Hand and Seale of Armes of such Baron or Personage); all Juglers Tynkers Pedlers and Petty Chapmen wandering abroade; all wandering persons and common Labourers being persons able in bodye using loitering and refusing to worcke for such reasonable Wages as is taxed or commonly gyven in such Partes where such persons do or shall happen to dwell or abide, not having lyving otherwyse to maynteyne themselves; all persons delivered out of Gaoles that begg for their Fees, or otherwise do travayle begging; all such persons as shall wander abroade begging pretending losses by Fyre or otherwise; to be Egipcyans, or wandering in the Habite Form or Attyre of Counterfayte Egipcians; shalbe taken adjudged and deemed Rogues Vagabondes and Sturdy Beggers.'

listed were then to be provided with 'convenient Habitacions and Abydinge Places throughout the Realme to settle themselves uppon to the end that they nor any of them should hereafter begge or wander about'. Further, the employable poor were to be worked according to their abilities. The completely helpless were to be provided for and those who worked were to have their efforts supplemented from the parish fund. Each parish was to appoint Overseers of the Poor to assess and collect a local poor tax. Individuals refusing to pay their weekly rate were to be gaoled until they complied. Those on relief who wandered from their parish-appointed place were deemed and declared vagrant, regardless of their age or physical condition.[37] By these statutes, the poor, the old and the disabled knew what they could expect in the way of support, as well as what was expected of them – obedience.

Fundamental to any discussion of old age is the question: How old is old? Determining a universal onset of old age is virtually impossible; it lacks formal milestones or legal bench-marks. The difficulty of the task is compounded further by the very personal and idiosyncratic pace of the ageing process. It would have been particularly inappropriate for early modern England with its wide range of incomes, from the fabulously wealthy to the utterly destitute; with its contrasting lifestyles, from the completely leisured to the ceaselessly labouring; and with its diverse climates, from the wind-blown coasts to the mosquito-ridden fens. Each of these conditions would have hastened or prolonged the physical characteristics of advanced old age – stooped backs, wrinkled skin and frail bones – and, in the iconographic world of early modern England, what one looked like went far in determining what one was. William Harrison, in his *Description of England* (1587), makes his famous point about the gentry: those who 'bear the port, charge and countenance' of a gentleman, become gentlemen.[38] The same, it has been argued elsewhere, is true for the poor, with their strenuous lifestyle, sparse diet and generally inadequate accommodation: one becomes old when one looks old.

For the rural poor of our two cases studies, the elderly poor were considered old at approximately age 50. A common practice was to award honorific titles, such as 'Mother', 'Father', or simply 'Old', to certain individuals once they reached old age, as a mark of the community's regard. In Cratfield, Suffolk, where this tradition continued throughout the seventeenth century, such titles were generally first affixed to the name of the elderly person – at least in the parish records – at or near age 50. As we shall see, this is approximately the same age when those who were to become 'the aged poor' first started collecting some form of public assistance. A lifetime of arduous labour for men and women, plus the likely onset of menopause in women, seemed to have

---

[37] (39 Eliz. I. C. 4). The sick poor were, with licence and adequate financing, allowed to travel to Bath or Buxton 'for Ease and Releife of their diseases'.

[38] Harrison, *Description of England*, p. 114.

conspired against the rural villager to produce visual clues that led to their public recognition as 'old' at or near age 50.[39]

The question of who should care and provide for the elderly poor – their families or their communities – has been vigorously debated. First raised by Peter Laslett, his 'nuclear-hardship' hypothesis assigned the burden of support to the 'collectivity', in the form of the parish and community.[40] Others, most notably David Thomson, have followed Laslett's lead, arguing for the primacy of state-funded relief, and extending the discussion into the relative merits of the Old versus the New Poor Laws' treatment of the aged.[41] Pat Thane, however, has challenged this orthodoxy, arguing instead for the strength of familial care.[42]

This book engages directly with the questions raised by Laslett, Thomson and Thane. It argues that survival for the poorest elderly inhabitants required the resources of both their community and their kin, as well as the aged's own efforts at self-sufficiency. The answer to the Thane/Thomson debate is therefore 'Both', and then some. The study also explores the question of whether this experiment in national poor relief was successful. The answer appears to be both 'Yes' and 'No'. It was not successful in the modern sense of providing retirement and complete support. However, it was never intended to do so, and, as it is argued below, the Old Poor Law was quite successful (at least in those areas where it operated) on its own terms of providing meaningful assistance towards survival.

Given its complexity, it may only be at the level of micro-history that historians can disaggregate the pieces which shaped England's local responses

[39] L. A. Botelho, 'Old Age and Menopause in Rural Women of Early Modern Suffolk' in L. Botelho and P. Thane, eds, *Women and Ageing in British Society Since 1500* (London, 2001), pp. 43–65.

[40] P. Laslett, 'Family, Kinship and Collectivity as Systems of Support in Pre-Industrial Europe: A Consideration of the "Nuclear-Hardship" Hypothesis', *Continuity and Change* 3 (1988): 153–76.

[41] D. Thomson, 'The Decline of Social Welfare: Falling State Support for the Elderly since Early Victorian Times', *Ageing and Society* 4 (1984), pp. 451–82, and his 'Welfare of the Elderly in the Past: A Family or Community Responsibility?' in M. Pelling and R. M. Smith, eds, *Life, Death and the Elderly* (London, 1991), pp. 194–221. For other studies that downplay the role of the family in the support of the elderly, see: M. Evandrou, S. Arber, A. Dale and G. N. Gilbert, 'Who Cares for the Elderly? Family Care Provisions and Receipt of Statutory Service' in C. Phillipson, M. Bernard and P. Strange, eds, *Dependency and Interdependency in Old Age* (London, 1986), pp. 150–66; J. Robin, 'The Role of Offspring in the Care of the Elderly: A Comparison Over Time, 1851–1881', *Ageing and Society* 4 (1984): 505–15; D. Thomson, '"I am not my father's keeper": Families and the Elderly in Nineteenth-Century England', *Law and History Review* 2 (1984): 265–86.

[42] P. Thane, 'Old People and their Families in the English Past' in M. Daunton, ed., *Charity, Self-Interest and Welfare in the English Past* (New York, 1996), pp. 113–38; her 'The Family Lives of Old People' in P. Johnson and P. Thane, eds, *Old Age from Antiquity to Post-Modernity* (London, 1998), pp. 180–210. See also P. Johnson, 'Historical Readings of Old Age and Ageing' in Johnson and Thane, *Old Age*, pp. 1–18.

to the poor. Consequently, this study employs two case studies in order to, in the words of Keith Wrightson, 'make concrete and accessible the abstractions and generalizations of historical interpretation'.[43] The villages of Cratfield and Poslingford, both in Suffolk, were reconstituted from parish registers for a two-hundred-year period.[44] Drawing together and linking scattered pieces of information about a family, such as their baptisms, marriages and burials, reconstitution outlines a community's key demographic characteristics, such as family size and age at first marriage.[45] My objective, however, was not to establish a wide range of demographic parameters, but instead to identify individuals over the age of 50.[46] Not all elderly inhabitants would register a vital event in the parish; therefore all extant documents were examined to identify other aged inhabitants. Eventually, 337 individuals were located – 105 from Poslingford and 232 from Cratfield – and 'biographies' were created that contained each person's documented history, often from baptism to burial. In addition to identifying particular people, these biographies permitted a sensitive investigation of the circumstances surrounding their old age, gaining an understanding of the limitations placed upon their range of old age options and illuminating the contexts of their lives.[47]

The two villages, while both small and rural, are located in contrasting parts of Suffolk (see Map 1). Poslingford, and its hamlet Chipley, were on the edge of the cloth-producing Stour Valley, straddling the Essex/Suffolk border. Even with Chipley's addition, the population was small, cresting at just over 200 at the start of the seventeenth century. Unlike its immediate neighbours Clare and Cavendish, Poslingford still had a foot in agriculture, providing food-stuffs to towns tied solely to waged employments in the cloth trade. It was one of many such villages that ringed the Suffolk cloth towns; yet it was directly affected by the fickleness of cloth production. Many of its poor survived by spinning, and those whose livelihood still came from the soil were held hostage to cloth, as their cloth-spinning customers could not buy what they produced

---

[43] K. Wrightson, 'The Social Order of Early Modern England: Three Approaches' in L. Bonfield, R. M. Smith and K. Wrightson, eds, *The World We Have Gained. Histories of Population and Social Structure* (Oxford, 1986), p. 202.

[44] Cratfield Parish Register, Suffolk Record Office, Ipswich (hereafter SROI), FC62/A6/23, beginning 1539, and Poslingford Parish Register, Suffolk Record Office, Bury St Edmunds (hereafter, SROB), FL615/4/1, beginning 1559.

[45] Wrightson and Levine's *Poverty and Piety* is the best-known example of reconstitution, but see also C. [Davey] Jarvis, 'Reconstructing Local Population History: The Hatfield and Bobbington Districts of Essex, 1550–1880', unpublished Ph.D. thesis (Cambridge University, 1990), for methodological refinements.

[46] In order to ensure total coverage during the end of the seventeenth century, the reconstitutions were carried forward until 1750, thereby encompassing those who died after 1700.

[47] See L. A. Botelho, 'Provisions for the Elderly in Two Early Modern Suffolk Communities', unpublished Ph.D. thesis (Cambridge University, 1996), pp. 67–87.

during times of declining trade. At the end of the day, Poslingford rose and fell with the state of English textiles. This arrangement left its stamp on Poslingford's population, with its marked polarization of wealth. It also left its stamp on its politics. The individuals who were clustered at the top of the economic hierarchy were the same individuals who formed the closed, ruling oligarchy of village. Most inhabitants found themselves gathered at the lower end of the subsidy returns, many of whom scrambled with each other for charitable relief and public aid. The village's collective theology was strictly speaking within the bounds of conformity. In other words it was not reported for religious nonconformity, but this may have been more a product of local sympathies and their unwillingness to draw attention to themselves than actual practice. The chief inhabitants clearly favoured the hotter sort of Protestantism, with one seventeenth-century vicar, Francis Abbott, proudly proclaiming his distaste for the prayer-book, as well as singling out from the pulpit 'adultresses', including the wife of the 'chiefest parishioner' to whom he addressed these words:

> when your husbands are gone abroad then you send your comrades, and then you play wantons, naughty plucks and whores, and then you defile the marriage bed and then the cuckoo's eggs are laid in the poor man's nest and the poor man is fain to bring up the bastard brood by the sweat of his brows, and you are not ashamed to come in to the house of God with your whorish face.[48]

During the seventeenth century, religious conformity in Poslingford may have taken its own form and not have coincided precisely with that prescribed by the Church of England. For the poor who had to navigate the politics of the parish, a shared religious affinity with the local elites, rather than that of the established church, may have been the deciding factor in whether or not they collected regular relief. Cratfield, too, had its own set of circumstances that influenced those on parish provisions. Slightly larger than Poslingford, with a population of just over 300 for most of the seventeenth century, Cratfield was a prosperous rural parish in the northeastern corner of the county, not far from the market town of Beccles. Its wealth sprang directly from its dairy and cheese production and its ties to the London market for foodstuffs. Economic prosperity was distributed fairly evenly throughout the parish, and manorial

---

[48] The above is drawn from Calendar of State Papers: Domestic Series (hereafter CSPD), 17 October 1634; 6 and 13 November 1634; 19 February 1634, pp. 269, 319–21, and CSPD, 16, 23 and 28 April 1635, p. 185. In the end, Abbott was both excommunicated and imprisoned as a result of his enthusiasm for moral reform and undiplomatic speech. Eventually he was freed, but was told to preach anywhere *but* Poslingford. None the less, he returned to Poslingford as vicar where he remained until 1644, despite another brush with authority. CSPD, April 1635, pp. 185, 189, 195; CSPD, 13 June 1640, p. 423. For more on Abbott, see Botelho, 'Provisions', pp. 150–3.

control was virtually non-existent from the beginning of the sixteenth century. Consequently, a loose and rather large group, always between eight and ten, of independent, sturdy yeoman formed the 'chief inhabitants' of the parish, directing both its finances and its poor relief. Religiously, it too tended towards the slightly hotter forms of Protestantism, but nowhere near the degree of Poslingford, and the village weathered the storms of both the Reformation and the Civil Wars without obvious trauma.

These two communities resemble each other in population and geographical size. Both were non-nucleated villages, without a concentrated population centre. They shared a large intellectual and political context within which they functioned; yet they differed significantly in how they responded to these outside influences and how they structured their particular communities. Their shared attributes are crucial, however. By understanding the many contexts (Chapter 1) that made up the early modern world, we are able to chart the ways in which Poslingford's and Cratfield's different social, religious and economic compositions affected each community's approach to, and provision for, its elderly members.

Chapter 2 is a detailed investigation of each village's distinctive interpretation of the Elizabethan Poor Laws. It suggests that in areas suffering from economic deprivation, such as Poslingford, the allotment of public relief was particularly discriminatory in nature, and that a shared religious affinity was the selection mechanism which separated the subsidized from the truly destitute. In other words, when there were more poor people than available relief, those chosen to receive aid shared their religious convictions and behaviours with the parish officers. Chapter 3 explores the tenuous world of the marginally poor. These elderly people neither paid the rate nor collected a weekly pension. Crucial to their well-being, if not survival, was the availability of some type of outside assistance, either in the form of an unmarried, stay-at-home daughter, as in the case of the poor village, or in the more affluent Cratfield, the presence of miscellaneous relief from the parish chest. Chapter 4 speaks to the central issue of the book: Were the Elizabethan Poor Laws adequate for the complete support of the aged dependent poor? The evidence from Cratfield and Poslingford strongly suggests that a parish pension, even when supplemented with other funds and the support of kin, was not large enough to cover an elderly person's daily expenses. Despite their unquestioned worthiness to receive charity, assistance and support – indeed, even with a moral obligation for others to assist them – the lives of the aged poor were still ruled by the common dictum under which the bulk of European society laboured: if one did not work, one did not eat.

Through these chapters we gain one of the first extended explorations of old age in early modern England. While historians are familiar with the concept that the elderly should be respected for their age and honoured for their wisdom, little is known about how the elderly spent their final years, except perhaps among the social elite. This study offers a counterbalance: it moves beyond theory to the specifics of daily life, while at the same time focusing on the humblest members of English society, the poor. 'Daily life' was more often composed of the shifting winds of parish politics and the movements of one's own children than it was of national policy and dynastic strategies. By using the small scale of the parish, we have been able to recapture at least some of those mercurial cross-winds of the politicized parish. The many subtle variables – such as health, skills and family that shaped the lived experience of an old age in poverty – would have been lost or obscured if viewed on a larger stage. Consequently, what emerges is a detailed look at village life as the community worked to assist the aged poor, and the aged poor worked to help themselves.

2

The parish's relief of the poor

The history of England's statutory relief of the poor has a long and distinguished past.[1] In its fundamental form of 1601, it stated that the worthy poor were to be housed and provided with a weekly pension; poor children and bastards were to be apprenticed; the labouring poor were to be given work; and the wilfully idle, those who according to common perception 'lick the sweat from the true labourer's brows', were to be punished and forcefully employed.[2] The entire structure of relief was to be underwritten by a weekly rate and managed by especially appointed officers, the overseers of the poor.

Much too has been written about the implementation of these laws. The traditional wisdom is that a series of crises in the 1650s prompted parishes not yet assessing a rate to do so.[3] More recent studies date this sequence of events later, after 1650.[4] One critic of this 'current orthodoxy', Steve Hindle, extends his historiographical criticisms to include the profession's equation of the advent of poor rates with the advent of pensions. He does so by demonstrating the widespread funding of pensions through traditional means, and reminds us that the statutes themselves 'granted overseers "discretion" to impose or not impose rates "as the time serveth"'.[5] Hindle's point is an important one.

---

[1] The study of the English Poor Laws has been undertaken by the leading scholars of many generations, including the Webbs and Steve Hindle. However, Paul Slack's meticulous analysis in *Poverty and Policy in Tudor and Stuart England* (London, 1988) remains the leading authority. The 1601 Elizabethan Statute (43 Eliz. I. C. 1) sets out the basic principles of relief in a form that remained fundamentally unchanged for 250 years.

[2] As quoted in A. L. Beier, 'Vagrants and the Social Order in Elizabethan England', *Past and Present* 64 (1974), p. 10.

[3] This view is drawn from the influential article by Tim Wales, 'Poverty, Poor Relief and the Life-Cycle: Some Evidence from Seventeenth-Century Norfolk' in R. M. Smith *et al.*, eds, *Land, Kinship and Life-Cycle* (Cambridge, 1984), pp. 369–81.

[4] S. Hindle, *The Birthpangs of Welfare: Poor Relief and Parish Governance in Seventeenth-Century Warwickshire* (Dugdale Society Occasional Papers No. 42, 2000), pp. 3–4; P. Slack, *From Reformation to Improvement: Public Welfare in Early Modern England* (Oxford, 1999), p. 67.

[5] See Hindle's *Birthpangs* for an extended discussion of non-rate-based pensions. The quote is drawn from *Birthpangs*, p. 4. See also his 'Dearth, Fasting and Alms: The Campaign for General Hospitality in Late Elizabethan England', *Past and Present* 172 (2001), pp. 44–86 for relief in kind, and not in cash, during periods of dearth.

However, this study contends that too much emphasis has been placed on the role of pensions, obscuring the continued importance of charity, and the poor's own efforts at self-help, in the survival strategies of the poor. Pensions were undoubtedly important, but they did not stand alone.

For the worthy poor, assistance was more varied than the pension and other provisions set forth in statutes and proclaimed across the realm. It included individual gifts to the poor that were managed and disbursed by the church-wardens. Likewise, it included the unquantifiable and historically elusive face-to-face charity, the gifts of bread and beer at back gates and kitchen doors, that formed a vibrant, ongoing stream of assistance. Pensions were, without question, an important element of the relief scheme, but they were not its sole platform. What emerges with clarity in the following chapters, however, is that poor relief was a community-wide effort and not the designated sole responsibility of community, kin or parish.

The decomplex nature of English poor relief resulted from the interplay between two factors: the growth of government at both the central and local level and the evolution of the churchwarden as a parish officer whose brief also included the relief of the poor. During the fifteenth century, parishes became adept at managing local affairs, announcing royal proclamations, and collecting national taxes, subsidies and grants. The sixteenth century witnessed the solidification of these responsibilities as part of an expansion of government that clearly established the sinews of authority from the country's smallest administrative unit, the parish, to its heart and head at the court and at Westminster.[6] Local authorities became responsible for an impressive array of public functions, none more important than the compulsory taxation for the relief of the poor.[7] Placed in the hands of the newly created office of the overseer of the poor, whose responsibilities also included the administration of those revenues, this position required sensitivity to the particular circumstances of both the haves and the have-nots. Indeed, the often consulted guide, *An Ease for Overseers* (1601), stressed repeatedly that the overseer must use his discretion in both the levying of the rate and the disbursement of

---

[6] B. Kumin, *The Shaping of a Community: The Rise and Reformation of the English Parish, c. 1400–1560* (Aldershot, 1996), pp. 241–55. The importance of the parish as the key unit of decision making and administration was greatest in the countryside. The very size of urban communities necessitated additional levels of administration and a different forum for decision making. P. Slack, *The English Poor Law, 1531–1782*, Studies in Economic and Social History (Basingstoke, 1990), p. 18; his *Reformation to Improvement*, p. 5; and S. Hindle, *The State and Social Change in Early Modern England c. 1550–1700* (Basingstoke, 2000). Cf. J. H. Thomas, *Town Government in the Sixteenth Century*, Reprints in Economic Classics (1933; repr. New York, 1969); and E. Trotter, *Seventeenth Century Life in the Country Parish, with Special Reference to Local Government* (London, 1968), pp. 1–4, for a traditional and protestant-centric view of the development of the parish as the unit of local government.

[7] S. Hindle, 'Exclusion Crisis: Poverty, Migration and Parochial Responsibility in English Rural Communities, c. 1560–1660', *Rural History* 7 (1996), p. 126.

relief.[8] The result was a constant process of negotiation between overseer and inhabitant, as well as overseer and poor, making the implementation of the Elizabethan Poor Laws the centre and very embodiment of parochial politics, and consequently, no two parishes would be precisely the same.[9]

Of much earlier origin was the transformation of churchwarden from minor provider of church-related goods and services to royally recognized civic administrator. This metamorphosis was neither sudden nor unopposed, but was necessitated by the growing number of pious bequests given to the church, for the upkeep of both the church fabric and the parish's poor, that had to be invested, administered and supervised.[10] 'In this process', explains Beat Kumin, 'the appointment of wardens and the creation of independent parish funds went hand-in-hand. Gifts for specific purposes needed some kind of supervision, and in turn only an independent administration guaranteed a legally distinct status of these parochial funds.'[11] By the mid-fourteenth century, churchwardens were not only firmly established in that role, but deeply embedded in the fabric of village life as senior men of the parish.[12] By the end of the sixteenth century, overseer and churchwarden worked simultaneously to relieve the burdens of poverty from the lives of their poor parishioners and from the shoulders of their ratepayers.[13]

---

[8] The setting of the rate could be a time of disorder and even violence in the community, especially if one felt disproportionately taxed. S. Hindle, 'Exhortation and Entitlement: Negotiating Inequality in English Rural Communities, 1550–1650' in M. Braddick and J. Walter, eds, *Negotiating Power in Early Modern Society: Order, Hierarchy and Subordination in Early Modern Britain and Ireland* (Cambridge, 2001).

[9] The idea of negotiated parish politics centred on the issue of relief is a theme explored in much of Steve Hindle's recent work. For example, see his *Birthpangs*, *passim*; 'Exclusion Crises', *passim*; and 'Power, Poor Relief, and Social Relations in Holland Fen, c. 1600–1800', *The Historical Journal* 41 (1998): 67–96.

[10] Resistance to the growth of lay leadership came primarily from the clergy, who quite accurately viewed this secularization of local power as a threat to their own authoritative position within the village. Hindsight reveals the nearly impossible nature of this opposition. L. A. Botelho, 'Provisions for the Elderly in Two Early Modern Suffolk Communities', unpublished Ph.D. thesis (Cambridge University, 1996), pp. 202–3; Kumin, *Shaping of a Community*, pp. 20–2.

[11] B. Kumin, 'The Late Medieval English Parish, c. 1400–1560', unpublished Ph.D. thesis (Cambridge University, 1992), pp. 13–14.

[12] See Kumin, *Shaping of a Community*, pp. 241–5 for an overview of the administrative structure of the late medieval parish, especially the wide-ranging role of churchwarden. See Eric Carlson's 'The Origins, Function, and Status of the Office of Churchwarden, with Particular Reference to the Diocese of Ely' in M. Spufford, ed., *The World of Rural Dissenters, 1520–1725* (Cambridge, 1995), pp. 164–207 for a discussion of the function and status of early modern churchwardens. Of related interest is Andrew Foster's essay, 'Churchwardens' Accounts of Early Modern England and Wales: Some Problems to Note, but Much to be Gained' in K. L. French, G. G. Gibbs and B. Kumin, eds, *The Parish in English Life* (Manchester, 1997), pp. 74–93, which discusses a number of methodological concerns associated with their use.

[13] The intermingled efforts of churchwarden and overseer to solve a common problem was part of a long-standing blurring between the boundaries of the civil and ecclesiastical parish,

The decision-making process of parochial poor relief reflects its dual provenance as both a legal obligation and a voluntary act. This complexity was compounded by the nature of early modern society: hierarchical and obsessed with order, two elements that were manifested in the relief of the poor.[14] Because of the nature of early modern authority, decisions by 'the better sort' were made on behalf of the rest. A great deal of power therefore lay in the hands of the few, with possibly the vicar's voice sounding a 'significant if not decisive' note.[15] This already explosive concentration of power was furthered by the cultural demand, and statutory obligation, to be discriminate in the distribution of relief. The great fear was that by being too 'generous' in relief one would multiply the numbers of poor instead of reducing the degree of poverty. Overseers were encouraged to 'endeavour to proportion the rates by the necessities of the poore, and not the poore by the direction of your rates'.[16]

For most parishes the power to set the rate and allot relief resided in the vestry, whose members referred to themselves as *the* inhabitants, *the* parishioners, or simply *the* town.[17] In Cratfield, this consisted typically of eight to ten men out of approximately 300 inhabitants, and in Poslingford it was often only five men out of just under 200. Representation on this scale was not atypical. Kineton, Warwickshire, for example, had eight men, plus the vicar, comprising the vestry in 1636, out of a community of 140 households.[18] Vestries also tended to be self-replicating, with the same men reappearing year after year. Four of Cratfield's chief inhabitants accounted for nearly

---

the overlap in the responsibilities of parish officials, and in the shared use of the church and churchyard to host both sacred and secular activities. Botelho, 'Provisions', pp. 203–6, 207. For the cultural continuation between the middle ages and the early modern periods see D. Palliser, 'Introduction: The Parish in Perspective' in S. J. Wright, ed., *Parish, Church and People: Local Studies of Lay Religion 1350–1700* (London, 1988), pp. 12ff., and R. M. Smith, '"Modernization" and the Corporate Village Community in England: Some Sceptical Reflections' in A. H. R. Baker and D. Gregory, eds, *Explorations in Historical Geography* (Cambridge, 1984), p. 177.

[14] The workings of order and hierarchy are found embedded in the work of many recent scholars of early modern history, just as it was embedded in the very fabric of early modern life. The following early works have set the tone for much of what has followed: S. D. Amussen, *An Ordered Society: Gender and Class in Early Modern England* (Oxford, 1988); Beier, 'Vagrants and the Social Order', pp. 3–29; K. Wrightson, 'Alehouses, Order and Reformation in Rural England, 1590–1660' in E. and S. Yeo, eds, *Popular Culture and Class Conflict 1590–1914: Explorations in the History of Labour and Leisure* (Brighton, 1981), pp. 1–27.

[15] Hindle, 'Exclusion Crisis', p. 142.

[16] *An Ease for Overseers of the Poore Abstracted from the Statutes* (Cambridge, 1601), p. 29. See Hindle, 'Exhortation and Entitlement'.

[17] For a regional study of a vestry's regulation and relief of the poor, see Hindle, 'Power, Poor Relief, and Social Relations', pp. 67–96, esp. pp. 94–5.

[18] Hindle, *Birthpangs*, p. 23.

one hundred (ninety-six) years' vestry experience between them, and in Poslingford, six men accounted for forty-nine years of office holding between them. In many parishes, the vestrymen also tended to be men with the highest weekly assessments and consequently their opinions mattered a great deal, both by virtue of their tenure on the vestry and by the strength of their economic contribution.[19]

To gain access to poor relief, the usual procedure in the seventeenth century was to apply, not to the overseer whose job it was to disburse it, but to those supervising relief, namely the churchwardens and vestrymen. In large and particularly urban parishes this could entail a written application, complete with the 'conventional obsequious phraseology', highlighting those aspects of one's past that might swing a decision in their favour.[20] In small parishes the application took the form of a face-to-face appeal between parties with a long familiarity, borne of their shared years of village living. The c.1660 ballad 'Of the Olde Man and his Wife' set to music the humiliating and desperate act of seeking charity:

> The olde man with his hat in hand
>   full many a leg did make
> The woman wept and wrong her hands
>   and prayd him for Christ his sake:
> Not so to send them back,
>   distressed and undone.[21]

Lifelong familiarity could have made such appeals virtually impossible to refuse if their previous interactions with the vestrymen had been positive. A lifetime of troubled relations, however, could as easily have been held against the petitioning poor, resulting in their dismissal, 'distressed and undone'.

The ability to collect formal assistance was determined by more than simple need. It also depended, in varying degrees, upon any or all of the following: catching the vestry's attention; eliciting sympathy; playing on old loyalties; emphasizing one's good points, such as long, proud years of labour; or promising to amend one's bad ways, such as an ongoing familiarity with the alehouse.

---

[19] For vestry longevity and disproportionate size of the rate in the Lincolnshire fen, see Hindle, 'Power, Poor Relief, and Social Relations', p. 79.

[20] See J. Boulton's carefully reconstructed application process for the large London parish of St Martin-in-the-Fields, 'Going on the Parish: The Parish Pension and its Meaning in the London Suburbs, 1640–1724' in T. Hitchcock, P. King and P. Sharpe, eds, *Chronicling Poverty: The Voices and Strategies of the English Poor, 1640–1840* (Basingstoke, 1997), pp. 26–33, which included a number of alternative strategies for gaining relief, such as abuse and playing both sides against the middle.

[21] *A Most Excellent New Ballad, of an Olde Man and his Wife, Which in their Olde-Age and Misery . . . Disdained and Scornfully Sent Away Succourlesse and How the Vengeance of God was Justly Shewed upon them for the Same* (London, 1600).

'Countless value judgements and the nods and winks of personal acquaintance', Pam Sharpe reminds us, 'must have affected the way in which relief was administered at a personal level. Likewise, local religious and political differences could have affected the complexion of giving within the overall structure.'[22] In other words, need alone was not enough, for without finding favour with the vestry one risked not receiving aid. Once aid was awarded, the pensioner's relationship to the vestry was ongoing and far from static. The pension rolls were periodically reviewed, sometimes weekly, and the threat of deselection, especially for unquiet behaviour, was always present, if seldom demonstrated so coldly and clearly as by the parish officers of Salford, Warwickshire, who warned one pensioner that if he continued to 'demaen and behave himself uncivilly and unreverently' he would 'have no contribution at all'.[23]

Few people questioned the effectiveness or appropriateness of the power invested in the vestry. The justification behind one seventeenth-century proposal to dissolve all existing vestries and re-establish them with new members was not motivated by egalitarian concerns, but rather hierarchical ones: the wrong sort of men had come to dominate. 'First that all vestrys be dissolved and none but the Ministers and Gentlemen of the best Estates, Quality and Reputation be chosen.' Judging from one of Cratfield's early sixteenth-century senior parishioners, John Everard, this complaint may have had some merit. In just twenty years he was charged with illegally alienating copyhold land, not cutting his trees that blocked the road, not clearing his ditches, nor repairing his houses, plus fighting in public, and stealing a horse and four cows. Yet he was a leading member in both church and guild affairs. The same seventeenth-century proposal also complained about the closed nature of these meetings, again not on democratic grounds.[24] Proper supervision of the vestry meetings, he reasoned, would 'prevent their spending the Poores money at the tavern which expence in the said Parish cannot account to less than £200 per annum'.[25] This allegation found an echo in the words of Alexander Strange who censored his vestry for secretly calculating the assessment 'not only in private houses but sometimes in alehouses'.[26]

[22] P. Sharpe, '"The Bowels of Compation": A Labouring Family and the Law, c. 1790–1834' in Hitchcock et al., Chronicling Poverty, p. 87.
[23] Quoted in Hindle, Birthpangs, p. 24. Boulton has found few examples, such as the one cited here, of a rider placed on relief. However, given the selection process, such stipulations may have been universally assumed and therefore unnecessary to state. See Boulton, 'Going on the Parish', p. 83.
[24] Ken Farnhill, 'Religious Policy and Parish "Conformity": Cratfield's Lands in the Sixteenth Century' in French et al., The Parish in English Life, p. 222.
[25] Huntington Library (hereafter HL) Ellesmere Collection, MS EL8572, undated proposal for dealing with poverty by providing more responsible vestrymen, c. 1649–86.
[26] As quoted in Hindle, 'Exclusion Crisis', p. 137. For examples of other vestries who met in public houses, see Hindle, 'Exhortation and Entitlement'.

In many parishes, those whose names were entered on the relief roll, or who collected money from the parish's endowed charities, had somehow successfully navigated the perilous waters of the select vestry and their closed meetings.

This is one of the first extended studies of the detailed workings of rural poor relief. Four potentially significant points emerge: (1) the critical role of the local economy; (2) the danger of simple comparisons between communities; (3) the contributions of churchwardens; and (4) the importance of non-pension relief. First, the parish officers were keenly aware of their community's financial particulars and its economic prospects, and consequently structured their internal affairs accordingly. Cratfield, with its relative wealth, was able to keep a healthy budgetary surplus, yet was also comfortable with a degree of 'deficient spending' on behalf of the poor, knowing that there was a steady stream of income from the rents of the town lands and the deep pockets of its yeoman inhabitants to more than adequately cover the debt in the following year. Lacking fear of financial ruin, the overseers and churchwardens were more capable of responding to unexpected crises. Poslingford, conversely, with its precarious economic position, could not afford the luxury of debt, and they rarely entered into it on behalf of the poor. The result was limited flexibility in the scope of relief and little official aid to the poor when times were tougher than usual.

Land-based versus wage-based economies were the critical distinctions between the communities, and thus in the strategies employed for the relief of the poor. Poslingford's primary source of wealth was the skill and strength of its people in the famously unstable cloth trade. Civic funding had little else to draw upon and consequently it offered relatively little relief. Land, however, was the basis of Cratfield's wealth. It produced a steady and dependable income and, given the village's marketing links to London, it was also lucrative. With the gradual development of a sizeable collection of town lands, by the start of the sixteenth century Cratfield found itself not only able to draw reliably from the purses of the rateable men, but also to count upon annual rents from parish property. At the most basic level, the local economy determined the extent and size of the available assistance. Cratfield was able to cover a wide range of needs, at a fairly generous level; it had the financial health to do so. Poslingford, with its declining economic health, was plagued by the poor, and hindered by its very poverty from doing much to alleviate it.

The second point follows directly from the above: there are grave dangers in simple community-to-community comparisons of figures such as the number of pensions or their amounts. If that had been done here, Poslingford and Cratfield would be cross-county cousins: they are not.

Third, in all but the poorest parishes, the churchwarden may have played an important role in aid to the poor throughout the early modern period. Traditionally the source of charity, they continued in this role long after the establishment of the overseer of the poor. In parishes such as Cratfield, the churchwarden was the source of a wide range of miscellaneous relief, as well as employment. Fourth, and finally, the contribution of the churchwardens in relief of the poor, as distinct from rate-based aid, highlights the importance of non-pension components in the budgets of the poor. More elusive than the recorded gifts of the town were the countless acts of private charity, family assistance, and the poor's own efforts. The very complexity of parochial poor relief suggests that the historiographical preoccupation with rate, pensions and overseers is arguably more important to historians than to history.

Each parish needed to strike its own balance, typically in an unarticulated process, between voluntary charity, charitable bequests and organized relief. Despite the opinion expressed by Strange in a blistering open letter, or perhaps sermon, to his parish that named charity lands as 'the readyest meanes to impoverish a towne and make it at length unable to releeve their poore because of the multitude of such persons as dayly presse into the parish', as well as the warnings of the Warwickshire bench of 1675 that 'no stock or former gift to the poor of the parish shall be a cause to lessen the levies', each community measured the burden of poverty, weighed up its ability to give charity, assessed its inclination to do so, and determined levels of taxation accordingly.[27] The composition of each parish's complete relief scheme varied one from the other in significant and deep-seated ways, while staying within the parameters of a theoretically uniform poor law.

While emphasizing aid to the aged, this chapter analyses the full range of recorded relief in both Cratfield and Poslingford. It must be noted, however, that a fundamental aspect of survival, namely informal charity, was seldom recorded and the extent of its contribution can be only speculated. In offering a survey of parochial poor relief, rate-based relief has been artificially divided from that administered by the churchwardens in an attempt to weigh the components and to assess which were sensitive to outside forces, such as the local economy and disease. Our goal is to provide the necessary knowledge for the detailed examinations of the lives of the aged poor that follow. What clearly emerges is the importance of local context and cultures in the shaping of each parish's response to the poor. Equally important, it demonstrates that the politics of the parish were played out in its poor relief, a political negotiation from which the elderly poor were not excused.[28]

---

[27] As quoted in Hindle, 'Exclusion Crisis', p. 134 and Hindle, *Birthpangs*, p. 21. As with all such legal pronouncements, they would not have been made if the proscribed behaviour was not a common practice.

[28] See Hindle, *Birthpangs*, p. 10.

Cratfield

Cratfield, with its heavy rich soil and its thriving dairies, was a typically prosperous High Suffolk village, characterized by a large number of yeoman farmers and a tradition of independent local government. Yet despite its relative wealth and comfort, it could not escape the all-pervasive problem of early modern England: poverty.

The first line of defence throughout Europe was the organization of charity, and in Cratfield, payments to the poor are found in some of the earliest surviving village records. The town book of 1534 notes money given 'for the relefe of Kempe hys wyfe and ther chylderene'.[29] Similar disbursements occurred periodically until the late 1530s and early 1540s when the trickle of assistance swelled into a stream of relief.[30] Cratfield, it appears, hosted one of a number of precocious poor relief schemes that sprang up across England, but seemed to be concentrated in the southeast. Norwich, York, Cambridge, Colchester and Ipswich were assessing local poor rates from the 1560s, well ahead of parliamentary directives, and organizing comprehensive and creative schemes for the maintenance and employment of the poor.[31] A number of rural parishes, also in the southeast, had implemented scaled-back versions of the same, but none as small as Cratfield has yet been identified.[32]

A significant portion of Cratfield's sixteenth-century relief scheme was funded in a typically rural manner, using a wide range of activities that also served to bind the community together, such as ales and Plough Monday. It also used to good effect the monies it received from pre-reformation pious will bequests and, in particular, grants of land. By the start of the sixteenth century the size of the village's land portfolio and the manner of its manage-

---

[29] Cratfield, TB, SROI, FC62/E1/3 (1534). Boxford, Suffolk, also contains a number of early sixteenth-century payments to the poor from their churchwardens, including the well-known incident of their sale of nearly £5 of church treasure: 'So ys now Rec. with the XXXVs of plate money iij li xiijs in Redy mony which remaynth in the hands of John porter chyrche warden to bestowe it Among the poore people as he shall se nede.' P. Northeast, *Boxford Churchwardens' Accounts, 1530–1561* (Suffolk Records Society, Vol. 23, Woodbridge, 1982), p. 57. According to Beat Kumin, however, 'there are . . . so few direct payments to the poor in parish accounts before the sixteenth century, in spite of occasional episcopal appeals for adequate parochial provision'. Kumin, *Shaping a Community*, p. 61.

[30] Cratfield's early sixteenth-century payments to the poor foreshadowed many categories of poor people later recognized in the Elizabethan Statutes, including those such as Kempe who appears to be overburdened by his children. For examples, see: Cratfield CWA, SROI, FC62/A6/13, 17 (1547, c.1550) and Cratfield TB, SROI, FC62/E1/3. See also Northeast, *Boxford*, p. 52.

[31] Slack, *Poverty and Policy*, p. 123 and his *Reformation to Improvement*, pp. 29–55.

[32] M. K. McIntosh, 'Local Responses to the Poor in Late Medieval and Tudor England', *Continuity and Change* 3 (1988), p. 233.

ment gave Cratfield's poor relief scheme some of the look and feel of an urban parish.[33]

Prior to the election of the overseers of the poor, the churchwardens oversaw the distribution of this revenue into a comprehensive system that included sporadic pensions to named individuals from the mid-1550s, 'collects for the poore people' in 1557, and finally, from 1570 onwards, fifty-two week pensions, such as that given to Widow Cady and William Caswick at 12d a week. Because of the famously uneven nature of early modern record keeping it is impossible to explore the inner workings of this early pension system at anything more than an individual basis, which has been done in a separate chapter for the aged poor.[34] The idiosyncrasies of the churchwardens' accounts do allow, however, for an examination of its funding and the general nature of its disbursements.

To explore the type of early relief provided by the churchwardens is also to explore the nature of its funding. Together they reveal much about the culture of the parish. Churchwarden-supplied assistance was divided into two fundamental types: that which had to be repaid and that which was an outright gift. Loans of various types were available up to quite sizeable sums, and by definition were expected to be returned. Outright gifts to the poor were funded from three sources: private and individual acts, such as will bequests; communal activities, such as village 'drinkings'; and corporate holdings, such as the revenues from town lands.[35]

The first known loan was for 10s in 1538: William Pantry was to repay that sum by Candlemas and 'Wylliam Ferror the elder ys become suerty for the sayde Xs to be payed at the forsayd daye'.[36] The practice of securing the loan was unusual, as most loans 'by the consent of the towne' were unsecured, despite their sometimes very sizeable amounts. In 1660, James Brundish received an unsecured loan of £4, to be repaid in four years. Half of this was immediately spent on apprenticing his son to Goodman Hayward, while the remaining money was simply 'given' to James.[37] Loans from the churchwardens

[33] K. French, 'Parochial Fund-Raising in Late Medieval Somerset' in French *et al.*, *The Parish in English Life*, pp. 118–23.

[34] See Chapter 4, this volume.

[35] See also Boulton, 'Going on the Parish', p. 24.

[36] Cratfield CWA, SROI, FC62/A6/4 (1538). For examples of loans given by the churchwardens of Cratfield, see: Cratfield CWA, SROI, FC62/A6/4, 63, 69, 93, 99, 108, 166, 203, 235, 252, 271 (1538, 1577, 1583, 1595, 1598, 1602, 1633, 1650, 1656, 1660, 1664–65). See also C. Hill, 'The Secularization of the Parish' in his *Society and Puritanism in Pre-Revolutionary England* (London, 1966), p. 424; and P. Slack, 'Poverty and Politics in Salisbury 1597–1666' in P. Clark and P. Slack, eds, *Crisis and Order in English Towns, 1500–1700* (London, 1972), p. 178. For the role of loans among kin, see D. Cressy, 'Kinship and Kin Interaction in Early Modern England', *Past and Present* 113 (1986), pp. 51–2.

[37] The loan does not seem to have been repaid, though Brundish continued to receive relief well into the 1680s. Cratfield CWA, SROI, FC62/A6/252 (1660). See also Cratfield CWA, SROI, FC62/A6/285, 286, 306 (1666, 1666, 1671) for examples of Brundish's additional relief.

could be tightly linked to the overseers' pension, with one playing off the other in an intricate web of assistance. In 1598, William Orford's complex arrangements with the parish were summarized at the bottom of an overseer's accounts:

> Memorandum that Orford receyved 13d from the third day of March untill the 16th day of Aprell being Ester day, which cometh to 7s. Then he requested to borrowe 7s to by him such things as he wanted the which seid 7s was lent to him by the consent of the townesmen in consideration whereof he agreed to abate evere week 4d of his stipend until he had made restitucion of the seid 7s so[me] he borowed for this cause he receyced weekly from Ester day until the 6th day of August, by 10d a weke. So that it being just 16 weekes from Ester day until the 6th of August he hath but 10d a week in those 16 weeks receyved just 13s 4d. And hath repayde in that meane whils 5s 4d. And doth owe stil 20d of the seid 8s so borowed. As[?] well therfore that it being 22 weeks from the third day of March until the 6 of August and 2 dais 14d a week for the space 6 weeks and 10d a weke for the space of 16 weks cometh just to 20s 4d.[38]

This was not the only loan which William Orford received, nor the only time he was on a stipend. The parish's generosity may perhaps be in recognition of Orford's previous standing as a churchwarden, in a rare churchwarden-to-pauper drop in status.[39]

Loans may be considered charity with an edge, as interest appears to have been routinely charged, but the churchwardens also disbursed money that did not need to be paid back.[40] One time-honoured source of such gifts were personal and individual will bequests to the poor. Of the eighteen known testamentary charitable bequests in Cratfield, the first was made by John Sancroft in 1531, who gave 4d to 'tenne of the powrest house holders of the townys of Laxfield and Cratfield', and the last was a generous 40s in 1683 from the wealthy John Goldsmith.[41] The other gifts represent a wide range of

---

[38] Cratfield, CWA, SROI, FC62/A6/99 (1598).

[39] William Orford served as churchwarden in 1568 and 1569, and he was rated at £5 worth of goods in the 1566 subsidy. His fall to poverty is discussed more fully in Chapter 4, p. 107, this volume. See also Cratfield CWA, SROI, FC62/A6/63, 69, 85, 104, 106 (1577, 1583, 1590, 1599, 1600) for a few examples of the relief received by Orford before his death in 1599, at about 80 years of age.

[40] L. A. Botelho, ed., *Churchwardens' Accounts of Cratfield, 1640–1660*, Suffolk Records Society, Vol. 42 (Woodbridge, 1999), pp. 44, 92, 96.

[41] The eighteen will bequests are found in: Will of John Sancroft, Cratfield, 1531, SROI, R10/192; Will of John Warner, Cratfield, 1538, SROI, R13/83; Will of Richard Balrye, Cratfield, 1545, SROI, R15/243; Will of Richard Broadbanke, Cratfield, 1548, SROI, R16/309; Will of Margery Penninge, Cratfield, 1550, SROI, R17/320; Will of Elizabeth Smith, widow, Cratfield, 1572, SROI, R25/338; Will of John Newson, Cratfield, 1585, SROI, R30/449; Will of Richard Smith, husbandman, 1589, SROI, R32/242; Will of John Whislecrofte, Cratfield, 1590, SROI, R33/250; Will of William Newson, yeoman, 1616,

monies given and poor relieved, from James Fryer's three-penny funeral dole in 1658 to Richard Broadbanke's 1548 gift of 20s 'to poore maydens maryages that be of honest behavyor and condycyon'.[42] Not all will bequests were recorded, nor were all recorded gifts honoured. For example, John Sancroft's gift was not noted by the churchwardens, either through oversight, or because the estate was unable to honour his will due to debt or an unwilling heir.[43] However, it is reasonable to assume that many such gifts made their way to the poor through the activities of the churchwardens, despite the laxity of their bookkeeping.[44]

Will bequests, while unquestionably playing an important role in permitting the churchwarden to relieve the poor, could not have underwritten the scale of church-based assistance available in Cratfield. They were problematic from the administrative point of view as well. First, they were irregular, predicated as they were upon the death of some philanthropic soul, an impossible occurrence to predict. Second, they were of varying sums, making it impossible to estimate parochial income in advance. Other sources of funding were equally problematic, such as Banbury, Oxon, relying on the combined income from the 'weekly collection and monies gathered at Communions, punishment of drunkards, tipsters and swearers . . . besides the constant contributions of many charitably affected' to keep their community chest full.[45] Rather than passively awaiting the passing of a generous inhabitant, many communities took decisive steps to regularize their affairs by augmenting the value and size of the communal holdings through seasonal and community-based fund raising.

SROI, R33/250; Will of Lewis Borrett, yeoman, Cratfield, 1620, SROI, R53/152; Will of Sir Thurston Smyth, gent, Cratfield, 1647, SROI, W87/71; Will of John Rous, gent, Cratfield, 1670, SROI, W101/34; Will of Elizabeth Rous, widow, Cratfield, 1677, SROI, R72/232; Will of Margaret Rous, widow, Cratfield, 1678, SROI, R75/329; Will of James Fryer, Cratfield, 1658, PRO PROB 11/293, fols 168–9v; Will of John Williams, Cratfield, 1655, PRO PROB 11/253, fols 401–3; Will of John Goldsmith, Cratfield, 1683, PRO PROB 11/357, fol. 123.

[42] Will of James Fryer, Cratfield, 1658, PRO PROB 11/293, fols 168–9v; Will of Richard Broadbanke, Cratfield, 1548, SROI, R16/309.

[43] An example of a contested will drawn from the southern part of the county involved the 'puritan' gentry family, the Appletons. Thomas Appleton's Will of 1603 in Little Waldingfield, Suffolk, bequeathed ten loads of wood to the poor, but was later disputed. Finally, his son, Isaacke Appleton, bequeathed four tenements adjoining the churchyard for the use of the poor, claiming they had been purchased by his late father for 'the lyke charitable uses'. Will of Isaacke Appleton, Little Waldingfield, SROB, K1/1.

[44] While nothing appears in the churchwardens' accounts to this effect, the account book of Robert Warner of Wickhambrook, Suffolk, records the settling of his father's Cratfield estate, including a £3 bequest to the poor. Account Book of Robert Warner, SROB, 2841, fol. 74v.

[45] PRO State Papers Domestic 16/191, fol. 19, The Mayor, and others, of Banbury, to the Council, 13 May 1631. Also quoted in *Banbury Corporation Records: Tudor and Stuart*, The Banbury Historical Society, Vol. 15 (Oxford, 1977), p. 152.

Church ales were one of England's most traditional and festive forms of fund raising, as well as community building. The basic premise is simple: 'people who worshipped together drank together'.[46] Ale was brewed, yeasty cakes were baked, and the neighbouring parishes were invited to come and enjoy the day, and of course purchase their vitals at an artificially high price, in full knowledge that in the not too distant future their home parish would host its own ale and the visit would be reciprocated. Thus were the boundaries of the wider community re-enforced and revenues raised.

In the 1490s, church ales were hosted by Cratfield, or its neighbours, between five and six times a year, and raised substantial sums of money. This pattern continued into the early sixteenth century. But by the early 1530s, Cratfield's ales netted only minor profits and were silently discontinued.[47] Most of this income was spent on the church fabric, the painting of images, or providing liturgical items, such as a 'holy water sprynckle'.[48] But ales and their profits were not restricted to the church; they were also held to benefit an individual or a specific cause. Bride ales could be given on behalf of a newly wedded couple to help ensure a good start in married life; help ales were given to assist a needy individual. The latter were a socially sensitive form of poor relief: they allowed the recipient to retain a sense of self-worth, since the needy individual was responsible for making and selling a product, and thus was not considered to be an idle recipient of charity. Help ales also allowed donors to give at their own discretion, or provided them with a face-saving avenue for not giving at all. In 1490, Cratfield hosted what appears to have been a help ale for Geoffrey Baret.[49]

Similar to church ales were the activities and collections taken on behalf of the church on Plough Monday. Plough Monday was devoted to 'the cere-monial blessing of ploughs in readiness for the opening of the earth and the resumption of the working agricultural year'.[50] It was a 'patently pagan' fertility rite, traditionally held on the first working day after Christmas. Apart from the 'sensyng of Powlles' by priests, the plough was sometimes harnessed to the young men of the village, who would plough up the ground in front of the house of anyone refusing to contribute at least a small token towards the parish

[46] French, 'Parochial Fund-Raising', p. 131.
[47] The total generated by church ales ranged from between £3 15s 7d in 1494 to only 8s 3d at the last known event, Pentecost 1535. Botelho, 'Provisions', pp. 226–7.
[48] Amounts spent on images within the Cratfield church could be substantial: for example, £9 13s 4d was spent painting the image of Our Lady in 1491. W. Holland, *Cratfield: A Transcript of the Accounts of the Parish, from A.D. 1490 to A.D. 1642, with Notes*, ed. J. J. Raven (London, 1895), p. 18. See also French, 'Parochial Fund-Raising', pp. 124–6.
[49] J. M. Bennett, 'Conviviality and Charity in Medieval and Early Modern England', *Past and Present* 134 (1992), pp. 19–41; Holland and Raven, *Cratfield*, p. 18.
[50] D. Cressy, *Bonfires and Bells: National Memory and the Protestant Calendar in Elizabethan and Stuart England* (London, 1989), p. 17; R. Hutton, *The Rise and Fall of Merry England. The Ritual Year 1400–1700* (Oxford, 1994), pp. 16–17.

church. East Anglian churches, according to Eamon Duffy, might also have a 'plough-light' before the rood or Sacrament. The church in Cawston, Norfolk, still has a plough galley with a 'magnificently carved beam' bearing a fertility prayer and concluding pun about the fund-raising nature of plough ales:

> God spede the plough
> And send us all corne enow
> our purpose for to mak
> Be mery and glade
> Wat Goodale this work mad.[51]

Whether or not a light stood in front of the high altar or before the rood in Cratfield's church, the parish certainly held profitable Plough Monday activities. The first recorded collection was in 1491, a new 'plowhe' was purchased in 1545, and they continued long after their prohibition in 1548.[52] In some cases, the poor seem to have benefited directly from such proceeds. In 1597, both John Olde and Olde Harsom were paid a shilling 'the sundaie after plough mundaye'.[53] By the seventeenth century, Plough Monday seems to have lost its pagan elements, as well as the parish's support, since it too was dropped as a fund-raising measure.

One traditional method of raising money that was not discontinued as part of the reformation of society, but was continued and indeed built upon, was the parish's endowed collection of land and property. Corporate in nature, these rents would finance much of the village's affairs, and the churchwardens' poor relief.[54] The core of Cratfield's holdings were placed in the hands of the village during the second half of the fifteenth century. One of the earliest gifts was that from its parish priest between 1439 and 1444, Sir John Caryell. Originally called the town house and close, this designation was soon given to another set of properties, and Caryell's gift became the schoolhouse.[55] Two more sets of property were given to the village in the 1460s, both by John Fyn in his will of 1461.[56] The first, known both as 'Benselyns' or 'the towne house',

[51] E. Duffy, *The Stripping of the Altars: Traditional Religion in England 1400–1580* (New Haven, CT, 1992), p. 13. See also N. Pevsner, *Buildings of England: North-East Norfolk and Norwich* (London, 1962), p. 112.

[52] Cratfield was not alone in retaining its Plough Monday activities after their prohibition in 1548; Cressy cites several communities which were still generating such profits in the late Elizabethan period. Holland and Raven, *Cratfield, passim*; Cressy, *Bonfires and Bells*, p. 17; Duffy, *Stripping of the Altars*, pp. 460–1; Cratfield CWA, SROI, FC62/A6/4, 12 (1538, 1546) and Cratfield TB, SROI, FC62/E1/3, *passim*.

[53] Cratfield CWA, SROI, FC62/A6/97 (1597).

[54] Ken Farnhill also notes this in 'Religious Policy', p. 223.

[55] Cratfield Deeds, FC62/L1/18. The change of name is confirmed by comparing the rent for the town house at the chancel end (unmistakably Caryell's house in Cratfield CWA, SROI, FC62/A6/23 (1554)) with that for the schoolhouse in Cratfield CWA, SROI, FC62/A6/36, 37 (1561, 1562).

[56] Farnhill, 'Religious Policy', p. 219.

was of substantial size and for many years it was managed through a separate set of accounts before eventually being incorporated into the churchwardens' accounts in the 1560s.[57] The second grant in that year was of the church house and close, which were by the early sixteenth century valued at 11s and 4s a year, respectively.[58] Elizabeth Baret was responsible for the largest series of gifts to the parish, as she eventually alienated all the land she inherited: first, from her parents John and Rose Baret upon the death of her brother Thomas, and second, from her late husband Richard Rogers. The first gift, in 1498, was a tenement known by the family name, Baret. The second alienation was five years later, in 1503, to the local guild. Called Swan, this was a parcel of land in excess of three acres. The guild also received, in the same year, the gift of Rose Larks, whose proceeds funded the guild chaplain.[59] It was not, however, until the well-endowed guild dissolved itself in 1541 that the churchwardens' landed endowment grew to its impressive size.

Cratfield's guild, dedicated to St Thomas the Martyr, was already in place by 1478 when John Gown left 40s for the purchase of a chalice. Its activities probably included light-keeping, and it certainly had its own chapel and priest. Processions led by the guild banner and followed by a feast in the guild-hall were also one of its enterprises.[60] The guild's impact on the poor of the community was both direct and indirect. While it recorded no payments to its poor members, it was, like the churchwardens, a ready source for loans, including 5s lent in 1536 to William Smith, cooper, which was only repaid on his death in 1542.[61] Similarly, John Scherman borrowed 4 marks in 1534 and Edmund Myllys was lent 6s 8d in 1537, both of which were jointly for-given by the guild and the town in 1538.[62] Unlike some other late medieval rural parishes, and indeed unlike the churchwardens, Cratfield's guild did not charge interest on these loans as a means of increasing their stock.

Ironically, it was the guild's indirect contribution to the poor of Cratfield that had the greatest impact. The guild slowly began divesting itself of property from 1537 when the guildhall was transferred into private ownership and the extensive property and mill of Rose Larks was transferred to the church-wardens in 1538.[63] This safeguarding technique was probably in response to the dissolution of the priory at St Neots, which held both the advowson

<hr/>

[57] The original size of Benslyn's farm is unknown, but it comprised fourteen acres in 1510 and eighteen acres in 1534. Botelho, 'Provisions', p. 12.

[58] Cratfield, TB, SROI, FC62/E1/3; Farnhill, 'Religious Policy', p. 220.

[59] See K. Farnhill, 'A Late Medieval Parish Guild: The Guild of St. Thomas the Martyr in Cratfield, c. 1470–1542', *Proceedings of the Suffolk Institute of Archaeology and Natural History* 38 (1995), pp. 261–7 for a meticulous reconstruction of the late medieval land grants to Cratfield's guild.

[60] Farnhill, 'Parish Guild', pp. 261–7.

[61] Cratfield TB, SROI, FC62/E1/3 also contains the guild accounts for the years 1533–42.

[62] Cratfield TB, SROI, FC62/E1/3.

[63] The original 1503 Rose Larks endowment was thirteen acres and a mill; six acres and three rods were added later, and by the 1530s income from this property was in excess of

of the church and the manor of Cratfield Roos. Ken Farnhill has carefully traced the history of the Cratfield guild's land acquisitions, and its process of concealment, through a maze of muddled guild accounts, wills, manorial records and property deeds to reveal an extensive set of properties that yielded over £8 a year by the 1530s.[64] Thanks to the evasive actions of the guild wardens in the 1530s, the churchwardens received the vast majority of these holdings, whose income was in turn used for the relief of the poor.[65] By the mid-seventeenth century, the churchwardens' land-based income had grown to over £90 a year.[66]

The gift of the old guildhall in 1553 was one of the most tangible aspects of the disbanded guild's legacy to the aged poor. The house was originally donated to the guild in 1502 by the priest John Rusale, and the adjoining land of one acre and one rod was added later through purchases of either church or guild. With the ill-wind of dissolution blowing in the 1530s, the guildhall was given, not sold, to John Thurketyll in 1537 in order to prevent the property from reverting to the heirs of the original benefactors. On the death of Thurketyll, the property was returned to the use of the parish in the form of an almshouse.[67] In a funding strategy employed more often by urban parishes than by rural ones, Cratfield's churchwardens acquired and managed a substantial and lucrative portfolio of landed investments.[68]

Cratfield was fortunate; it had an almshouse. Marjorie McIntosh's work on local responses to the poor suggests that few elderly people had recourse to the sheltered accommodation provided by these institutions.[69] A place in

130s a year. Cratfield TB, SROI, FC62/E1/3; Cratfield Deeds, FC62/L1/3, FC62/N1/4–5, FC62/L1/18.

[64] Cratfield TB, SROI, FC62/E1/3.

[65] For the process of concealment, see Farnhill, 'Religious Policy', pp. 225–6.

[66] The large proportion of Cratfield's churchwardens' income generated by rents, or 'gifts of the dead', at the beginning of the sixteenth century was either unusual, demonstrating traits associated more typically with urban areas, or it marks an early shift in parochial funding strategies from rates to investments, a shift which Burgess and Kumin place at the end of the fifteenth century. In 1652, the churchwardens recorded an income of £95 10s 8d; in 1654 £92 16s 1d; and in 1656 it was £101 8s 11d. Cratfield CWA, SROI, FC62/A6/211, 217, 240 (1651, 1653, 1656–57). C. Burgess and B. Kumin, 'Penitential Bequests and Parish Regimes in Late Medieval England', *Journal of Ecclesiastical History* 44 (1993), pp. 619, 626–7.

[67] Cratfield Deed, SROI, FC62/L1/15; Farnhill, 'Religious Policy', p. 220. See also Chapter 4, this volume, and my 'Accommodation for the Aged Poor of Cratfield in the Late Tudor and Early Stuart Period', *Suffolk Review*, n.s. 24 (1995), pp. 19–31 for a fuller discussion of the living arrangements of Cratfield's elderly, including those in the almshouse.

[68] Katherine French's study of late medieval parochial funding in Somerset suggests that 'rural parishes generally did not rely on property rents or a policy of acquiring land; they were, at best, a minor source of income'. French, 'Parochial Fund-Raising', p. 120.

[69] When viewed nationally, Marjorie McIntosh suggests that only one elderly person from every two parishes would have found a place in a late medieval or Tudor almshouse. McIntosh, 'Local Responses', p. 216. See also P. Laslett, *The World We Have Lost. England Before the Industrial Age* (2nd edn, London, 1971), p. 262.

an almshouse, if one could be obtained, would have been an excellent way for poor people to live out the remainder of their lives, though frequently at the cost of personal liberty.[70] Rent was usually provided, along with a stipend, and perhaps a gown. The buildings themselves were generally well built and often located at the heart of the community, guaranteeing the occupants a continuing involvement with the village at large and casting doubt on Paul Slack's earlier assessment that 'a lonely old age was the lot of most of the labouring poor'.[71] The adjacent parish of Fressingfield built a new guildhall or townhouse in the first decade of the sixteenth century and a related property deed of 1509 illustrates the social nature of these town structures. It was to be used for 'the kepyng of all church ales, gildes, yerdayes, burynges and other drynkynges necessary to the profyte of the said chirch or parishe', and built 'for the more reverens of God and in avoydyng of etynge and drynkyng and other abusions in the chirch'.[72] Cratfield's guildhall probably served this same function.

Another parish property, Cratfield's former guildhall, was centrally located, standing 'in the church yard'.[73] Its bake-oven and outbuildings nestled against the west chimney and at one time formed the community's bakehouse, known as 'the gyldhall kytchen'.[74] Despite the cost of the 'mendinge of twoue ovens at the howse', they were also sometimes a minor source of parish income. In 1559, for example, Wylliam Bocher paid 4s for the rent of the ovens.[75] Built

---

[70] Competition for a place in an almshouse could be quite fierce. Vacancies were infrequent and they were strictly for the 'worthy poor'. Once resident, the expectations were often quite demanding. See M. K. McIntosh's *A Community Transformed. The Manor and Liberty of Havering, 1500–1620* (Cambridge, 1991), p. 282 for a discussion of how 'their [almspeople's] conduct and deference were closely supervised by the almshouse bailiff.

[71] Slack, *Poverty and Policy*, p. 85. Furthermore, McIntosh suggests that almshouses may have also been used as a place where some kind of 'informal' care could be given to the more 'fragile' members of society. V. B. Redstone, 'Chapels, Chantries, and Gilds in Suffolk', *Suffolk Institute of Archaeology and Natural History* 12 (1906), p. 11; Cratfield Deed FC90/L3/8, also quoted in N. Evans, 'Inheritance, Women, Religion and Education in Early Modern Society as Revealed by Wills' in P. Riden, ed., *Probate Records and the Local Community* (Gloucester, 1985), p. 57; Cratfield CWA FC62/A6/40 (1563); McIntosh, 'Local Responses', p. 220; W. Newman Brown, 'The Receipt of Poor Relief and Family Situation: Aldenham, Hertfordshire, 1630–90' in Smith, *Land, Kinship and Life-Cycle*, p. 414; and M. Barker-Read, 'The Treatment of the Aged Poor in Five Selected West Kent Parishes from Settlement to Speenhamland (1662–1797)', unpublished Ph.D. thesis (Open University, 1988), p. 85. See T. Sokoll, 'Old Age in Poverty: The Record of Essex Pauper Letters, 1782–1834' in Hitchcock *et al.*, *Chronicling Poverty*, p. 137.

[72] Evans, 'Inheritance, Women, Religion and Education', p. 57.

[73] 'Paid to John Thredkell for a new gate next to the guildhall in the church yard.' Cratfield CWA, SROI, FC62/A6/309 (1677).

[74] Cratfield CWA, SROI, FC62/A6/17 (c.1550).

[75] Community bakehouses may well have been a common feature in this region of Suffolk, although, by the mid-seventeenth century, Cratfield was buying its communion bread from

in the fifteenth century, possibly on the site of an older and smaller building, the original structure had large public rooms on its two levels, with the remaining one-third of each floor dedicated to housing.[76] Additional alterations occurred shortly after its construction, and possibly the subdivision of the east and west rooms of the ground floor took place during this period, further increasing its residential potential to between five and seven almspeople (see Figure 2.1).[77]

Responsibility for the upkeep and maintenance of the old guildhall was shouldered by the churchwardens and carefully documented in their accounts. The roof was regularly rethatched and the ovens and hearth repaired. Likewise, workers were paid 'for triming of the dore and the windowes and for nalles and for the sell' in 1603, while the 1616 accounts record two days' labour to Simond Chrispe and his helper for 'layeinge the gystes and parting the rome for the widdowe cady'.[78] The accounts also record Widow Cady's reimbursement of her personal expenditure towards this remodelling: 'for iij plankes and a wyndow that was to parte the Gylde hall, 4s.'[79] Even at the close of the

---

the neighbouring parish of Laxfield. Botelho, *Churchwardens, passim*. Laxfield's bakehouse is still standing, and it shares a common wall with the guildhall. In Cratfield, the west external chimney was unaltered at the time of the Society for the Protection of Ancient Buildings' report in 1960 and a bake-oven was clearly identified at that time. Cratfield CWA, SROI, FC62/A6/17, 48 (c. 1550, 1569 or 1570), and P. E. Locke, *Report on the Town House, Cratfield, Suffolk. Prepared for the Society for the Protection of Ancient Buildings* (London, 1960), p. 3. For parish revenues gleaned from bakehouses, as well as brew works, see French, 'Parochial Fund-Raising', p. 123.

[76] The guildhall also had two attics which ran the length of the building and were approached via the stairwell that encircled the central chimney. These attics acted as parish storage, as in the case of Widow Cady's 'househould stufe' which was removed 'up unto the guyldhall chamber'. Cratfield CWA, SROI, FC62/A6/157. Evans, 'Inheritance, Women, Religion and Education', p. 57; *Society for the Protection of Ancient Buildings*, p. 4; and unpublished letter from Stanford, Broom and Stanford Auctioneers, Valuers and Estate Agents to the Trustees of Cratfield's Town Estate, dated 19 April 1961, p. 1.

[77] The dual nature of guildhalls, operating as both meeting place and residence, is not surprising. Guildhalls, particularly after the suppression of religious guilds, were frequently used as almshouses or village workhouses. For example, the Horringer, Suffolk, guildhall became the local workhouse, and in Bardwell, Suffolk, the guildhall of St Peter became an almshouse. *Society for the Protection of Ancient Buildings*, p. 4; M. W. Hervey, *Annals of a Suffolk Village being Historical Notes on the Parish of Horringer* (Cambridge, 1930), p. 75; F. B. Warren, 'A Pre-Reformation Village Gild', *Suffolk Institute of Archaeology and Natural History* 11 (1903), p. 109; and H. F. Westlake, *The Parish Gilds of Mediaeval England* (London, 1919), p. 63.

[78] Cratfield CWA, SROI, FC62/A6/111, 137, *passim* (1603, 1616).

[79] Cratfield CWA, SROI, FC62/A6/138 (1617). This may well be the 'lightly partitioned' subdivision of the ground floor described in the report of the Society for the Protection of Ancient Buildings. It may have been the result of friction between inhabitants, as was the case in Maidstone, Kent, when 'a brick partition' was erected through the centre of the structure 'to secure harmony between two occupants'. Barker-Read, 'Treatment', p. 78.

Exterior Plan

Legend
- - - Additional
Construction

First Floor Plan

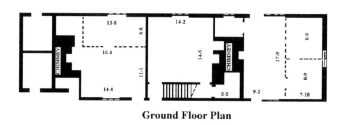

Ground Floor Plan

Figure 2.1 Cratfield's almshouse architectural plans

seventeenth century, this building was still known as the 'gild hall', it still housed 'the pore folckes', and was still maintained by the churchwardens.[80]

By the start of the seventeenth century, the assistance offered by the churchwardens and paid for primarily from the town estate was fundamental to the survival of the poor in general and the elderly in particular. Yet, due to the relatively static nature of this funding, the churchwardens were unable to meet the demands of the increased levels of poverty: while the parish officers may themselves have been sensitive to the plight of the poor, their sources of revenue were not. The role of churchwarden and the money from the town lands therefore shifted from being the primary source of support for the poor to supplementing that raised by a rate and distributed by overseers.

The accounts of the overseers of the poor do not survive until 1625, when the rates, pensions and casual relief records are bound together in a single volume. A payment of 6d to Joshua Stubard 'for makinge the overseers booke' in 1606, however, assures us that the statutes had been enforced from at least that date.[81] While 'overseers' by name are not mentioned in earlier documents, their activity may be partially reconstructed from the churchwardens' accounts. For many years the churchwardens also recorded expenditure by the overseers, but often in more detail. For example, the overseers of 1660 record 5s given to John Stannard under the catch-all heading of 'sickness and distress', while the churchwardens describe that same 5s as being paid to 'ould Stannard being not well'.[82] Therefore, we know that 'sickness' and not simple need lay at the root of John Stannard's momentary poverty. While the churchwardens' accounts allow the construction of relief histories for particular individuals prior to 1625, they do not allow for rigorous examination. Consequently, the analysis that follows relies upon the post-1625 documents and represents the seventeenth-century structure of Cratfield's formal and statutory poor relief.

As the statutes directed, the parish's formal scheme consisted of two components: those who paid a rate in support of the poor, and those who were poor and in receipt of relief. The ratepayers, predictably, included local office holders, men like John Williams, John Smyth de Stubbards, Edmond Tollifer and Robert Milles.[83] John Williams, who was typical of many male ratepayers, began paying the rate at age 39. Rates were also collected from a handful of wealthy widows, whose formal relationships with the office of overseer began

[80] Cratfield CWA, SROI, FC62/A6/173, 231, 240, 362 (1637–38, 1656, 1656–57, 1699).

[81] Cratfield CWA, SROI, FC62/A6/116 (1606).

[82] Cratfield OSA, SROI, FC62/A2/1 (1660) and Cratfield CWA, SROI, FC62/A6/252 (1660).

[83] Socially, the ratepayers included: fifteen will makers; fourteen churchwardens; nine chief inhabitants; nine yeoman; eight overseers; seven constables; four gentlemen; four tailors; and one each: linen weaver, glazier and draper. There were also widows of four yeoman; two gentlemen; one carter and the linen weaver. Cratfield OSA, SROI, FC62/A2/1 (1660, 1672, 1679, 1645, 1668, 1686).

late in life, typically in their late fifties.[84] Once rated, men and women were faced with the same legal obligations, and their careers as contributors followed the same course.

Once in the rate book, most householders remained there for some time: men for an average of twenty-four years, and women for a sixteen-year average, an impressively long tenure given their late start. Unlike pensions, which gradually increased with age and their recipients' frailties, the monthly assessment was tied to wealth, probably land, and was not indexed firmly to age. All but six of Cratfield's forty-six elderly ratepayers were still funding the poor well past their fiftieth birthday, some at levels outstripping their far younger counterparts.[85] Interestingly, they seldom remained ratepayers until death; most paid their final rate seven years before they died. Poor rate payments were not scaled back gradually, but were instead abruptly stopped. Was this the point where land, property and authority were handed over to the younger generation, perhaps in exchange for a secure old age?[86]

Some parishes determined rates by yardland, and assessments varied in the mid-seventeenth century, but 3s a yardland could be considered typical. Other villages based their rate on property, such as 3d in the pound used in parts of seventeenth-century Warwickshire or 5–6d in the pound in mid-eighteenth-century Buckinghamshire.[87] Cratfield, too, assessed the poor rate according to

---

[84] There were four female ratepayers (Mary Broadbank, Frances Fiske, Ann Williamson and Frances Rouse). Their average age at first payment was 58.

[85] The six in question were: Gregory Rouse, died at age 75; Robert Warner, 63; Simon Warren, 51; William Stannard, 60; John Stannard, 51; and Simon Collier, 86.

[86] Much of the evidence we have of the elderly transferring land in exchange for support is found in manorial records. For a thoughtful discussion of the historiography of manorial court records and maintenance contracts see R. M. Smith's 'The Manorial Court and the Elderly Tenant in Late Medieval England' in M. Pelling and R. M. Smith, eds, *Life, Death and the Elderly: Historical Perspectives* (London, 1991), pp. 39–61. See also E. Clark, 'Some Aspects of Social Security in Medieval England', *Journal of Family History* 7 (1982), pp. 307–22; C. Dyer, 'Changes in the Size of Peasant Holdings in Some West Midland Villages, 1400–1500' in *Land, Kinship and Life-Cycle*, p. 289; and Z. Razi, 'The Myth of the Immutable English Family', *Past and Present* 140 (1993), pp. 3–44. Cf. the superficial treatment of the care of the elderly in the English manor in S. R. Burstein, 'Care of the Aged in England from Mediaeval Times to the End of the Sixteenth Century', *Bulletin of the History of Medicine* 22 (1948), pp. 738–46. Old age arrangements made on behalf of an elderly widow are typically found in last wills, with Margaret Spufford's *Contrasting Communities: English Villagers in the Sixteenth and Seventeenth Centuries* (1974; repr. Cambridge, 1987) being hugely influential, but see my '"The Old Woman's Wish": Widows by the Family Fire? Widows' Old Age Provision in Rural England', *Journal of Family* 7 (2002), pp. 59–78 for a critical evaluation of her methodology and an alterative reading of widows' old age provisions.

[87] Hindle, *Birthpangs*, p. 19; HL, Stowe Collection, MS STG Manorial Box 5, folder 34, Wooton Underwood, Buckinghamshire, Overseers Rates, 1756–57. For complaints against the use of yardland to assess the rate on the grounds that it did not reflect one's true worth, see Hindle, 'Exhortation and Entitlement'.

one's annual worth at somewhere between 3d and 4d to the pound. While the precise mathematics of Cratfield's overseers is lost – there was obviously some level of discretion exercised, since individuals of roughly, but not exactly, annual worth were required to pay the same monthly assessment – it appears that the long arm of local taxation stretched far across the social scale, with monthly payments ranging from Goodman Tilles' single penny to Robert Mynne's 5s 8d.[88] Unlike other parishes, especially those with a fairly comprehensive tax base, there seems to have been little trouble in collecting the rate, or with those who felt that they bore an unjustifiably large portion of it. It appears to have been successfully collected as a matter of course.[89]

The ease of collection was probably due to Cratfield's general state of economic well-being. Most of the community could pay their share without undue hardship, grumbling or protest. In 1674, for example, two-thirds of all Cratfield householders were paying rates for the relief of the poor and by the close of the century the percentage of ratepayers was seventy-five.[90] Yet seventeenth-century Aldenham, Hertsfordshire, rarely had more than 45 per cent of its resident householders contributing to the rate and the Kineton Hundred, Warwickshire, could only muster a combined average of 31 to 38 per cent in 1639.[91] The number of ratepayers in Cratfield rose and fell around an average of forty-five households, peaking at fifty-five in the 1650s and seldom falling below forty.[92]

Unlike the situation in Poslingford at the end of the seventeenth century, or in parts of Warwickshire at mid-century, the hierarchy of ratepayers was not as neatly defined.[93] In 1690, for example, there were no pronounced clusters either at the top of the scale, 4s 6d a month, or at the bottom, 4d a month. Instead, there were two ratepayers at nearly every level of assessment. The lack of a dominant group of ratepayers was even more evident in the early years of the century, with the bulk of the rate, both numerically and proportionately, carried by those at the lower levels of assessment. The composition of the rate attests to Cratfield's overall prosperity.

[88] Cratfield OSA, SROI, FC62/A2/1 (1652, 1678). *An Ease for Overseers* provides some examples of when such discretion should be exercised, pp. 15–16.
[89] Hindle, 'Exhortation and Entitlement'.
[90] The Hearth Tax return records seventy-one households, both rich and poor. The rate book for the same year lists forty-seven rated households. *Suffolk in 1674, Being the Hearth Tax Returns* (Suffolk Green Books, No. 11, Vol. 13, Woodbridge, 1905), p. 85; Cratfield OSA, SROI, FC62/A2/1.
[91] Newman Brown, 'Receipt', p. 409; Hindle, *Birthpangs*, p. 20.
[92] Dearth, such as those found in the 1590s, 1630s and 1640s, can sometimes account for peaks in the size of the rate. J. Walter, 'The Social Economy of Dearth in Early Modern England' in J. Walter and R. Schofield, eds, *Famine, Disease, and the Social Order in Early Modern Society* (Cambridge, 1989), p. 117, fn. 120.
[93] Hindle, *Birthpangs*, pp. 20–1.

Cratfield's wealth naturally made it a parish from which JPs solicited assistance and cash to aid more impoverished and distressed areas.[94] The parish's frequent contribution to parishes and towns overcome by poverty, with buildings in disrepair or destroyed by fire, speaks strongly of the overall wealth of the community and its relatively high level of disposable income.[95]

Perhaps the most important way that the town's wealth manifested itself, certainly so in the eyes of the poor, was its ability to keep the overseer's purse well stocked with coin, but also the self-assurance to allow the parish chest to run into arrears occasionally, knowing that it could be restocked at virtually any time. Information on income is available for sixty-one years in the seventeenth century, during which time the departing overseers presented their replacements with a sizeable average surplus of 32s. When viewed over time, a pattern of funding becomes clear. A large surplus was quickly produced, generally through a temporary increase in the amount of rate paid per person and sometimes, such as in the 1650s, by an increase of ratepayers. This positive balance was carried forward for several years before it slowly dwindled away, year by year, until the fund was depleted and the town in debt. The current overseers would supply the needed income from their own pockets, typically financing the parish's poor relief for a year or two, before the town's rate was again momentarily increased, not only to reimburse the 'previous overseers', but once again to create a cash surplus.[96]

None the less, the ever-escalating cost of poor relief made its demands upon the pockets and purses of the ratepayers. Contributions were increased in

---

[94] Among the village's many contributions towards the relief of Bylthburgh's poor include two in 1599, one in 1602 and two more in 1603. In the same manner the poor of Walberswick, Suffolk, were assisted annually between 1631 and 1633, as well as in 1636. Lowestoft and Bungay received help at least once in 1636 and 1665, respectively. Other examples of Cratfield's financial generosity include 2s sent to help repair the hospital in Norwich in 1616 and a seemingly endless number of briefs for damages caused by fire, including those of Dorchester, 1614; Brundish, 1656; Bury St Edmunds, 1652; Glasgow, 1655; Hengrave, 1656; Peterborough, 1656; Saffron Market, 1656; Southwold, 1659; and a massive £10 to Southwold again in 1659. Cratfield CWA, SROI, FC62/A6/101, 102, 107, 109, 111, 157, 159, 166, 169, 171, 275 (1599, 1602, 1603, 1630, 1631, 1634, 1635, 1636, 1665–66). See also payments 'for relieving the inhabitants of the City of Lincoln who were much impoverished by the plague'. Holland and Raven, *Cratfield*, pp. 167, 144. Cratfield CWA, SROI, FC62/A6/137, 210, 215, 239, 246, (1616, 1651, 1652, 1657, 1659).

[95] R. W. Herlan, 'Poor Relief in London during the English Revolution', *Journal of British Studies* 18 (1979), pp. 37–9, 45, and his 'Relief of the Poor in Bristol from Late Elizabethan Times until the Restoration Era', *Proceedings of the American Philosophical Society* 126 (1982), pp. 223, 226; and V. Pearl, 'Social Policy in Early Modern London' in H. Lloyd-Jones, V. Pearl and B. Worden, eds, *History and Imagination. Essays in Honour of H. R. Trevor-Roper* (London, 1981), p. 125.

[96] For the twelve years of debt, the overseers averaged 20s a year deficit. Cratfield OSA, SROI, FC62/A6/1 (1626, 1658, 1659, 1660, 1662, 1663, 1664, 1677, 1687, 1691, 1692, 1693).

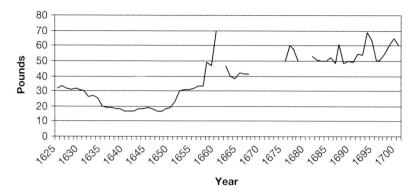

Figure 2.2 Cratfield poor relief: value of annual expenditure

response to the growth of poverty and the damaging effects of inflation. The price of poor relief soared in Cratfield during the years prior to the 1660s, matching the movement of inflation throughout the country, to a plateau from which it never descended.[97] The cost of supporting Cratfield's poor continued to increase after 1650, but not with the intensity of the first half of the century (Figure 2.2).

The overseers and chief inhabitants were not mere civic-minded worthies, but economically successful men in their own right, and they developed a financial strategy for the parish in light of their experience. The annual surplus maintained by the overseers during most of the seventeenth century was more than a mark of their economic prosperity and Christian charity; it also served the very useful purpose of acting as a buffer between estimated expenditure and actual costs. With no reason to expect that prices would rise year after year, the rate was assessed using the previous year's spending as a guide to current needs. However, the demands of the poor were generally greater than had been anticipated, and their impact was absorbed by the surplus. Therefore, increased spending was shadowed a year or two later by increased taxation: the surplus made it possible for the poor to continue to be assisted without the village resorting to a supplemental rate.

While the statutes stipulated a particular form of relief depending upon the type of pauper, such as employment for the able-bodied and willing worker, parishes frequently found it more effective, or simply easier, to provide for the poor in their own way. In Cratfield, for instance, few attempts were made at employing the poor to work, and those appear to have failed.[98] The

[97] R. B. Outhwaite, *Inflation in Tudor and Early Stuart England* (2nd edn, Basingstoke, 1982), p. 14.
[98] See Chapter 4, this volume, pp. 128–31. Cratfield CWA, SROI, FC62/A6/112, 116, 117, 171, 173, 329, 333, 334 (1604, 1606, 1607, 1636, 1637, 1656, 1680, 1680). See Trotter,

churchwardens' accounts record at least seven instances where 'a stock' of hemp or thread was purchased 'to set' someone to work. This includes 10s 'to the tannar for leather for Ruben Tallowin to sett him aworke'.[99] The attempt failed and, by the following year, Ruben Tallant was regularly employed at 10s a quarter as the church sexton. Yet there is no evidence of the proceeds being recycled into the overseers' purse. This does not imply that the parish was opposed to employing the poor: the churchwardens themselves were the usual source of employment in the form of odd jobs and errands.[100] It does illustrate the difficulty that many other parishes found in setting the poor to work profitably.[101]

Instead, like many other communities across England, Cratfield chose either to pension its unemployed or to provide a string of miscellaneous payments to its underemployed and labouring inhabitants. For example, in 1692, while in his mid-thirties and able-bodied, John Downing received 6s a month for his family of four and for lame Elizabeth Milles. Likewise, Catherine, the wife of Robert Pacy, received 1s a week in 1656 when she was 46 years old. They had four children between the ages of 6 and 19.[102]

Apart from a few short-lived attempts at employment for particular individuals, the structure of Cratfield's poor relief expenditure was twofold: pensions and miscellaneous relief. Pensioners, those in receipt of 'ordinary' relief, were paid a weekly sum by the overseers. This could vary throughout the course of the year, and it certainly changed over the course of a pensioner's life. The miscellaneous relief category, the 'extraordinary' payments made by the overseers, reached a much wider audience. This side of Cratfield's debit ledger was organized by type of expenditure rather than the individual. Overseers provided gifts of cash and firewood, the payment of medical services and annual rents, the cost of pauper apprenticeships and the 'schooleing [of] 4 towne boyes', as well as the catch-all category of 'sickness and distress'.[103]

Seventeenth Century Life, p. 62 for examples of other parishes employing the poor. Daniel Defoe, in his *Giving Alms No Charity and Employing the Poor. A Grievance to the Nation, Being an Essay upon this Great Question* (London, 1794), p. 17, viewed these schemes as taking work away from the honest labouring poor and giving it to vagrants, 'enriching one poor man to starve another, putting a vagabond into an honest man's employment'.

[99] Cratfield CWA, SROI, FC62/A6/171 (1637).

[100] The following two chapters illustrate the importance and function of parish-generated odd jobs in the life of the elderly poor.

[101] Hindle, 'Power, Poor Relief, and Social Relations', p. 86. See also A. L. Beier, 'The Social Problems of an Elizabethan Country Town: Warwick, 1580–90' in P. Clark, ed., *Country Towns in Pre-Industrial England* (Leicester, 1981), pp. 75–6, and his 'Poor Relief in Warwickshire, 1630–1660', *Past and Present* 35 (1966), p. 82; Herlan, 'Relief of the Poor in Bristol', pp. 216–17; and V. Pearl, 'Social Policy', pp. 119–26.

[102] Cratfield OSA, SROI, FC62/A2/1 (1692, 1656). For other examples see Cratfield CWA, SROI, FC62/A6/310, 330 (1672, 1679).

[103] There were a number of early sixteenth-century educational efforts, such as the will provision of John Warne in 1540 to have his wife Agnes arrange for the teaching of reading

Some gifts of cash, however, were on condition that the applicant promised 'to aske noe more' of the town.[104]

During the seventeenth century, four expenditure types emerged as the focus of Cratfield's poor relief scheme: pensions; rents (typically quarterly); firewood; and medical treatment. Needy individuals, such as William Browne, might receive 20s for 'howsefarme' in 1626, but not a weekly stipend. Alternatively, one might qualify for both a rent payment and a pension, as in the case of Widow Cady. She was paid by the overseers 10s for her rent and 8d a week for her maintenance.[105] Weekly pensions were always the overseers' greatest responsibility, not in terms of their numbers, but in their draw upon the parish's finances. Throughout most of the seventeenth century, the weekly stipend accounted for about half of all expenditure.[106] Other parishes, including Poslingford in the late seventeenth century, spent nearly all of their revenues on pensions, such as the 90 per cent average in Kineton Hundred, Warwickshire, and St Martin-in-the-Fields, London.[107] Charity was therefore left mainly in private hands and through private acts. Cratfield's relatively low spending on the pension, in conjunction with its otherwise extensive poor relief programme, speaks quite eloquently of its economic good health.

Aid from the overseers was also a highly sensitive type of relief, unlike that provided from churchwardens' fixed-income endowments, reacting to changes in demography, economics and morbidity.[108] The 1650s immediately capture our attention: 82 per cent of the total budget was spent on pensions. It was a difficult time for Cratfield, as both overseers and churchwardens stepped in to assist 'in regard of the cheapness of comodityes and the hardness of the tymes'.[109] The number of pensioners rose sharply in 1650 to eleven, and then dropped sharply to a low of six between the years 1653 and 1657, before beginning another sharp rise. The large sums of money spent during the latter half of the 1650s foreshadowed the 1690s. Similarly, the 1650s were also a time of high mortality in the parish, especially from 1654 onwards, with burials more numerous than baptisms (Figure 2.3).[110]

---

and writing to their sons. The first mention of a schoolmaster, however, was in 1559, and he was to be paid 20s a quarter, with another reference to the same in 1562 at 30s, at virtually the same income as the guild priest. Farnhill, 'Religious Policy', p. 225. It raises the question of whether it was the same individual, continuing his same functions.

[104] Cratfield CWA, SROI, FC62/A2/1–363, *passim*; Cratfield CWA, SROI, FC62/A6/316 (1674).

[105] Rents were also paid for the elderly poor in Boxford. Cratfield OSA, SROI, FC62/A6/1 (1626); Northeast, *Boxford*, p. 53.

[106] It averaged 54 per cent between 1625 and 1700.

[107] Hindle, *Birthpangs*, p. 16; Boulton, 'Going on the Parish', p. 24.

[108] This breakdown of expenditure raises an interesting and as yet unanswered question: Why did food disappear as a form of public relief? It only appears in the overseers' accounts during the 1630s.

[109] Cratfield CWA, SROI, FC62/A6/240 (1656).

[110] Botelho, 'Provisions', Appendix 1, p. 374.

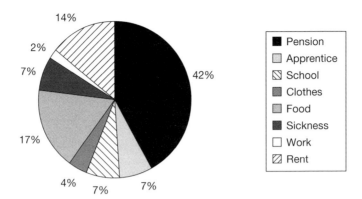

Figure 2.3a Cratfield's poor relief, 1630s

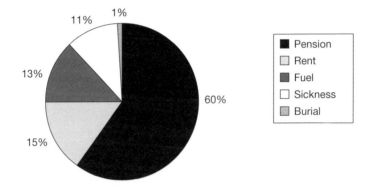

Figure 2.3b Cratfield's poor relief, 1640s

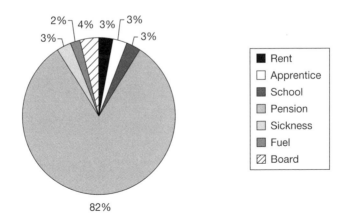

Figure 2.3c Cratfield's poor relief, 1650s

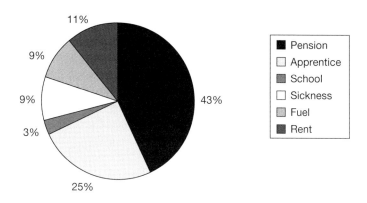

Figure 2.3d Cratfield's poor relief, 1660s

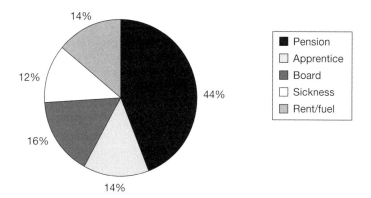

Figure 2.3e Cratfield's poor relief, 1670s

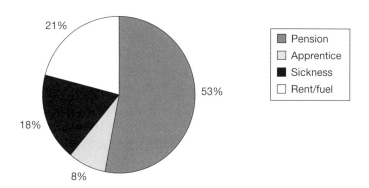

Figure 2.3f Cratfield's poor relief, 1680s

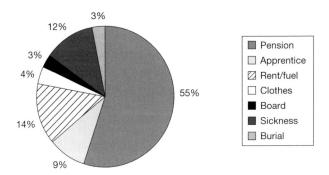

Figure 2.3g Cratfield's poor relief, 1690s

Disease, in a number of forms, was probably responsible both for Cratfield's high expenditure on poor relief and high mortality during this time.[111] Smallpox was moving throughout southeast England in the late 1640s and early 1650s. Ralph Josselin, in nearby Essex, commented in his diary on the number of deaths in 1645 as a result of smallpox and he was still discoursing upon the 'wonderful sickly time' when 'many died very suddenly' in 1652.[112] Just a few years later, the ague or intermitting fever (perhaps typhoid) struck the southeast with great force during the autumn months of 1657. Again, Josselin noted its presence: 'their was never a more sickly time generally in England than now', a month later adding that 'feavours . . . fil many places with pale faces'.[113] A later account by Dr Willis of this fever emphasized the vulnerability of the aged to its 'contagion and deadliness'. He wrote:

> About the month of August, this Feaver began to spread far and near, among the people, that in every Region and Village many were sick of it; but it was much more frequent in the Country, and smaller Villages, than in Cities or Towns. It was still like an intermitting Feaver, unless that it seemed more infectons than that is wont, and with more cruel fits, and shorter intermissions, and therefore was called the New Disease: besides, it underwent the note of a certain malignity, and gave knowledg of its Contagion and Deadlieness; insomuch, that it crept from house to house, infected with the same evil, most of the same Family, and especially those familiarly coversing with the sick, yea, old Men, and Men of ripe Age, it ordinarily took away.[114]

[111] See O. P. Grell and A. Cunningham, eds, *Health Care and Poor Relief in Protestant Europe 1500–1700* (London, 1997) for a wide-ranging discussion of such relief.
[112] A. Macfarlane, ed., *The Diary of Ralph Josselin, 1616–1683*. Records of Social and Economic History, n.s. iii (London, 1976), pp. 116, 284. Also quoted in M. Dobson, *A Chronology of Epidemic Disease and Mortality in Southeast England, 1601–1800*, Historical Geography Research Series No. 19 (London, 1987), pp. 50–1.
[113] Macfarlane, *Josselin*, p. 407. Dobson, *Chronology*, p. 53.
[114] T. Willis, *Dr. Willis's Practice of Physick* (London, 1684), p. 138. Also quoted in M. Dobson, *A Chronology of Epidemic Disease and Mortality in Southeast England, 1601–1800*, Historical Geography Research Series No. 19 (London, 1987).

This fever returned, along with an influenza epidemic, to the southeast in the following year, and again struck hardest at the 'weak and sickly'. The decade was rounded out by the return of influenza, not only in the southeast but throughout the country.[115]

The 1650s were certainly a 'wonderful sickly time' in Cratfield, and the elderly were particularly hard hit during these years: seven died in 1654 and another four in 1659, as opposed to the average of two elderly deaths a year.[116] Marginal notes in the parish register highlight the vulnerability of the aged during this 'time of great sickness'.[117] 'Edmond Milles was buried the four and twenty day of December anno dom 1654. He was a very old man well on to five score yeres of age.'[118] Ann Wilton, buried July 1659, was recorded as 'a widdow nowe a hundred yeares of age'.[119] The relatively little spent directly on sickness and medical attention during this decade indicates the size of the problem faced by the overseers: many people were too sick to be provided for through the small cash hand-outs typical of payments to those in 'sickness and distress'. They and their families needed the more complete support of a parish pension.

Fuel and rent were other prominent and consistent elements of parish-provided relief.[120] Apart from the 1650s when all other spending was subsumed by weekly stipends, nearly 20 per cent of the parish's budget was spent on rent and firewood.[121] The overseers conflated the two categories under a single heading in the late seventeenth century; however, the records through the 1660s indicate that about equal numbers of poor received each type of gift. Sickness, the fourth identified concern of the overseers, was neither as dominant as pensions nor as consistent as rent and fuel. Payments for sickness were not confined only to those who suffered from epidemics and mysterious fevers: women in childbed, limbs broken from a fall, physical disability and the frailties of old age were also found under this ill-defined rubric of 'sickness

---

[115] Dobson, *Chronology*, p. 54.

[116] Cratfield PR, SROI, FC62/D1/2.

[117] There are many payments for illness throughout the 1650s, but 1651 seems particularly hard hit, including a 10s payment 'given to pore Pacie in the time of Great Siknes'. Cratfield CWA, SROI, FC62/A6/211; Cratfield PR, SROI, FC62/D1/2.

[118] In fact, Milles was 84 years old when he died. Cratfield PR, SROI, FC62/D1/2.

[119] See also the burials of Agnes Warren and Mary Broadbank in 1656: Agnes Warren was reputedly 'a woman above fouer score yeares of age' and Mary Brudbanke was thought to be 'a greate deale above ffower score yeares of age'. The ages of Ann Wilton and Agnes Warren are unknown, but Mary Broadbank was only 69 years old when she died. Cratfield PR, SROI, FC62/D1/2.

[120] Fuel in the form of firewood may have come directly from the town farm of Rose Larks or Sallow Pightell. In 1650, the town book records a lease of both these properties to Thomas Broadbank with the proviso that he remove only six loads of wood, the rest to be for the use of the town. Cratfield TB, SROI, FC62/E1/3 (1650).

[121] The average, without the figures for the 1650s, was 18 per cent of poor relief spending. Including the 1650s lowers the percentage to sixteen.

and distress'.[122] Important as such payments were to their recipients, the amount needed to meet this expense would have been unpredictable even one year in advance. The remainder of services provided by the overseers of the poor were also exposed to unpredictable demand. The apprenticeship of pauper children, clothes for the poor and the burial of the poorest paupers were tied as closely to changes in demography, economics and morbidity as were payments to the sick and distressed.

The lives of the poor were extremely sensitive to adverse changes in any or all of these categories, and particularly those of the elderly poor. It was as if, to the aged, the faceless forces of population pressure and ill-health had hands as shaky as their own. For the indigent elderly and youngest paupers alike, life was often perilous. Improved security, perhaps even stability, was available to a few paupers of any age who were lucky or deserving enough to be awarded a weekly pension.[123]

The pension was the staple of the dependent poor's budget, a steady and often sizeable stream of cash in an often undependable and uncertain world. It would be hard to underestimate its importance to those who received it. From the time of Cratfield's first recorded pension in the 1550s (as opposed to *ad hoc* cash payments), both the number and the amount of pensions grew steadily throughout the sixteenth and early seventeenth centuries: from one or two recipients a year to eight in 1625 and from 3d a week to over 3s a week in the seventeenth century; during the first three decades of the century 3d a week was the standard starting rate for most pensions; during the 1640s, however, it jumped sharply to an average of 1s a week.[124]

During the sixteenth and very early seventeenth centuries, most pension recipients were old people, frequently 100 per cent of the total. From 1610, however, this was no longer true. While the actual number of old age pensioners did not fall, but rather stayed at a remarkably constant three or four a year, their share of the total number of pensions grew smaller and smaller with each passing year.[125] This illustrates vividly the changing nature of poverty during the seventeenth century, and the growing number of poor people and families who were unable to support themselves. Consequently,

---

[122] Examples of such payments, whose details were recorded by the churchwardens, include the 4s given to Widow Tallant in 1659 'when her daughter lay in' or the three visits and 10s 6d spent 'to pay the surgon for his [Samuell Milles] daughtars' leg'. Cratfield CWA, SROI, FC62/A6/220, 246 (1655, 1659).

[123] See Chapter 4, this volume, pp. 110–15 for a further discussion of the benefits of weekly pensions.

[124] See Chapter 4, this volume, p. 111, fn. 25. The size of the weekly pension varied remarkably between parishes. For example, the Kineton Hundred in Warwickshire had pensions ranging from 3d to 2s a week in 1639, with an average pension of 6d a week. Hindle, *Birthpangs*, pp. 14–15.

[125] S. R. Ottaway has found the same pattern for much larger towns in the eighteenth century in 'Providing for the Elderly in Eighteenth-Century England', *Continuity and Change* 13 (1998), p. 403. SROI, FC62/A6/212, 246 (1651, 1659).

entries such as 'to Samuel Garvis towards clothing his children, 5s 6d' and 'to younge Goodwife Mills towardes a coate for her child' became more common (Figure 2.4).[126]

The obligation to the poor was not always easy, and each ratepayer felt its burden. The cost of poor relief rose steadily and substantially, yet as we have already seen, the number of ratepayers was not significantly increased.[127] As Figure 2.5 clearly shows, each ratepayer was forced to take up a greater share of the poor relief budget, as the number of ratepayers called upon to support a single pensioner fell dramatically during the last half of the seventeenth century. In other words, a single ratepayer provided a larger portion of an individual pension. During the crisis years of the 1650s, Cratfield increased its tax base and, as a result of this major redistribution of wealth, the support of a single pensioner was spread among nine ratepayers. Having weathered the local crises of the 1650s, the tax base was again reduced.

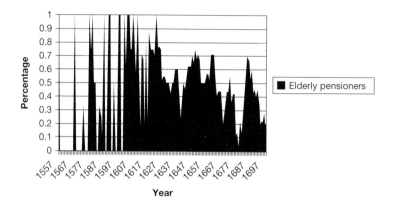

Figure 2.4 Cratfield pensioners: percentage of the elderly

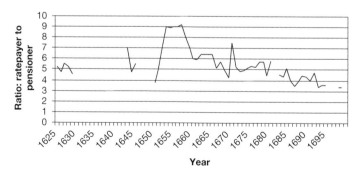

Figure 2.5 Cratfield: number of ratepayers to one pensioner

[126] Cratfield CWA, SROI, FC62/A6/330, 310 (1679, 1672).
[127] See Chapter 4, this volume, p. 138 for annual costs of maintaining the aged poor.

Yet not all poor people were pensioners. In Cratfield at the end of the seventeenth century, a sizeable minority were marginally poor, defined here as those who collected miscellaneous relief but not a pension or who neither paid the rate or received any formal relief. The type of assistance they received spanned the available range, except of course the pension. Parishes in Warwickshire at a slightly earlier date ranged between a 1: 6 and a 1: 4 ratio of pensioners to marginally poor.[128] The particulars of this type of poverty as played out in the lives of the elderly are explored below.

Given the religious tone of much parish life, the penal nature of Cratfield's approach to poverty seems very small compared to the 'godly' cities, towns and villages of early modern England, such as Salisbury, Dorchester or Sudbury.[129] The village did not have its own workhouse or bridewell, and neither did its immediate neighbours. While the bridewell in Beccles was not prohibitively distant, it was rarely called upon by Cratfield's overseers.[130] The only mention of the house of correction was in 1611, after 3s 5d was spent 'to carry the poor people that was taken in the privy watch and carried to Beccles'.[131] The parish favoured the more traditional punishment of the village stocks and the courts.[132] The wandering poor who had passes were given relief and sent away.[133] A number of neighbouring poor, such as Goody Miller of Peasonhall, were 'removed' and returned home.[134] However, the local and troublesome poor like Anne Wright consistently received assistance, even into old age.[135] She

[128] Hindle, *Birthpangs*, pp. 15–16.

[129] Slack, *Poverty and Policy*, pp. 148–56. See also D. Underdown, *Fire From Heaven: Life in an English Town in the Seventeenth Century* (London, 1993).

[130] The Quarter Sessions of April 1681 ordered the construction of a house of correction and a workhouse in Beccles 'for the benefit of this division', at a cost of £600. Quarter Sessions, April 1681, SROI, 105/2/10.

[131] Another privy watch was conducted in 1631, but no mention was made of the house of correction at that time. Holland and Raven, *Cratfield*, pp. 139–40, 166.

[132] The stocks: Cratfield CWA, SROI, FC62/A6/45, 333 (1566, 1680). Unfortunately, the accounts seldom record the names of those against whom an action was taken in court, or why.

[133] The churchwardens' loose accounts are well supplied with examples. Cratfield CWA, SROI, FC62/A6/1–363.

[134] On 22 June 1631 3d was 'given unto ould Browne for conveynge awaye of vagrants to the next Constable'. It is interesting to see the elderly poor used as the escort for such removals, rather than the more robust constable. Cratfield CWA, SROI, FC62/A6/158, 331 (1631, 1679).

[135] The parish did not seem to strictly enforce the late seventeenth-century settlement laws and did not remove those elderly who were chargeable, or 'likely to be chargeable' in order to avoid paying for their maintenance and burial. See K. Snell, 'Parish Registration and the Study of Labour Mobility', *Local Population Studies* 33 (1984), pp. 34–7. Snell addresses this issue of old age as part of a general critique of David Souden's use of parish registers to study migration. See also D. Souden, 'Movers and Stayers in Family Reconstitution Populations', *Local Populations Studies* 33 (1984), pp. 11–28. I am indebted to Dr Jeremy Boulton for this reference.

was one of Cratfield's most notorious idlers, whose life is well documented through a sequence of bastard bearing, poor relief, excommunication and visits to the parish stocks. The parish register records the birth of her bastard daughter Elizabeth, who was baptized 'by Mr Richard Sherman the 18th day of September 1603', as well as recording her own burial with the words, 'Widow Wright was buried the 28th of December [1614] being excommunicated 12 yeares and to her end'. Furthermore, at least one of her visits to the stocks was chronicled by the churchwardens when they paid 2d 'for bread and beere to Anne Wryght when she was in the stocke'.[136]

From a range of sources, the churchwardens and overseers of Cratfield were able to assist a variety of needy people, both those in occasional need and those in chronic despair, throughout the sixteenth and seventeenth centuries. A place in the almshouse would relieve the overseers of the responsibility of paying that aged individual's rent. Income generated from rents of lands and houses found its way into the hands of the poor in the form of cash, clothing and fuel. The churchwardens were the funnel through which all recorded charity was poured and the overseers administered only those monies collected from the weekly rate. Poor relief in Cratfield, then, consisted of a generous mixture of parish-provided pensions, gifts, loans and odd jobs from the churchwardens, and little threat of life in the workhouse.

Poslingford

By the mid-seventeenth century when most of the parish's records are extant, Poslingford was poor and its relief system was shaped by that poverty.[137] Few inhabitants possessed enough wealth to qualify for the rate, and consequently taxation generated little income. Furthermore, there were more people in need of relief than the overseers could maintain, and those who managed to find a place on the relief rolls were aided at extremely modest levels. In short, the nature and content of Poslingford's poor relief was very different from Cratfield's, despite common statutory obligations.

Consequently, the overseers' funding pattern varied significantly from that in Cratfield. Rarely did the overseers overspend and allow their account to fall into arrears. Undoubtedly this was a deliberate and important strategy, for unlike the more wealthy Cratfield, there were few untapped reserves available to rectify an overdraft. Some of Poslingford's ratepayers were clearly pushed to the point of potential hardship. The overseers were undoubtably aware that their spending could not exceed their means. The increasing contributions of this small group of men were just adequate to meet the cost

---

[136] Cratfield PR, SROI, FC62/D1/1; Cratfield CWA, SROI, FC62/A6/117 (1607).
[137] Most of Poslingford's parish documents date from 1663 and the survival of the town book.

of care, and most overseers managed to hand over a small sum to their replacements.[138]

Poslingford's poverty was reflected in a number of different ways, but perhaps nowhere more forcefully than in the tiny percentage of the population in a position to shoulder the cost of their neighbours' relief. The size of the financial contribution to the rates is known for most years after 1663,[139] but the number of its contributors are limited to the returns of 1669, 1687, 1696 and 1700.[140] The 1687 rate is unusual, suggesting that a staggering 95 per cent of the population was called upon to assist in what could only have been a crisis.[141] In this instance, both the rich and the marginally poor contributed to the relief of the destitute, including both the richest men and those worth only 10s and rated at ¼d a month. Even in this year of crisis and extended rating, the importance of the three richest men was unquestionable, since they accounted for 43 per cent of that year's contribution. The severity of Poslingford's polarization of wealth, illustrated in Table 2.1, is further underlined when the lowest group of ratepayers is subdivided further to reveal that fourteen, or 38 per cent, of these thirty-six households were worth £10 or less.

Table 2.1 Distribution of Poslingford ratepayers by annual worth, 1687

£100+	£99–£75	£74–£50	£49–£25	£24–£1	**Total**
3	0	2	8	23	36

By the 1690s, between 20 and 35 per cent of the village, but mostly just its three wealthiest families, carried the financial burden of the poor. The situation described in 1599 in Brailes, Warwickshire, would have been all too familiar to the vestrymen of Poslingford: 'There is not any man within our parish that we think able to spare a penny a weeke, but he is at a weekely paiment and yet we feare that diverse of our poore must be suffered to begg among us until more forraine help be had.'[142] Furthermore, from 1688 the ratepayers of Poslingford were stretched even further, since constabulary costs

[138] Between £1 and £2 was transferred to the new overseers annually.
[139] The amount collected by the rate was not recorded in the following years: 1668, 1673, 1674, 1675, 1682, 1683, 1684, 1690, 1691, 1692, 1693, 1697, 1698. Poslingford OSA, SROB, FL615/7/1.
[140] Only in 1687 do the overseers actually name the thirty-eight ratepayers and indicate the amounts of their assessment. In 1669, 1696 and 1700 the number of rates collected was recorded, but without individual names.
[141] The population percentage is derived from the base population of 190 in 1674. See Botelho, 'Provisions', pp. 119–23. The widening of the rate base in response to crisis may have been an unusual action. See Hindle, 'Exhortation and Entitlement'.
[142] As quoted in Hindle, *Birthpangs*, pp. 11–12.

were incurred when individuals were escorted to the bridewell in Clare or returned to their place of settlement.[143] Unlike Cratfield, where the long arm of local taxation reached far down the social ladder to raise revenue and spread the cost of poor relief widely, Poslingford's ratepayers were clustered around the upper rungs of their social and economic hierarchy.

Despite its small tax base, the village's middling sort and elites were still forced to meet the ever-rising cost of poor relief. The annual collection, assessed at 2 to 3d per pound, rose from an average of £17 12s in the 1660s, to an average of slightly over £19 in the following decade, to £23 15s 3d in the 1680s, and finally to an annual average of £26 11s 6d in the 1690s. Surprisingly at first, the cost of poor relief continued to rise in the second half of the seventeenth century, *after* the period of greatest inflation. This persistent escalation in the cost of relief was undoubtedly linked to the concurrent decline of the cloth trade. Despite a national reprieve from spiralling inflation, Poslingford's economic difficulties continued to place enormous pressure on the village's ratepayers.

Fortunately for Poslingford's poor, relief came from a variety of sources and was not based solely upon the rate. Lacking sixteenth-century sources, we have no examples of traditional revenue raising. Did the parish, for example, host church ales and May Day dances? Did its youth collect monies from the area's thriving wool merchants during Hocktide and on Plough Monday? Certainly, the organized charities of the seventeenth century were a continuation of earlier charitable impulses. One seventeenth-century alternative to the rate was for the overseers to reinvest the proceeds from pauper employments, although spinning and related pursuits seldom generated a profit.[144] Mary Durant must have worked long and hard on her parish-provided labours in order to hand over £2 12s 7½d to the overseers in 1676.[145]

Another potential source of funding was the Easter communion offering. The poor received 3s each in 1685, the only year in which such contributions were recorded.[146] However, the town book of another Stour Valley cloth village survives and records the annual receipt of the 'comeunyon monye' to be given to the indigent.[147] The gifts of Little Waldingfield's Easter

---

[143] The overseers' accounts records: £1 16s 10d to the constable in 1688; £2 16s 9d in 1689; £2 6s 1d in 1696, plus payments to three weeks' extra collection paid by John Eagle and 15d for a warrant; £1 12s 5d in 1699; and £4 5s 7d in 1700. Poslingford OSA, SROI, FL615/7/1 (1696). Money was also given directly to the constables in Clare such as the 2s spent for mending the stocks. See below (pp. 66–7) for a discussion on the penal nature of Poslingford's poor relief.

[144] See pp. 131–2 for a discussion of Poslingford's putting the poor to work.

[145] See Poslingford OSA, SROB, FL615/7/1 (1673) for a complete account of Durant's work stock purchased at the parish's expense. See p. 66 for other instances of pauper employments, especially as they highlight the parish's concern for an ordered society.

[146] Poslingford CD, SROB, FL615/7/1 (1685).

[147] Little Waldingfield, Suffolk, is only ten miles to the east. Little Waldingfield Parish Records, SROB, EL 158 (1629–1867).

communicants were as regular as the holy day itself, averaging nearly £2 a year.[148] However, in terms of the treatment of the poor, Easter-time giving must be seen as symbolic of Christian charity and the seven acts of mercy, and not as effective poor relief. A final, if sporadic, means of increasing the parish purse was to sell the personal effects of recently departed paupers and to keep the proceeds as a partial repayment for the relief they had received earlier. In 1699, Widow Metcalfe died and all of her worldly possessions were sold. Subsequently this 9s profit was funnelled directly into the overseers' accounts, and not given to her daughter.[149] While paupers' possessions generated relatively little cash, overseers throughout the country were quick to exploit even the smallest sources of revenue in their constant battle to fund poor relief.[150]

The bulk of the overseers' meagre income was split between four major categories of relief whose composition changed significantly between the 1670s and 1680s, signifying a realignment of the overseers' priorities. In the 1660s and 1670s, rent, fuel, illness and pensions were the leading areas of public concern and parochial relief. In the 1680s and 1690s, rent, fuel and pensions continued as major expenses, while payments due to illness were curtailed sharply and replaced by gifts of clothing. The switch from medical care to waistcoats and shoes reveals a fundamental change in relief as the community struggled to match an increase in poverty. While the vestry minutes do not survive and we have no direct insight into the decision-making process of the chief inhabitants, it is arguable none the less that less medical attention did not reflect a healthier population, but marked a shift towards providing the most basic and fundamental necessities, clothing the naked (Figure 2.6).[151]

An even more rudimentary redirection of resources occurred at this time. Spending on weekly stipends increased dramatically and nearly doubled between the 1670s and 1680s. This altered pattern of spending likewise reflects changed priorities, prompted no doubt by a growing poverty problem. Until the 1670s, the pension consistently accounted for just over 40 per cent of all

---

[148] For example, in 1634 £1 14s 4d of the overseers' income came from communion money; £1 17s 6d in 1635; and £1 12s 6d in 1636. Little Waldingfield TB, SROB, FL645/1/2, n.p.

[149] At the time of her mother's death, a warrant was issued for the arrest of the daughter. Poslingford PR, SROB, FC62/D1/2; Burials, 29/5/1699; Poslingford OSA, SROB, FL615/7/1 (1700). Boulton, 'Going on the Parish', pp. 35–6.

[150] Even wealthy Cratfield, on occasion, made use of this form of revenue: 'receyved for the Widow Casswickes goods which wer sould, 15s 1d'. It would appear that even the poorest of Cratfield's poor, like Widow Casswick, had more personal goods than their counterparts in Poslingford. Cratfield CWA, SROI, FC62/A6/157 (1630).

[151] Little Waldingfield (Suffolk), however, had a long-standing tradition of giving the poor both cloth and money as part of parish relief. Little Waldingfield PR, SROB, FL645/1/2, passim. See also H. Clive, Beyond Living Memory. The Story of a Suffolk Village (privately printed, 1979), p. 36.

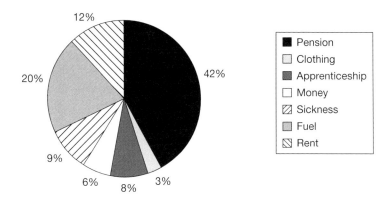

Figure 2.6a Poslingford's poor relief, 1660s

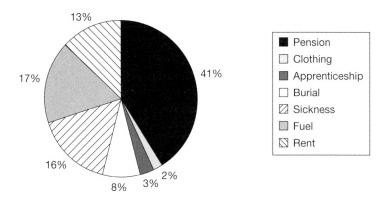

Figure 2.6b Poslingford's poor relief, 1670s

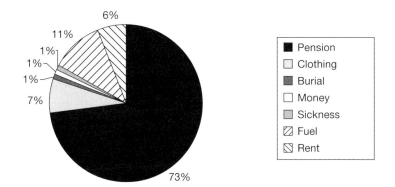

Figure 2.6c Poslingford's poor relief, 1680s

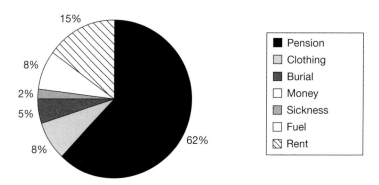

Figure 2.6d Poslingford's poor relief, 1690s

relief spending. This rose sharply, to over 70 per cent of the budget in the 1680s, as the parish struggled not to increase the size of the relief roll, but simply to maintain those already there.[152] By the final decade of the century, the majority of the parish's resources were overwhelmingly directed towards funding weekly stipends and aimed at providing the most basic of needs.[153]

Accommodation was, and is, one of the most basic concerns of the poor. The Elizabethan Poor Law recognized this need, and directed the local over-seers to respond appropriately. The Act of 1572 required parishes to provide 'convenient habitacions and abyding places' for the poor, even if that meant the expense of erecting new buildings.[154] Instead of constructing cottages or tenements, both Poslingford and Cratfield paid the rent on existing homes. For example, the Poslingford overseers paid 13s 4d 'for the rent of Corder's house'.[155] They also paid the expenses of a small number of lodgers, such as Elizabeth Greene who collected her 'rent for 28 weekes ending the 22d of Apprille 1677 at 6d a weeke'.[156] Housing was at a premium in this parish of widely scattered dwellings and its scarcity was reflected in its high rents, as well as the parish's overriding of the period's well-established aversion to the taking in of lodgers.[157] By the late seventeenth century, the annual cost of a single lodger in Poslingford was £1 6s, slightly higher than Wrightson and Levine's estimates of £1 a year for a family of five in early modern Terling.[158]

Fuel, like accommodation and clothing, was another pressing problem for the poor and one of the overseers' highest priorities. Lack of fuel struck the

---

[152] The pension comprised an average of 73 per cent of the budget in the 1680s.

[153] In the 1690s it dropped slightly to 60 per cent of the overseers' expenditure.

[154] 14 Eliz. I. C. 5.

[155] Poslingford OSA, SROB, FL615/7/1 (1663).

[156] The average price of a room was 6d a week. Poslingford OSA, SROB, FL615/7/1 (1677).

[157] Hindle, 'Exclusion Crisis', pp. 128–9, *passim*.

[158] The Terling figure was calculated for the 1690s. K. Wrightson and D. Levine, *Poverty and Piety in an English Village: Terling, 1525–1700* (2nd edn, Oxford, 1995), p. 40.

elderly with particular fierceness, as it does in the twentieth-first century. Death by hypothermia stalks many of the aged poor in the modern world, and judging from the elevated mortality rates of the old during the winter months, it was a threat in the past as well. Wrigley and Schofield's work at the national level reveals substantially elevated rates of elderly mortality during this time. They also stress the benefits that only slightly warmer winter temperatures could produce in terms of increased life expectancy.[159] Winter was unquestionably a difficult season for many, and Poslingford's overseers responded by distributing fuel, faggot by faggot, to the most needy in the community.[160] Wood was relatively scarce in this community, as western Suffolk faced the 'persistent problem' of 'timber famine'.[161] Therefore, it needed to be purchased on the open market, unlike Cratfield where it was provided annually from the town lands. Poslingford's allocation of fuel, virtually one stick at a time, was therefore done as a result of necessary frugality and not due to a niggardly nature.

Until the shift in their priorities, the overseers' spending on medical matters in the 1660s and 1670s made up a significant portion of the overseers' budget. The average proportion of poor relief funds devoted to medical care ranged between 9 and 16 per cent. The cost of a sick pauper could be extremely high, especially if they had been taken ill away from home. In 1680 the overseers recorded: 'For fetching her [Widow White] when from Hevingham where she laye sick 3s 6d and to her in that sickness which was about September, 1680 8s 6d, in all 12s.' The parish also paid for her nurse, and in her case, the cost of burial as well.[162]

The elderly were just as frail as those in Cratfield, still prone to shaky hands and broken limbs. But the relatively youthful nature of Poslingford's poor undoubtedly meant that younger people absorbed the bulk of the overseers' medical resources, and the attention of Clare's barber surgeon.[163] Local nurses and midwives were often paid to assist mothers in childbed. In impoverished circumstances a new child could bankrupt a family's budget. The birth of John

---

[159] E. Wrigley and R. Schofield, *The Population History of England, 1541–1871. A Reconstruction* (1981; repr. Cambridge, 1993), pp. 384–94. Cratfield also responded to the poor's winter-time needs. The churchwardens gave 1s 'to John Myllses wife to releve her and her children in the snowie weather'. Also that year, Widow Thurton was given 1s when 'she complained so of want in the snowie weather'. Cratfield CWA, SROI, FC62/A6/306 (1671).

[160] For examples of firewood being distributed by faggots, rather than by loads: Widow Borley's '11 faggots at 4d the faggot' in 1694 or Elizabeth Mascoll's thirty faggots in 1698. Poslingford OSA, SROB, FL615/7/1 (1694, 1698).

[161] Slack, *Reformation to Improvement*, p. 47.

[162] Poslingford OSA, SROB, FL615/7/1 (1680). See below (pp. 63–4) for more about Widow White.

[163] The first mention of a barber living in Clare is the undated, late sixteenth-century lease to Patrick Hyghehie, barber. Clare Deeds, SROB, FL501/11/50.

Smith's new baby, for example, threw his household into disarray. The overseers gave 'to John Smith's wife in the time of her lyeing in: to goodie Coppin for nursing her 6s; and in money, wood, commodittie and shoes for her children and to Coppin's wife and Ranson's wife for looking to her children and to Pratt for going to her husband to the 13th of February 1683, in all £7: 2: 1¼.'[164] Likewise, illness or disability could also result in momentary poverty, forcing individuals to seek aid and assistance until they could recover and resume work. The lameness of John Metcalfe's wife in 1678, for example, cast the entire household on to relief.[165]

As we have seen, bandages gave way to stockings, medicines to petticoats, as the 1680s marked the rapid decline of spending on illness and witnessed increased expenditure on hats, shoes, jackets and aprons. Clothing was a valued commodity, as Wrightson and Levine found in Terling when they charted the descent of a particular 'kyrtell' through the hands of three generations of women.[166] It was also expensive. New shoes in Poslingford cost 3s 6d and shifts 2s 6d.[167] Used clothing also had an important role to play in helping the poor balance their budgets, enabling families to afford to both feed and clothe their children. But children grew and clothing wore out. Even the apparel of pauper children needed replacing. Poverty-stricken and overburdened with children, the overseers placed Widow Borley's child with Thomas Copping. His bill for three years' expenses illuminates what was considered appropriate attire for a poor child. He spent 5s 8d for two 'shiftings [?]'; another 2s for a bodice; 1s for stockings, and 2s 8d for shoes. Copping also purchased one apron for a shilling and a cap for 2s 6d. A further shilling was spent on neckcloths; 1s more for pattings [?]; 4s for two 'wooley aprons'; 1s 6d for a hat; and an unknown amount for '5 yards and a halfe of wooley for a mant'.[168] The cost of clothing a pauper child only *adequately* for a three-year period was at least 22s. Fewer items of clothing were provided to adult paupers, who were better able to rework old clothes and less likely to damage what they did own. Even the rich, such as Lady Margaret Hoby, reworked older clothing rather than necessarily purchasing new items: '[I] was busie all the day about the mending and sortinge [of] linan.'[169] Therefore, adults tended to

[164] Poslingford OSA, SROB, FL615/7/1 (1684).
[165] Poslingford OSA, SROB, FL615/7/1 (1678).
[166] Wrightson and Levine, *Poverty and Piety*, p. 40. See also M. Spufford, *The Great Reclothing of Rural England: Petty Chapman and their Wares in the Seventeenth Century* (London, 1984). For the place of clothing in the budget of the poor, see Chapter 4, this volume, pp. 147–8.
[167] The price for shoes was calculated for 1685 and that of shifts, 1688. Poslingford OSA, SROB, FL615/7/1 (1685, 1688).
[168] According to the *Oxford English Dictionary*, a mant is a large and long outdoor wrap for women. *Compact Oxford English Dictionary* (2nd edn, London, 1989), p. 1033. Poslingford OSA, SROB, FL615/7/1 (1699?).
[169] M. Hoby, *Diary of Lady Margaret Hoby, 1599–1605*, ed. D. M. Meads (London, 1930), pp. 96, 128.

receive single items of apparel or small sums of cash. Payments such as the 8s 'for cloathing of the Widow Borley' or the 3s 4d spent in 1686 for new shoes for Susan Green were more typical of spending on adults than were the long lists of items given to children.[170]

Unquestionably, the pension was the most substantial part of the overseers' budget, even before the watershed years of the 1670s. It was also the most ready source of cash for the parish's needy. The number of pensioners in Poslingford, both young and old, was remarkably constant throughout the second half of the seventeenth century. Indeed, economic difficulties undoubtedly prevented the number of pensions from increasing over time and prohibited the overseers from being as sensitive to outside influences as they were in Cratfield. Three or four individuals were pensioned each year, of which only one or two were over the age of 50.[171] In other words, only 2 per cent of the total population received regular relief, from a poor population that could reach as high as 80 per cent of the entire community. The remainder of the poor – 48 per cent at the close of the seventeenth century – were somehow surviving with only the occasional charitable donation. As we have seen, this was a far greater number of poor people without pensions than in most communities. Clearly, only a very small number of those in need of help received it. Once on relief, however, the younger pensioners, those with families, received a fairly high level of support, 19d a week on average. The aged pensioners, or, as contemporaries sometimes called them, 'collectioners', felt keenly the bite of discrimination, averaging a mere 8d a week.

Poslingford was poor, and bearing in mind that it was two-thirds the size of Cratfield, the amount spent on poor relief was small. The parish spent an average of only £25 19s a year between 1675 and 1700, as compared to Cratfield's £54 9s 11d for the same period.[172] The ratio of ratepayers to pensioners was 2.5: 1 in 1669 and in the crisis year of 1687, 9.3 ratepayers to one collectioner. These two years represent two contrasting extremes. The next two figures are more representative: 1696 required 4.75 ratepayers to support a single collection and 1700 had a ratio of 3.5 to one. The relative weighting of ratepayer to pensioner was comparable to Cratfield, but the fact remained that Cratfield's greater number of ratepayers allowed them to support greater numbers of poverty-stricken villagers.

In short, most needy people would have to look elsewhere for aid, since the overseers rarely gave supplemental, non-stipendiary gifts.[173] Unfortunately, options were few. The only organized alternative source of assistance was

---

[170] Poslingford OSA, SROB, FL615/7/1 (1695, 1663).
[171] These figures are based on an estimated population of 190.
[172] See Chapter 4, this volume, p. 138.
[173] Few monied disbursements were recorded in the 1660s and 1680s, 5 and 1 per cent respectively. A total of only 28d was disbursed in the 1670s, and no miscellaneous cash payments were awarded in the 1690s.

Poslingford's endowed charities. By the latter half of the seventeenth century, Poslingford had at least eight established charities for the relief of the poor.[174] An additional six bequests to the poor were found in wills, many of which pre-date the surviving parish records.[175] For example, we know that Thomas Golding's bequest of 1575 to the poor of Poslingford and Clare was paid out in Clare because a record of its street-by-street list distribution survives for 1595.[176] It is quite likely, therefore, that the Poslingford portion of the bequest was paid as well. Furthermore, three of the established charities can be traced to their will bequests, including Silvester Strutt's gift of £6:

> into the hands of the churchwardens and overseers for the poore people of Poslingford aforesaid to be imployed and disposed for a stocke for the use and benefitt of the said poore people as to the discretion of the said churchwardens and overseers for the poore people of Poslingford aforesaid shall seeme meete and convenient.[177]

The eight known endowments were not all of equal size or duration, nor were they all immediately disbursed.[178] John Harne's gift may have been set forth in his will, which does not survive, but his efforts to relieve the poor of Poslingford were limited. His gift of 20s was dispersed in a single year, 1671, and divided, between twenty-two individuals, into amounts that ranged from

---

[174] The eight recorded donors in the town book are: William Cadge, late of Clare; George Golding of Lynn's Farm; Jane Strut, widow; Mistress Ashfield; Mister Strutt; John Harne; Thomas Linn; and Frances Golding, spinster.

[175] Will of Alice Golding, widow, Poslingford, 1606, SROB, R2/46/201; Thomas Strutt, yeoman, Poslingford, 1563, SROB, R2/32/61; Robert Elyotte, singleman, Poslingford, 1601, SROB, R2/44/492; Frances Golding, spinster, Poslingford, 1664, SROB, R2/63/305; Silvester Strutt, yeoman, Poslingford, 1637, SROB, W1/93/73; William Russell, yeoman, Poslingford, 1617, SROB, W1/74/50; Thomas Golding, Poslingford, 1575, PRO PROB 11/57 fols 380–1; George Golding, Poslingford, 1595, PRO PROB 11/86 fols 202–3; Thomas Golding, Poslingford, 1620, PRO PROB 11/149 fols 378v–379; George Golding, Poslingford, 1626, PRO PROB 11/149 fols 387–387v.

[176] Alice Golding, widow, left 20s in 1606 to be paid to the poor one month after her death. Will of Alice Golding, widow, Poslingford, 1606, SROB, R2/46/201. Likewise, Thomas Strutt stipulated that 'yerely after my decease so longe as my lease of Poslingforde hall shall continue, distribute and geve unto the poore people of Poslingford fyve shillings at such tym of the yere as by him [his executor] shalbe thought most convenient'. Will of Thomas Strutt, yeoman, Poslingford, 1563, SROB, R2/32/61. Golding left 40s to the poor in Clare, Cavendish, Glemsford, Sudbury and 26s 8d in Poslingford. Clare CD, SROB, FL501/11/15; Thomas Golding, Poslingford, 1575, PRO PROB 11/57 fols 380–1.

[177] Will of Frances Golding, spinster, Poslingford, 1664, SROB, R2/63/305; George Golding, Poslingford, 1626, PRO PROB 11/149 fols 387–387v; and Silvester Strutt, yeoman, Poslingford, 1637, SROB, W1/93/73.

[178] While in Cratfield such bequests to the poor were administered by the churchwardens, in Poslingford they were under the joint control of the overseers and churchwardens, and their activities were recorded separately from the other town accounts.

2s to 4d.[179] Frances Golding's substantial endowment of money and wood, on the other hand, was delayed for nearly six months while the contents of the will were verified. The town book for December 1665 records the following memorandum:

> Frances Golding spinster ante to Thomas Golding esquire of Poslingford dyed in Poslingford and was buryed there the eleventh daye of July in the yeere 1665 and was a good benifactor to the church and poore of Poslingford for by hur last will and testament she gave to Mr Robert Rash then vicar of the towne forty shillings and to him and his sucksessers forty shillings a yeere as longe as the world endure by whomme to be payed and at what times refferances being had to hur will it will appeere she lickwise gave to the poore in monye twenty shillings and as much woode to them as came to six pound teens shillings six years which many and woods was distributed among the poore according to her will upon the one and twenty days of December in the Yeere 1665 to the poore hereafter named.

The names of twenty-three individuals and the size of their gifts faithfully follow this entry.[180] These endowments all appear to be directed to poverty in the wider context, and not limited to those in receipt of parish pensions. Regardless of whether the donors actually made such stipulations, their gifts were given only to those 'which receive not collection'.[181] Between them, they reached between thirteen and twenty-five impoverished households a year. However, the amounts they disbursed were small, in most cases only a few pence a year. Poslingford's charities cast a wider relief net than did its overseers and they were able to assist many more people, though at pitifully low levels.

The churchwardens were another potential source of relief. In Cratfield they were an important element of the poor's budget, dispensing jobs, loans, clothing and cash. In Poslingford they did little to alleviate the problems of the needy, not even by providing interest-bearing loans. Admittedly it would be foolish to dismiss the possibility of relief payments by the churchwardens simply because they are seldom recorded among their expenditures.[182] Masons,

---

[179] Poslingford CD, SROB, FL615/7/1 (1671). Thomas Linn's gift was a single payment in 1683/4, recorded only because the churchwardens originally forgot to enter charity payments for a six-year period. They were recorded *en masse* in 1683. Poslingford CWA, SROB, FL615/7/1 (1683).

[180] Poslingford TB, SROB, FL615/7/1 (1665).

[181] Two examples of overlapping payments occurred in 1676 when Susan Green and Widow Jaggary each received pensions and charity. Poslingford CD and OSA, SROB, FL615/7/1 (1676). Cadge's bequests to the poor were quite extensive, including a charity in Bury St Edmunds and Clare where he left, by his will of 1668, £10 p. a. for a schoolmaster to instruct ten poor boys and £15 p. a. for clothing eight widows aged 45 or older. Clare CD, SROB, FL501/11/165–186; Bury St Edmunds CD, SROB, GB519/25; and Poslingford OSA, SROB, FL615/7/1 (1685).

[182] One occasion when they contributed directly to the relief of the poor: 'given out of the towne many to the poor, 7s 6d'. Poslingford CWA, SROB, FL615/7/1 (1679).

glaziers and the repair of the church bells figure prominently in these records, as do expenses for prayer-books, preaching hoods and diocesan visitations.[183] Yet cash payments and jobs for the poor rarely featured in their accounts, and their responsibilities apparently did not include poor relief.

As we have seen, the role of churchwardens again highlights the differences between the two villages. Poslingford's town house, for example, was primarily the responsibility of the overseers and not the churchwardens. The building's earliest mention coincides with the first surviving overseers' document. In 1663, the overseers spent 5s 6d 'for mending the towne house' and a further 6s 6d 'for straw and haching and haching stufe'.[184] These efforts must have been in desperation, because the following year the entire structure was pulled down and replaced. New timbers were purchased by the overseers, old ones salvaged by the parish, and further assistance came from the constable of Clare, who was paid £5 18s 8d 'for tenbes [timbres] and worke for bulding the towne house'. Potter daubed, Borley thatched, and Edward Burton made the 'hookes and henges and nayles'. The structure rose quickly, and the finishing touches were added by the mason when he completed the new stock hearth and oven.[185]

Its immediate use was evidenced by a series of minor repairs recorded in 1666 and 1679.[186] 'An account of the reparis of the town house (wherein How lives) done by Mr Grigg' in 1685 states that the marginally poor Thomas How lived there, and that he was also behind with his rent.[187] In the same year How paid 11s of his £1 10s rent and worked off the remainder repairing the town house.[188] Again, Potter daubed and Borley thatched, and the mason

---

[183] All references are to Poslingford CWA, SROB, FL615/7/1. For work on the steeple and presumably for masons (1669). For glazers (1668). For bells (1668). For prayer-books (1663, 1679, 1685). For Master of Arts hood (1679). For visitation articles (1667, 1668, 1676).

[184] Poslingford OSA, SROB, FL615/7/1 (1663).

[185] Poslingford OSA, SROB, FL615/7/1 (1664).

[186] In 1679 the churchwardens also contributed 2s 7d towards the repair of the town house. Poslingford CWA, SROB, FL615/7/1 (1679).

[187] It was not unusual to lease the town house to private individuals, while reserving rights of access for civic duties. This practice, according to Robert Tittler, was common 'when fiscal shortfalls made the upkeep of civic halls insupportable from civic revenues'. Poslingford's choice of tenant, Thomas How, may not have proved to be the most fiscally reliable. How lived on the brink of poverty, receiving miscellaneous relief from the overseers and from a variety of charities in 1671–78, 1680 and 1686. Presumably, he was still living in the town house in 1687, the year of the exceptionally large poor rate, as he was assessed 'for the town lands' worth £4 10s, and required to contribute 2¼d a week towards the relief of the poor. R. Tittler, *Architecture and Power. The Town Hall and the English Urban Community, c. 1500–1640* (Oxford, 1991), p. 70; Poslingford OSA, SROB FL615/7/1, *passim*, and Poslingford Poor Rate, SROB, FL615/7/1 (1687).

[188] Thomas How dug the clay and helped the carpenters, dauber and mason. Poslingford TB, SROB, FL615/7/1 (1685).

applied his craft. Ralph Griggs, the richest man in the parish, laid out £2 10s 2½d towards the cause, plus 'beer for all'. Even the churchwardens contributed 12s 6d 'for repairs of the town house'.[189] The overseers' accounts also record additional repair work in 1693 by both the carpenter and mason, and another more substantial series of repairs in 1695.[190] The town house was truly a municipal charity.[191]

The full range of the town house's functions is unknown, but it did serve as sheltered accommodation for the aged poor.[192] The role this building played in the lives of the poor becomes clear when we look at the life of Widow White. Widow White collected a few pence of charity each year in the mid-1660s.[193] However, the year 1667 was a time of particular hardship for her. The parish paid to apprentice her daughter Sarah, and the widow herself received money from the charities and the overseers, plus a pension of 2s 9d.[194] The parish even tried to establish the widow in business, arranging for her to run the Goldings' mills. It was an experiment in self-help that quickly failed.

[189] Poslingford CWA, SROB, FL615/7/1 (1685).

[190] Poslingford OSA, SROB, FL615/7/1 (1693, 1695).

[191] The same 1685 memorandum also includes 15s 'disbursed to Mr Seffery for drawing of the new feoffees'. Poslingford CD, SROB, FL615/7/1 (1685).

[192] Examples of those probably accommodated in the town house are as follows. Old Henry Collin collected an assortment of poor relief before 1664, at which time 2s 6d was paid 'for removieng of Henry Collin', presumably to the town house, since he continued to receive relief, charity and a pension until he died in the parish in 1667. See the Poslingford town book, Mistress Ashfield and Master Strut charity, 1663, and the overseers' accounts for the same year and for 1664. Poslingford TB, SROB, FL615/7/1 (1663, 1664). Surprisingly, the parish register does not record his burial. However, the churchwardens list the cost of the coffin at 7s. Poslingford CWA, SROB, FL615/7/1 (1667). Collin's widow continued as a dependant of the parish. Henry Collin's 'removal' clearly was not that associated with the laws of settlement. Similarly, the churchwardens paid for 'removeing of the widdow knights thinges' in 1663, and again, like Collin, she continued to receive parish assistance. Poslingford CWA, SROB, FL615/7/1 (1663) and Mistress Ashfield and Master Strut's charity, Poslingford CD, SROB, (1664). Widow Jaggary may well be another instance of removal into the town house. She followed her husband on to miscellaneous relief and in 1676 the parish paid 'for removinge of her and providing of work for her'. She is not recorded as having died in the parish, but her children continued on in the community, receiving relief themselves. Since the destination of these particular removals was not specifically identified as the town house, we must allow for the possibility that these moves were simply into different accommodation. For examples, see: Poslingford OSA, SROB, FL615/7/1 (1676) and the charity accounts of George Golding; Strutt and Ashfield, and Golding late of Lynn's, Poslingford CD, SROB, FL615/7/1 (1674, 1675, 1676).

[193] In 1665, Widow White collected 1s from the charity of 'George Golding of the farme called Lynnes in Poslingford', and in 1666 she collected another shilling from the combined fund of Ashfield and Strutt. Poslingford CD, SROB, FL615/7/1 (1665, 1666).

[194] Sarah was apprenticed to John Fuller of Cavendish. Poslingford OSA, SROB, FL615/7/1 (1667) and Poslingford CD, SROB, FL615/7/1 (1667). She was later sent to the house of corrections.

In 1669, the overseers paid £5 12s 6d to Mr Golding 'for the rent of his mills for a yeere and a quarter ending at Lady [Day] 1669 for the Widow Whitt'.[195] In the final blow to her autonomy and in what must have been humiliating circumstances, Widow White's few possessions were collected and paraded through the street as she was relocated to the town house.[196] Henceforth, the widow's dependence was complete. She received both pensions and miscellaneous relief until she died in 1680.[197] The town house was the last stop on a trail of dependency.

Parish 'removals' were not always as compassionate as Widow White's. As a symptom of its 'parochial xenophobia', the parish was quick to record in 'a paper booke . . . the names of strangers' and to move along those who might become chargeable to the parish.[198] The overseers, for example, spent over 10s 'settling Abraham Kerrington at Belchamp St Paul, [Essex]'. Horses were hired and agreements were reached with the townsmen of both Clare and Belchamp in the process of returning Kerrington to Belchamp, just six miles to the south.[199] Given the often large sums involved in supporting the poor and burying them when they died, it is not surprising that parishes quickly tried to remove potentially burdensome individuals. Pregnant women were especially targeted because of the double burden to the parish they represented. Mary Coppin, who had an illegitimate daughter by Samuel Leach, was promptly sent away.[200] The cost of an illegitimate child, such as Mary Coppin's, could strain an already overburdened village like Poslingford to its limits.

---

[195] Poslingford OSA, SROB, FL615/7/1 (1669).

[196] 'For carriage of the Widow Whitt's goods to the towne house.' Poslingford OSA, SROB, FL615/7/1 (1669). Dr Steve Hussey's Essex work confirms the sense of humiliation experienced by the elderly when their pitifully few possessions were exposed for all to see as the overseers moved them to the workhouse. While Widow White was not being sent into a bridewell-like institution, that same sense of public shame was undoubtedly present. S. Hussey, '"An Inheritance of Fear": Old Women in the Twentieth-Century Country Side' in L. Botelho and P. Thane, eds, *Women and Ageing in British Society Since 1506* (London, 2001), pp. 186–206.

[197] Widow White did not live in the town house for the rest of her life; she was 'removed' again in 1673 at the expense of the churchwardens. A full reconstruction of Widow White's poor relief career is as follows: Poslingford OSA, SROB, FL615/7/1 (1667, 1669, 1671, 1672, 1675, 1676, 1677, 1678); Poslingford CWA, SROB, FL615/7/1 (1673); Poslingford CD, SROB, FL615/7/1 (1665–80).

[198] Quote from Hindle, 'Exclusion Crisis', p. 127; Poslingford CWA, SROB, FL615/7/1 (1671). By the nineteenth century it appears that instances of removal were more common in the threat than in the event, since most parishes were content to strike informal arrangements between themselves. The cost of removal and the effects of disturbing informal support structures were often greater than simply paying out-parish support. Sokoll, 'Old Age', pp. 138–9.

[199] Poslingford OSA, SROB, FL615/7/1 (1696). This is an extremely unusual case, since Abraham had served as churchwarden in Poslingford in 1669 and would normally have been considered as possessing a settlement.

[200] The dating of either one or both of these documents may be wrong, or the baptism

However, not all potential charges to the parish were driven out before it was too late. Christian Hudiball was not normally resident in Poslingford, but the cost of her labour and childbirth was still borne by the parish. The overseers recorded:

> For Christian Hudiball and her child paid Henry Simonds in the tim of her lying in 14s; paid the midwife 2s 6d; paid Henry Simonds for two weekes keeping 4s 6d; paid Henry Simonds for eight weeks houserome 4s; paid hur selfe for 8 weekes at 12d per weeke, 8s; for my journey to Bumpsted and Bridwell, 2s for a journey to Yeldham, 2s; for my and John Eagles journey to Chelmsford assessions, 14s; paid the clerk of the assessions, 3s 6d; paid the cryer of the court, 4d paid for keeping of hur child after shee went away, 9s 6d; at the last assessions at Chelmsford gave the counselars, £1: 1: 6; paid the clerk 3s 6d; paid the cryer 4d; paid Thomas Rule for keeping the child one week 2s 6d; paid the widdow copping and goodwife rufe for carring of the child to Bumpsted, 1s 6d; for my journey and expences the last assessions, 13s 8d; [and] for my journey to Bumpsted to deliver the child, 1s.[201]

The amount recorded here is £5 4s 2d, or the approximate cost of supporting four elderly pensioners for a year.

Sometimes even whole families would eventually find themselves sent to the Bridewell, such as Widow White's children after her death in 1680. Two years later, the overseers' accounts record 8s spent on Widow White's daughter Hannah, for 'the time she was at Clare'. Her elder sister Sarah, who had previously been apprenticed to John Fuller of Cavendish in 1667, found herself ordered to follow her sister to the Bridewell twenty-two years later.[202]

The foundation date of this institution is unknown, but it was probably established sometime between 1575 and 1630, a period that Joanna Innes suggests was characterized by the spread of rural, market town bridewells.[203]

---

delayed, or Mary Coppin may have been simply a trouble-maker returned to haunt the parish. The parish register records the baptism of her illegitimate daughter on 21 November 1690 and the overseers paid 2s for her removal order dated 1689. Poslingford PR, SROB, FL615/4/1 and Poslingford OSA, SROB, FL615/7/1 (1689).

[201] Poslingford OSA, SROB, FL615/7/1 (1699).

[202] Also in 1689, the Poslingford's overseers' paid 10s 'to Goodman Martyn of the Bridewell for clothes for Hannah White', and Hannah received more clothing through the hands of Goodman Martin in 1693. Poslingford CWA, SROB, FL615/7/1 (1678); Poslingford Constables' Accounts, SROB, FL615/7/1 (1681–2); and Poslingford OSA, SROB, FL615/7/1 (1682, 1689, 1693).

[203] Poslingford's accounts open with the constables paying 10d 'for the house of corection' and in the following year, 1664, they sent a further 2s shillings to the Clare Bridewell. Poslingford Constables' Accounts, SROB, FL615/7/1 (1663, 1664). G. Thornton does not know when the House of Correction was established, but notes that it needed repairs by 1660. G. Thornton, *A Short History of Clare Suffolk* (London, 1963), p. 22. Paul Slack credits the Bridewell – not the poor rate – as 'England's first original contribution to European welfare strategies' in P. Slack, 'Hospitals, Workhouses and the Relief of the Poor in Early

The politics of the parish, the religious culture of the elites and the hard economic realities of the local economy may have inclined the parish to use the bridewell frequently. 'It is possible,' writes Innes, 'that those of "puritan" leanings may have been especially anxious to promote the establishment of bridewells: it is interesting that there appear to have been more bridewells in West Suffolk, a notably puritan district, than in any other county.'[204] Poslingford's use of the institution was in line with early seventeenth-century legislation authorizing 'bridewells to punish forms of behaviour which threatened to increase the burden borne by the parish'.[205] In Poslingford's case, it involved a group notorious for being easily stigmatized and unable to support themselves, small children and single women, but not the elderly.

Addressing the same desire for good order was the parish's attempts to provide work and a means of self-subsistence for its poor.[206] We have already seen that Mary Durant was hard at work in 1672 and 1673, and was able to contribute £2 12s 7½d to the overseers' purse in 1676.[207] Likewise, we have witnessed Widow White's endeavour to profit from the lease of Golding's mill.[208] Other attempts at pauper employment included providing 'the smith' with his materials and tools in 1685, and Widow Jaggary 'with work' and a wheel in 1676.[209] Poslingford's involvement with the cloth trade naturally resulted in spinning wheels being distributed to the poor, both young and old, male and female.[210] No one was as successful as Mary Durant, nor were wheels issued to all poor inhabitants, but their provision and use underscores the role of cloth production in the budgets of the poor and the parish's belief in the redemptive value of work.

Poslingford's endorsements of the bridewell system and parish-provided employments for the poor were matched by its use of the stocks and whipping posts, whose repair and maintenance testify to their use.[211] In this village both

Modern London' in Grell and Cunningham, *Health Care and Poor Relief*, pp. 235–51 and his *Reformation to Improvement*, pp. 20–1. See also J. Innes, 'Prisons for the Poor: English Bridewells, 1555–1800' in F. Snyder and D. Hay, eds, *Labour, Law, and Crime. An Historical Perspective* (London, 1987) for a clear and accessible account of the English bridewell.

[204] Innes, 'Prisons', p. 72.

[205] Innes, 'Prisons', p. 68.

[206] Despite the acknowledged good intentions of such schemes, according to Tim Wales, most parishes abstained from such projects. Wales, 'Poverty', p. 386.

[207] Poslingford OSA, SROB, FL615/7/1 (1676).

[208] See above, pp. 63–4.

[209] Poslingford OSA, SROB, FL615/7/1 (1676, 1685).

[210] For example, Widow Borley's boy was given a wheel in 1677 and Widow Gowlan, who was considerably his senior, was given one in 1690. For the distribution of spinning-wheels by the overseers: Poslingford OSA, SROB, FL615/7/1 (1676, 1677, 1690, 1699). See also M. Pelling, *The Common Lot: Sickness, Medical Occupations and the Urban Poor in Early Modern England* (London, 1998), p. 145 for spinning done by boys.

[211] Poslingford Constables' Accounts, SROB, FL615/7/1 (1664) and OSA, SROB, FL615/7/1 (1686, 1694).

punishment and work were seen as necessary tools in managing the poor. Finally, in a move more characteristic of urban areas, the parish responded to the Act of 1697 stipulating the badging of the approved poor of the parish. Six badges were purchased and distributed in 1699.[212] Given Cratfield's complete disregard for the statute, Poslingford's response indicates large numbers of wandering poor and strangers – like those found in the cities and towns – moving through the Stour Valley searching unsuccessfully for work in the textile trade, and the consequent need to identify clearly its own paupers.

The wheels and the whipping post, the bridewell and the badges, all set Poslingford's poor relief scheme apart from Cratfield. However, the most distinctive and perhaps most significant feature was the infrequency with which Poslingford's few pensioners directly received their stipends.[213] In Poslingford, pensions were usually paid to the collectioner through a third party. Of the thirteen known third-party overseers all but one were marginally poor, eight of whom also received relief from the town's endowed charities. This arrangement was clearly a case of the poor being paid to relieve the poor. What is less clear is whether the position of third-party overseers themselves was seen as a form of poor relief. Unlike nineteenth-century Essex, they were not related to their inmates.[214] It seems probable that this arrangement included accommodation as part of one's 'maintanaus', as housing allowances were never paid in combination with pensions.[215] These personal overseers, it would seem, were expected to provide most of the inmate's basic needs, food and maintenance. Only in exceptional circumstances would the parish provide supplementary assistance, such as, for example, the 3s given to Johnathon Copper on behalf of Martha Bastard with the words, 'to him extraordinary for her in the time of her sickness of the small pox'.[216] In most other situations, they were left to their own devices. The point of having these personal overseers was to reduce the cost of poor relief and provide accommodation in a parish with a shortage of housing, expensive rents and a poverty problem, a task which seemed to work well.

Poslingford's system of third-party overseers runs counter to much of the received wisdom in the field:

> The formation of such non-nuclear households seems to have rested on the initiative of the poor themselves. There is as yet no indication, for example, that the local authorities would ever have ordered an elderly widow to be placed in the

---

[212] Poslingford OSA, SROB, FL615/7/1 (1699?); Boulton, 'Going on the Parish', p. 34.

[213] Fifty-five per cent of the 112 annual pensions were distributed to a third party.

[214] Sokoll, 'Old Age', p. 136.

[215] Furthermore, those few individuals receiving pensions directly could receive rent relief as well.

[216] Poslingford OS, SROB, FL615/7/1 (1675).

household of a relative of hers. This suggests that under the Old Poor Law there was no interference on the welfare agencies with [. . .] your household you had chosen to live.[217]

Several aspects immediately catch our attention: the initiative in Poslingford appears to have come from the vestry and not the pensioner; that the aged paupers were living outside their kin set; and that the welfare agency did interfere most profoundly in household formation. One can only conclude that the Poslingford vestrymen were driven to such intrusive acts by the depth and desperation of their poverty problem, with perhaps the added and secondary benefit of controlling the behaviour of the poor.

The problems of large-scale poverty resulted in a poor relief system that was different from Cratfield's, as was the nature of its vestry. Poslingford's vestry was closed, with a virtually fixed list of members, and was deeply influenced by the resident puritan gentry family, the Goldings. Information survives for a thirty-three-year span and reveals that there were 132 offices, of which we know the identities of 103 officers. Significantly, town and parish offices were concentrated in the hands of twenty-one individuals, six of whom held office between six and eleven times each.[218] In other words, local power was clearly concentrated. Present too would have been the vicar of the 1630s, including the ecclesiastically censured, fire-breathing, name-calling-from-the-pulpit, just up from Cambridge, young Francis Abbott. If he was as hard on the poor as he was on his parishioners – at one time he called from the pulpit that 'If adultry, swearing, forswearing, drinking, Sabbath-breaking, cosening, cheating and such like, will bring a man to heaven, then there is none of my parish but shall go hither' – then the politics of the parish would have been very treacherous waters indeed.[219] Even the payments of the overseers were closely monitored and, in one case, the town refused to reimburse their expenditures, indicating that they did not agree with that overseer's definition of worthy poor.[220] The elite of Poslingford shouldered a disproportionate share of the poor relief funding and consequently their collective will carried a disproportionate weight in the running of its affairs.

It is time now to take up the vexed issue of poor relief and social control. In its early manifestation, historians explicitly linked such behaviour to the

---

[217] Sokoll, 'Old Age', pp. 146–7.

[218] Those holding office six times or more were: William Deekes, eleven offices; John Simpson, nine; John Metcalfe, nine; John Hart, seven; Zachariah Rowning, seven; Robert Rash, six.

[219] For an extended discussion of the puritan nature of Poslingford, see Botelho, 'Provisions', pp. 145–8.

[220] The overseer in 1698 was out of pocket for the 6s he 'paid Henry Simonds for keeping of Tattersole and his wife nine dayes which was not alowde me when I past my account the last year'. Tattersole shows up in 1699 as a third-party overseer for John Metcalfe. Poslingford OSA, SROB, FL615/7/1 (1698, 1699).

forces of puritanism at work in the parish, thanks in large part to the work of Keith Wrightson.[221] The bond between puritanism and social control has been convincingly broken, as work across the religious spectrum clearly reveals a national preoccupation with order and the reform of society. Yet the question remains: Did vestries exercise their power over poor relief in such a way as to dictate the behaviour of the poor? Evidence from across England, including Poslingford, suggests that when situations became difficult, when the local economy proved fragile, and any time an uprising threatened, vestries did indeed intend to control the behaviour of the lower orders, or as they saw it to impose order when chaos threatened.

Religion was not the driving force behind the quest for order in Poslingford; if it were there would have been more similarities between the poor relief schemes of both communities. However, given its all-pervasive and all-encompassing nature in early modern life, personal piety and outward behaviour may have been the culling mechanism or sorting device used to help select which poor among the many would receive regular relief. In other words, religious tendencies among the poor that matched those of the puritan vestry may have been a critical vector of selection. Some contemporaries would have laid the entire blame for Poslingford's limited poor relief at the feet of its puritan leaders, and not where it properly belonged, at the altar of textile decline. Dr Thomas Archer, rector of Houghton, Bedfordshire (c. 1580–1630) blamed puritans (his word) for the 1626 burglary of his church *precisely* because they stole the poor's money, along with his surplus and communion cloth. 'Chartie to the poor sure they had non', wrote Archer, 'but sutle like a fox braking in the church, they robe the pooremans box'.[222] Puritans, despite Archer's strident claims, certainly did not rob from the poor, nor were they alone in the desire for a quiet and orderly parish, but the puritan elite in Poslingford were forced to make hard decisions about who would be granted ongoing relief from a very small pool of funds. Manifestations of godly piety on behalf of the poor may have been crucial in obtaining the rare parish pension, and were undoubtedly an important consideration to the poor when transversing the politics of the parish.

---

[221] K. Wrightson, *English Society 1590–1680* (1982; repr. London, 1986), pp. 202–6 and his 'Two Concepts of Order: Justices, Constable and Jurymen in Seventeenth-Century England' in J. Brewer and J. Styles, eds, *An Ungovernable People* (London, 1980), pp. 21–46. The criticisms of this view are found in M. Spufford, 'Puritanism and Social Control' in A. Fletcher and J. Stevenson, eds, *Order and Disorder in Early Modern England* (Cambridge, 1987), pp. 41–57. For a discussion of the issues involved, see Slack, *Reformation to Improvement*, pp. 32–5, and for a concise historiographical summary, see Boulton, 'Going on the Parish', p. 20.

[222] Dr Archer MS, Bedfordshire RO, P 11/28/1, fol. 34v. I would like to thank the Revd Dr Judith Maltby for this reference. Some three hundred years later, this same opinion was echoed in a history of Sudbury: 'poverty was rife and the Puritans added to the gloom'. B. Wall, *Sudbury through the Ages* (Ipswich, n.d.), p. 19.

The range, as well as size, of relief available in Poslingford was relatively small, particularly given its large number of poor. Both young and old would first turn to a series of endowed charities for assistance, but this was given only at the very lowest levels of support. Furthermore, only a few would later be awarded the relative comfort and security of a parish pension. Finally, the weight of this entire structure was borne by a small proportion of the population, typically no more than 30 per cent.[223] It is no wonder that so few were singled out for substantial relief. The community simply could not afford to support more people. The old could expect a loss of independence as they grew frail and sought help. The town house sheltered one or two, leaving the rest to a third-party overseer system. The young, 'foreign' and potentially burdensome poor may well have found themselves forced out of the parish through a removal order, while the young, local and able were just as likely to spend their adolescence in the bridewell. Poor relief in Poslingford, then, consisted of an uncertain and precarious life at low levels of charitable relief, or a less precarious, but far from lavish existence as a dependant of the parish.

Conclusion

The early modern period witnessed an explosion in the number of poor throughout England and the Continent which eventually rendered traditional relief inadequate. England responded to its poverty problem with the establishment of a secular and statutory relief system based upon the parish. Yet in the words of Steve Hindle, 'parliamentary debate would "neither fill the belly nor cloathe the back", and it was only where the care of the commonwealth was translated from proclamation and statue into overseers' account books and parish doles that public welfare became a reality'.[224] But even within the unifying framework of the English Poor Laws, individual communities developed distinct schemes in response to their own particular poverty problem.[225] Cratfield and Poslingford provide an excellent illustration of differing strategies.

What is immediately apparent is the importance of local context in framing each parish's approach to easing the burdens of poverty. We have seen how the healthy local economy of Cratfield had a significant and positive ripple effect across the lives of the poor. The 'decayed' economy of the Stour Valley had an equally significant, although unquestionably negative, impact on

---

[223] See pp. 38–9 for comparisons to relatively more prosperous parishes with larger tax bases.

[224] Hindle, Birthpangs, p. 3.

[225] Katherine French has also found a great deal of variation between parishes' fund-raising activities in the late medieval period and the importance that local context played in the support of the church. French, 'Parish Fund-Raising', pp. 116, 141.

Poslingford's poverty-prone inhabitants. Yet poor relief was not simply the product of an economically driven equation.

> Economic factors will determine the ability to give and the need to receive, but will not guarantee charitable disposition nor prescribe the forms in which relief will be dispensed, considerations largely governed by non-economic, religious and cultural values.[226]

We have also seen how religious tendency and the intensity with which it was pursued, especially when Abbott commanded the pulpit, appears to have played a role in shaping the form of the available aid. Economics may set limits on the amount of assistance available, but when resources were tight such as in Poslingford and hard decisions needed to be made, the collective theology of the vestrymen may have been the determining factor in the administration of the relief programme.[227]

The role of local context in structuring each parish's relief scheme did not stop at the vestry door, but was carried on intensely within the often closed and private meeting house. Here was the true locus of parish politics and the heart of the matter for the poor themselves, aged and young alike. The larger forces of economics and religion sketched out the general form relief might take, which I have outlined above, but it was the individual relationships and personal politics at play behind the vestry doors that furnished the colour and details. There were three primary sets of personal relationships at work, at the same time as the vestry collectively constructed the relief rolls: (1) the pauper's personal relationship with the overseer of the poor, whose membership of the vestry was not guaranteed, but whose recommendation was often required; (2) the poor individual's relationship with the members of the vestry; and (3) the vestry's relationship with the overseer himself. The successful petitioner had therefore managed to avoid any number of potential pitfalls and unseen obstacles.

Put simply: just because they were poor did not mean they were stupid, unaware of the internal politics of their parish or unable to construct successful strategies to promote their petition, as the Essex pauper letters so powerfully attest.[228] Poor people would have been well aware that need was not enough and that their petition could fail. Given the systemic nature of early modern poor relief, I doubt that the poor, even the aged poor, believed they had a 'right' to relief, as Peter King and others have suggested for a later period.[229] 'Whether

---

[226] M. Rubin, *Charity and Community in Medieval Cambridge* (Cambridge, 1987), p. 15.

[227] For the argument against simple economic determinism and the pro-active nature of puritanism, see Slack, *Reformation to Improvement*, pp. 34–6.

[228] See Sokoll, 'Old Age', *passim*, for the fashioning of petitions. For the use of pauper letters in the study of poverty, see Sokoll, 'Old Age'; Sharpe, '"Bowels of Compation"'.

[229] Most proponents of this view draw their conclusions from eighteenth-century material and read these conclusions backwards into earlier years. T. Hitchcock, P. King and

pensions could ever be demanded as a "right" remains questionable,' explains Jeremy Boulton, 'since many applications for relief were probably rejected, and pensions could be cancelled on grounds other than purely objective deprivation or physical infirmity.' This view is echoed by Thomas Sokoll's scepticism of 'the achievements in the field of public assistance for the elderly poor during the period of the pre-history of the modern welfare state'.[230] They may have had an 'expectation' of aid, tempered by the *real politik* of parish life. Even if the aged did expect relief, they 'self-consciously *avoided* the language of entitlement, since the mere suggestion that the poor thought they had a right to relief might itself alienate vestry and magistracy alike'. If Sokoll is correct, 'expectation' was not transformed into 'right' until the end of the eighteenth century.[231]

The importance of local considerations in the formation of each parish's response to the poor is quickly becoming a historical commonplace, yet the importance of this data in evaluating groups of parishes is often ignored. Too often, comparisons are made between communities based on the percentage of pensions, the size of those pensions, or the size of the annual relief budget. Yet, as the extended treatment of Cratfield and Poslingford makes plain, comparisons without context are meaningless. On the basis of simple comparisons, Cratfield and Poslingford appear similar: at the end of the seventeenth century, both had about the same proportion of the population collecting a weekly pension, roughly 10 per cent. Further, they both taxed their rate-bearing households at similar levels; in Poslingford it was between 2d and 3d per pound, in Cratfield it was between 3d and 4d. To the uninformed, one might conclude that both parishes were on about equal footing. This we know was wrong. Looking at a different set of factors, placed in the light of local context, the worlds of wealth and poverty that separate these two villages quickly emerge. The bulk of Poslingford's relief burden was borne by only three men and was not spread more equitably across the community as it was in Cratfield. Viewed from a different angle, the cost of supporting one pensioner was typically shouldered between four households in Cratfield, yet this same weight was carried by only 2.5 households in Poslingford, where there were fewer people to help, and where more people needed it. The story of Poslingford as a village under siege by the poor is told in other ways. The ratio of pensions to miscellaneous relief was 1: 4.8 in Poslingford, yet it was nearly one-to-one (1:1.5) in Cratfield. Superficially, both villages appear to have the same size poverty problem. Yet, when these figures are viewed in light of

P. Sharpe, 'Introduction: Chronicling Poverty – The Voices and Strategies of the English Poor, 1640–1840', in Hitchcock *et al.*, *Chronicling Poverty*, pp. 10–12, and Sharpe, '"Bowels of Compation"', p. 87.
[230] Boulton, 'Going on the Parish', p. 37 and Sokoll, 'Old Age', pp. 145–6.
[231] Sokoll, 'Old Age', p. 147. See Hindle, 'Exhortation and Entitlement', regarding the 'discourse of entitlement', although our findings run counter to his conclusion that the aged's legal right was probably 'uncontroversial'.

Poslingford's strict enforcement of the settlement laws, we gain a completely different understanding of their troubles. Poslingford could support only its destitute inhabitants and many not quite so desperate went without a pension. However, the richer Cratfield could afford to pension the destitute, but also the not quite so desperate, as well as a wide range of marginally poor villagers. The true depths of Poslingford's problem are masked by a simple comparison.

The parish-specific formation of poor relief laid out above not only provides the context of poor relief in the lives of elderly villagers; it also offers one of the first extended examinations of how local relief was funded and how it was spent. Charity mixed potently with formal relief to secure the survival of the parish poor. What is missing from the mix, but was not part of organized relief, was 'self-help'. This too will become an important component in the lives of the elderly, and the following chapters attempt to reconstruct how all of these variables came together in the lives and budgets of real people. After 1795, this world of individually tailored poor relief – that form the heart of this study – would become part of the world we have lost.[232]

---

[232] Sharpe, '"Bowels of Compation"', p. 102.

3

The marginally poor

By a survaie of the towne of Sheffield made the second day of Januarie 1615 . . . it appearethe that there are in the towne of Sheffielde 2207 people; of which there are . . . 160 householders not able to relieve others. These are such (though they beg not) as are not able to abide the storme of one fortnights sickness but would be thereby driven to beggary.[1]

While describing Sheffield, this surveyor of the poor could have been rehearsing the inhabitants of any early modern English community: ratepayers, pensioners, and those in the middle who neither paid the rate nor received it. The neither-rich-nor-destitute survived through a precarious balance of resources and resided on the knife's edge of self-sufficiency. Economic depression, harvest failure, or even 'the storme of one fortnights sickness' could hurl such households into the hands of the overseers and on to the charity of their neighbours. Such an existence left precious little extra to be saved for old age. The poor, wrote Thomas More in *Utopia*, were 'ground down by unrewarding toil in the present . . . [and] worried to death by the prospect of a poverty-stricken old age – since their daily wages aren't enough to support them for one day, let alone leave anything over to be saved up when they're old'.[2]

The delicate position of the marginally poor resulted from a variety of causes, but two stand out as the primary culprits of economic insecurity. The first was the growing reliance upon waged labour that occurred throughout England during these years. As certain householders were driven to depend more heavily on earned income instead of more traditional forms of self-employment, they opened themselves up to the tumultuous upheavals and sudden pitfalls of a fledging cash economy.[3] The result was periods of unemploy-

---

[1] As quoted in J. Pound, *Poverty and Vagrancy in Tudor England* (London, 1971), p. 93.

[2] T. More, *Utopia*, trans. P. Turner (1961; repr. Harmondsworth, 1987), p. 129. See S. R. Ottaway, 'Providing for the Elderly in Eighteenth-Century England', *Continuity and Change* 13 (1998), p. 413.

[3] Economic instability was not confined to individuals, but plagued corporations and towns as well. Robert Tittler's study of urban town houses attests to 'that age of notoriously unstable economies'. R. Tittler, *Architecture and Power. The Town Hall and the English Urban Community, c. 1500–1640* (Oxford, 1991), pp. 51–77. Periodic poverty and cloth production were a common combination: 'trading hath declined, and the multitude hath

ment, or equally destructive underemployment, instigated by simple events such as illness at home or complex ones such as a trading slump abroad. Either could force wage-earners and their families to seek assistance from the parish and bring 'destitution [to] some of the self-supporting poor'.[4] Salisbury in the 1620s is a well-known example of how a 'decayed' cloth trade could combine with other outside factors, in this case plague, to toss many of the marginally poor on to full-time relief.

The second cause of poverty was inherently structural: the life-cycle.[5] The nature of early modern English society created points over the course of life when individuals would most likely need outside assistance. For example, in childhood it was extremely difficult to be self-sustaining, due either to sheer helplessness or low wages. Likewise, middle age was often a time when otherwise self-sufficient households were overburdened by children, and when the potential for asking the parish for assistance was great.[6] Old age could arguably be considered the weakest link in humanity's chain. The old could set themselves to fewer tasks hindered by the creeping frailties of late life, dimming eyesight, increasing deafness or decreasing strength. The occupations they did pursue were similar to children's, with similar remuneration.[7] Even when

continued still, we have been abated in our wages and have hungered for want of work by reason whereof we are bought into great extremity and want and not able to maintain our poor wives and children.' 'The Humble Petition of the Weavers of Braintree and Bocking, Essex', Essex Quarter Sessions Roll, Q/SR 266/121 (1629), as quoted in A. C. Edwards, *English History from Essex Sources 1550–1750* (Chelmsford, 1952), p. 44. See also G. Unwin's discussion of Suffolk cloth, local petitions and poverty in his 'The History of the Cloth Industry in Suffolk' in R. H. Tawney, ed., *Studies in Economic History: The Collected Papers of George Unwin* (London, 1927), p. 297.

[4] Dearth and 'the potential loss of the high harvest wage . . . combined with other savage price rises to send them [waged labourers] spiralling into poverty'. J. Walter, 'The Social Economy of Dearth in Early Modern England' in J. Walter and R. Schofield, eds, *Famine, Disease, and the Social Order in Early Modern Society* (Cambridge, 1989), pp. 77, 124. For Salisbury, see P. Slack, 'Poverty and Politics in Salisbury, 1597–1666' in P. Clark and P. Slack, eds, *Crisis and Order in English Towns*, (London, 1972), pp. 168, 173.

[5] R. Jutte, in his *Poverty and Deviance in Early Modern Europe* (Cambridge, 1994), pp. 36–44, provides a general introduction to the structural causes of poverty, drawing heavily on the English investigations of P. Laslett, W. Newman Brown and T. Sokoll. See also P. Laslett, 'Family, Kinship and Collectivity as Systems of Support in Pre-Industrial Europe: A Consideration of the "Nuclear-Hardship" Hypothesis', *Continuity and Change* 3 (1988), pp. 153–76; W. Newman Brown, 'The Receipt of Poor Relief and Family Situation: Aldenham, Hertfordshire, 1630–90' in R. M. Smith, ed., *Land, Kinship and Life-Cycle* (Cambridge, 1984), pp. 405–22; and T. Sokoll, 'The Pauper Households Small and Simple? The Evidence from Listings of Inhabitants and Pauper Lists of Early Modern England Reassessed', *Ethnologia Europaea* 17 (1987), pp. 25–42.

[6] T. Wales, 'Poverty, Poor Relief and the Life-Cycle: Some Evidence from Seventeenth-Century Norfolk' in Smith, *Land, Kinship and Life-Cycle*, pp. 351–404.

[7] M. Pelling, *The Common Lot: Sickness, Medical Occupations and the Urban Poor in Early Modern England* (London, 1998), p. 144.

the elderly were employed in more lucrative activities, their advanced years often resulted in decreased productivity and income. Robert Allen, writing in 1600, summed up the mechanism of life-cycle poverty: the 'diligent Bee or painefull Labourer [who] for want of necessary relief toward his great family and charge of children, specially in time of sicknesse, or in old age, or in time of dearth . . . pine away and perish.'[8]

The marginally poor came in several different varieties. In Cawston, Norfolk, they were divided between those who owned a cow or cottage and those who owned neither.[9] In Henry Arthington's *Provisions for the Poor* (1597) these individuals were those situated between the 'impotent poore' and 'such as may earn ther whole maintenance':

> The poore not being able to live by their labour, and yett fitte and willing to take paines, are of three sorts also
>
> 1. orphaned children above seven yeares olde.
> 2. such as be overcharged with children, having nothing to maintaine them but their hand labour.
> 3. such as fall to decay in their workes, by reson of theyr yeares, weaknesse or infirmities.
>
> All which ought to be relieved in part, as their necessitie shal require.[10]

In Cratfield and Poslingford the marginally poor were divided into two sorts: those who occasionally called upon the churchwardens and overseers for help with rent or a small influx of cash and those who never called upon the parish purse, nor did they ever contribute to it. In either case, they stood on the cusp of outright destitution where the smallest of setbacks could send them crashing on to the relief rolls.

Reconstructing the history of these people poses a particular set of challenges. Unlike pensioners whose names appear with a comforting repetition, the details of those who occasionally collected relief are jumbled across the pages of the overseers' records, leaving the historian to untangle the entries and form coherent pictures of real lives. For those 'painefull labourers' who hovered between collecting aid and giving it, the historian's challenge is still greater. While these individuals may have been beyond the horizon of the overseers, the marginally poor were none the less deeply involved in village life – performing odd jobs around the church, witnessing wills, having their children baptized – and the contours of their lives, even if sometimes only the barest outline, can be reconstructed only through a comprehensive

---

[8] As quoted in Slack, 'Poverty and Politics', p. 168.
[9] Wales, 'Poverty', p. 370.
[10] H. Arthington, *Provisions for the Poor* (London, 1597), also quoted in Wales, 'Poverty', pp. 268–9.

examination of all records. In either case, it is only through a biographical approach and the building of life histories that the lives of the aged and marginally poor can be understood. It also undoubtedly explains why the vast majority of research concentrates on pensioners.[11]

As with many aspects of poverty, the size of the marginally poor population varied between communities. This group accounted for only 1 to 2 per cent of the population of late sixteenth-century Hadleigh, Suffolk; 3 per cent of Havering, Essex, in 1564/65; 7 per cent of late sixteenth-century Sheffield; 12 per cent of London during the 'Revolution'; 17 per cent of Elizabethan Bristol; 25 per cent of England as a whole and 33 per cent of Aldenham, Hertfordshire, in the late seventeenth century; while in Elizabethan Warwick, 44 per cent were able to maintain themselves but not help others, while a further 18 per cent in that city were 'ready to decay into poverty'.[12] The contrasting sizes of the marginally poor populations of Cratfield and Poslingford underline the sometimes vast structural differences between communities. In the late seventeenth century, Cratfield hosted a fairly consistent 15 per cent of its population in this hazy world between economic good health and destitution. Poslingford, with its unstable economy, played host to a widely fluctuating number of marginally poor in the seventeenth century, between 39 and 79 per cent of its total population. By the close of the century, Poslingford's economy

---

[11] William Newman Brown's work on the poor of Aldenham, Hertfordshire, dedicates more time to what he calls the 'marginal' poor than do other historians, such as Ronald Herlan or Valerie Pearl, but the result is still unsatisfactory. Largely anecdotal, Newman Brown reports little more than the size of Aldenham's 'poor labouring men', though he does make clear that 25 per cent would eventually shift to a weekly pension. Herlan, on the other hand, does not explore the poor's movement from miscellaneous relief to pension, but instead makes an unsubstantiated claim that one in six of Bristol's poor would need occasional assistance. Meanwhile, Pearl's tightly focused investigation of London is not applicable to rural communities due to the unique conditions found in the metropolis. Both Herlan and Pearl mention the existence of the marginally poor, describe the nature of their relief, and move the discussion on to different topics. See Newman Brown, 'Receipt', pp. 405–422; R. W. Herlan, 'Relief of the Poor in Bristol from Late Elizabethan Times until the Restoration Era', *Proceedings of the American Philosophical Society* 126 (1982), pp. 225, 227; and V. Pearl, 'Social Policy in Early Modern London' in H. Lloyd-Jones, V. Pearl and B. Worden, eds, *History and Imagination. Essays in Honour of H. R. Trevor-Roper* (London, 1981), pp. 124, 129.

[12] M. K. McIntosh, 'Aid for the Worthy, Punishment for Idlers: Elizabethan Responses to the Poor in Hadleigh, Suffolk', unpublished paper, calculations based on figures provided in Table 1 and p. 4; M. K. McIntosh, *A Community Transformed. The Manor and Liberty of Havering, 1500–1620* (Cambridge, 1991), p. 284; R. W. Herlan, 'Poor Relief in London during the English Revolution', *Journal of British Studies* 18 (1979), p. 46; Herlan, 'Relief of the Poor in Bristol', p. 225; T. Arkell, 'The Incidence of Poverty in England in the Later Seventeenth Century', *Social History* 12 (1987), p. 47; Newman Brown, 'Receipt', p. 409; and A. L. Beier, 'The Social Problems of an Elizabethan Country Town: Warwick, 1580–90' in P. Clark, ed., *Country Towns in Pre-Industrial England* (Leicester, 1981), p. 59.

and number of marginally poor seems to have stabilized: approximately half of the entire village lived in uncertain and poverty-prone circumstances. Village life and the structure of society were very different between these two contrasting Suffolk communities.[13]

With increased age came increased chances for the personal budgets of Cratfield's elderly to break down, and for self-sufficiency to dissolve into debilitating poverty and public support (Figure 3.1).[14] At best, they faced even odds of maintaining a life-cycle above the threshold of poverty, since the elderly were twice as likely as the general population to need occasional help from the parish.[15] They were twice as likely to require a pension as well. This age-related downward spiral may well have happened in Poslingford, as it did elsewhere, such as in Norwich, but it was not recognized by those dispensing relief, and the economic structure of the elderly remained a virtual mirror image of the general population (Figure 3.2).[16] It was not that Poslingford's aged were necessarily better prepared financially for the effects of old age and less likely to need relief or later a pension, but rather that the overseers' lack of response was dictated by the financial constraints at work across the parish.

In either parish, the sorts of people who lived out their old age in marginal poverty were the small landholders, whose holdings did not generate enough surplus to produce a financial reservoir. They were usually working men, respected by their community, and who sometimes served it by holding the lesser offices, such as constable. Some were will makers with enough property and effects to warrant the cost of a last will and testament, but still their affairs were modest. The minor crafts were also represented among the marginally poor. Again, these were artisans of small means. In some ways, such men were distinctive within the ranks of the marginally poor because they pursued clearly defined means of production. A large number of marginally poor in general – and an overwhelming majority in Poslingford – were 'multi-occupation', without a primary mode of subsistence, but rather engaged in a series of non-

[13] See L. A. Botelho, 'Provisions for the Elderly in Two Early Modern Suffolk Communities', unpublished Ph.D. thesis (Cambridge, 1996), ch. 4, fn. 3, for a discussion of percentage calculations. The large size of Poslingford's marginally poor population is characteristic of cloth-dependent communities. H. French, 'Chief Inhabitants and their Areas of Influence. Local Ruling Groups in Essex and Suffolk Parishes, 1630–1720', unpublished Ph.D. thesis (Cambridge, 1993), pp. 69–70.

[14] The total number of those identified as marginally poor in Cratfield was 118.

[15] Thirty-seven per cent of Cratfield's aged were marginally poor, as compared to 15 per cent of the total population.

[16] There were a total of fifty-seven aged marginally poor in Poslingford. For 'downward mobility' with age, see Wales, 'Poverty', p. 380. In late sixteenth-century Norwich a person aged 60 or more 'stood between a one-in-three and a one-in-two chance of poverty'. Furthermore, according to Pelling, a poor aged person had a 25 per cent chance of becoming severely disabled. Pelling, *Common Lot*, p. 160.

Figure 3.1 Cratfield: elderly by status

Figure 3.2 Poslingford: elderly by status

specialized by-employments and economies of makeshifts.[17] In either case, the end results of their efforts were the same: marginal poverty and the constant threat of outright destitution.

How did the marginally poor survive old age? The answer was hard labour, economizing strategies, the kindness of strangers and kin, and the occasional draw upon the goodwill of the parish. In fact, the aged poor turned to their families and communities only after they had made every effort and exhausted all resources at their disposal. Even the oldest of the old were expected to be self-supporting 'until they were absolutely unable to do so'.[18] In Norwich in 1570, for example, the aged poor were expected to continue to work through all stages of old age and physical infirmity, including three aged widows in their seventies and eighties who were described by city officials as 'almost past work, that continued to spin white warp and Elizabeth Mason of 80 yere, a lame woman of one hand, & spin & wynd with one hande'.[19] 'Disability altered the

[17] See Pelling, *Common Lot*, pp. 169–72 for the multi-occupational aspects of employment among the aged poor, especially women. In Poslingford, only one marginally poor individual left a will and none served in parish office.

[18] Ottaway, 'Providing', p. 392, including quote. See also C. Gordon, 'Familial Support for the Elderly in the Past: The Case of London's Working Class in the Early 1930s', *Ageing and Society* 8 (1988), p. 309.

[19] Pelling, *Common Lot*, pp. 141–4, 161, fn. 26, and pp. 166–72 for a general discussion of older women's employment. See also the example quoted in Pelling of a woman with no hands and only one foot who continued to spin, *Common Lot*, p. 161, fn. 26.

extent of work done,' explains Margaret Pelling, 'rather than the fact of working.'[20] The aged's' desire to remain self-sufficient was as strong as society's expectation of it, and ran as a steady current throughout the lives of the marginally poor. However, the price was high, coming at the cost of shortened life expectancy. The harder they fought to remain off 'the dole' the shorter their lives, especially among women.

Neither ratepayers nor relief receivers

Those who neither paid relief nor collected assistance are a segment of the poor population about which we know very little; indeed they are virtually ignored in the historiographies of both poverty and social structure. We know even less of its elderly. Without question it is the methodological difficulties which discourage research. This type of marginally poor, those who neither received aid nor paid the rate, are particularly difficult to locate in the past, being defined – in a sense – by their absence from the very records of poor relief. Yet, as we shall see, they were still considered poor, albeit not destitute. Family reconstitution and individual biographies may be the best methodological approach to date; reconstitutions help identify those involved and biographies provide an organizing structure for otherwise unrelated data.

At any given time during the seventeenth century there would have been between three and four elderly people, such as Henry Worlich, living in Cratfield and categorized as 'not able to geve enything'.[21] Through careful planning and good fortune these people spent their final years in a state of selfsufficiency, undoubtedly buttressed by simple acts of kindness that made up so much of village living. In one sense, women were 50 per cent more successful than men in managing the trials of marginal poverty and keeping their households independent.[22] Yet, if success is framed in terms of life expectancy, women were doomed to failure by the experience, dying at much younger ages. Men, having managed to arrange their affairs to keep themselves out of deep poverty, could expect a long life, on average not dying until 79 years of age. For women, it was another story. Female self-sufficiency, at any age, was considerably more difficult in early modern society than it was for men, since women were consistently paid lower wages, and nowhere was a more difficult life truer than for those who laboured under the double burden of gender and

[20] Pelling, *Common Lot*, p. 160.
[21] As quoted in Wales, 'Poverty', p. 371. In Cratfield there were sixty-four individuals in both the sixteenth and seventeenth centuries who were identified as unable to pay the rate, but who also did not collect aid from the parish. For the purpose of analysis and purity of sample, we have confined our investigation to twenty-seven confirmed cases during the post-1625 period. See also Botelho, 'Provisions', p. 300, fn. 89.
[22] There were sixteen females to eleven males.

declining abilities. The effect it had on their lives was undeniable. Few lived to advanced old age, such as Ann Adam's 82 years. Most died considerably younger, at an average age of 64. In other words, men typically lived a full fifteen years longer. These men and women were drawn from the same elements of society: the minor crafts, the smaller landholders and the lower office holders. The startling gender differences in age at death therefore raise a series of important questions about the gendered nature of old age. Did age override gender? And, if so, under what conditions? Or, did the nature of being female in this society always colour the experience of being old? And, in the most extreme instance, did it cut life short? It appears that when self-help was the key to survival in Cratfield, as it was with the marginally poor, gender significantly shaped the experience of old age and length of life: women simply did not live as long.

The typical elderly and marginally poor person of Cratfield, therefore, was not the long-lived Ann Adams, nor was it the vicar Gabriel Eland and his widow, despite their technical adherence to the requirements of marginal poverty. Adams lived for an exceptionally long time, until age 82, and supported herself mostly through her own devices. Eland's social standing was disaggregated from his income, his education and moral authority counting for more than the amount of his living. 'The poorest curate or humble artisan,' explains Jonathan Barry, 'might not earn much more than an able-bodied labourer in his prime, yet still seem socially close to those better off.'[23] In Eland's case he was firmly entrenched as one of the elite, regularly signing documents, and often as the lead name, as one of the chief inhabitants of the town.[24]

Henry Worlich, a Cratfield native, best typifies this 'meaner sort' of person and one whose life outlines the contours of this particularly elusive group of poor. Born around 1608, he married Elizabeth Kirke, another native of Cratfield, in 1635, and had two sons: Richard, born in 1636 and Henry, born in 1640.[25] We do not know exactly how Henry held his family together, nor did he leave a will attesting to his final financial condition, but his name and activities feature in the village records. His early years of adulthood were bright enough, with all the makings of a promising civic career. He was first mentioned by the churchwardens in 1639, and by 1644 he had taken the first step on the well-worn path to higher office and the vestry by serving as Cratfield's constable. While constable, Worlich was paid 'to make upp the weekly rate the 17th of Apriell for two monthes', and was given £3 8d to share between 'constabll Henery Worlich and other poore men for ther charges

---

[23] J. Barry, 'Introduction', in J. Barry and C. Brooks, eds, *The Middling Sort of People. Culture, Society and Politics in England, 1550–1800* (London, 1994), p. 17.
[24] See, Chapter 2, this volume, p. 21 and L. A. Botelho, *Churchwardens' Accounts of Cratfield, 1640–1660*, Suffolk Records Society, Vol. 42 (Woodbridge, 1999), pp. 146–7.
[25] Cratfield PR, SROI, FC62/D1/2.

concerning the perlements cause' during the early years of the civil wars.[26] Clearly, he was not rich, but he was respected and showed promise in the eyes of his community.

In an incident that not only underlines the unstable nature of personal economics but also illustrates the power of parish politics, Worlich's star fell, possibly condemning him to marginal poverty for the rest of his life and certainly stopping short his upward social mobility. He ran foul of the vicar, Gabriel Eland. The parish register tells the story from Eland's view, with Eland's sense of righteous indignation:

> Henry Worlich had a child baptzd without aquainting the minister at the place rightly called and it is an userpation and an unlawfull invasion of any man so to performe, besidest the malice of mind of them that invite such invader to thrust sickle in to another's corn.[27]

Worlich had a child baptized illegally in his house and the vicar was indignant at the usurpation of his religious authority, not to mention the laws of England. The motivations behind Worlich's actions – be they religious, political or mixed – are unknown, although the results are clear: the abrupt and complete curtailment of Worlich's involvement in local affairs. He was seldom even mentioned in the village records between that day in 1645 and the day he died, nearly twenty years later.[28]

Two important points emerge from the life of Henry Worlich. First, it reveals the position of the marginally poor. Worlich was not rich, yet – at least initially – he was respected: his time as constable speaks eloquently of his modest but respectable position in local society. And, while he was not destitute or in need of repeated aid from the parish, he was still considered poor. The community's assessment of his worth was revealed by the church-wardens associating the young constable with '*other* poor men'.[29] Poor but not starving, potentially active but not prominent, Henry Worlich of Cratfield represents the self-supporting villager. His life also illustrates the very politicized world of the parish, and the power of the vestrymen. As a relatively young man with a small family, Henry Worlich seemed set to reach economic and political success. His appointment as village constable was the first door opened

---

[26] See Botelho, *Churchwardens*, pp. 16, 18–19, for more about Cratfield's involvement on behalf of Parliament during the civil wars, and pp. 57–69, *passim*, for Worlich's activities. Cratfield CWA, SROI, FC62/A6/176, 185 (1639, 1644).

[27] Cratfield PR, SROI, FC62/D1/2 (1645).

[28] The last mention of Worlich was in the year of his death when the churchwardens paid John Cross, the blind iron worker, 'for a lock for Henry Worliche's doore'. Worlich died in 1663. Cratfield CWA, SROI, FC62/16/191, 271 (1646, 1664).

[29] Cratfield CWA, SROI, FC62/A6/185 (1644), emphasis added. For views of the rank of the parish constable, see J. R. Kent, *The English Village Constable* (Oxford, 1986); and E. Trotter, *Seventeenth Century Life in the Country Parish* (London, 1968), esp. pp. 112–13.

by the influential local elite into their world of local governance. These men were powerful; they brokered deals and dispensed patronage. Their goodwill could go far towards ensuring one's success. Their displeasure could virtually ensure one's failure. Henry Worlich challenged the authority of one of their own and lost. If the displeasure of the vestry was so great that a man's upward mobility was checked on the spot, the amount of power they exerted over the very poor and humble must have been virtually absolute.

We know more details of Henry Worlich's life than we do about the others who spent their old age in low-level poverty. Parish reconstruction could only reveal the number of aged individuals living in this type of marginal poverty, but not the specifics of their provisions. Family reconstitution, however, suggests a potential means of staying above outright poverty: the presence of adult children in the village. Just over half of this group of elderly inhabitants had adult children living in Cratfield, as opposed to those collecting miscellaneous relief, of which only one-third had children living locally.[30]

As we lack household listings for either Cratfield or Poslingford, we cannot addresses the issue of co-residence and the household formation of the elderly, but we can draw upon the work of others to gain a sense of how the presence of adult children might have affected the living arrangements in rural Suffolk. Susannah Ottaway has worked intensely on Terling, Essex, and Puddletown, Dorset, with this question in mind. She found that about one-half of the men and one-third of the women, or approximately 40 per cent of the elderly, lived with their children. She suggests that co-residence happened 'often enough in this society that it would have been natural for needy, elderly parents to keep a child at home to help them, to ask a child to move back in with them, or to move into the home of a child'. As Ottaway rightly points out, even the 'passive help' of sharing expenses would have been significant.[31]

Few historians acknowledge what the elderly themselves knew well – the possibility of being mistreated by one's own children. This sixteenth-century cautionary tale illustrates the realities of an unhappy co-residence:

> There was a certain old man which let his son marry and to bring his wife and his children to dwell with him and to take all the house into his own hand and guiding. So a certain time, the old man was set and kept at the upper end of the table; afterwards they set him lower, about the midst of the table; thirdly, they set him at the nether end of the table; fourthly, he was set among the servants; fifthly, they made him a couch behind the hall door and cast on him an old sack cloth. Not long after, the old man died.[32]

---

[30] Fifty-eight per cent, or fifteen individuals, had adult children in the village. The 'children' of nine of these aged inhabitants had families of their own, three were married without children and three were single.

[31] Ottaway, 'Providing', pp. 394–5, quote p. 395.

[32] *Tales and Quicke Answeres, Very Mery, and Pleasant to Rede* (London, 1625?), repr. in P. M. Zall, ed., *A Hundred Merry Tales and Other Jestbooks of the Fifteenth and Sixteenth Centuries* (Lincoln, NB, 1963), pp. 316–17.

The greatest danger of mistreating an elderly parent lay in the example it set for the grandchildren, who would in turn repeat the treatment with their own aged parents. The author advised: 'Son, reverence and help thy father in his old age and make him not thoughtful and heavy in his life. . . . He that honoreth his father shall live the longer and, shall rejoice in his own children.'[33] Most children who sheltered and cared for their aged parent probably did so to the best of their abilities, but there were enough contemporary examples of mistreatment to indicate that the early modern aged parent would think twice before committing fully to such arrangements.

There are several ways, in addition to actual co-residence, in which a family presence may have been crucial in keeping this group of marginally poor from the depths of destitution. One possibility was that adult offspring were able to contribute financially to the budgets of their aged parents, and would have done so without jeopardizing the financial health of their immediate households. Alternatively, such children may have aided their parents, despite the damage it did to their own families. Such a redistribution of poverty would have ensured the survival of both groups, albeit at a lower level than without the presence of an aged parent. Yet another way that an elderly person may have benefited from living near his or her family was the presence of and sometimes co-residence with grandchildren. This arrangement, it appears, was not primarily about raising the child, although that could be true as well, but rather providing aid for the aged relative. Small hands and fingers would have been able to do a great many things around the house, just as small eyes and ears would have proved useful around the village.[34] Finally, the availability of kin undoubtedly aided the aged poor in a number of important but non-financial ways: help around and with the house, the sharing of meals, and a host of other simple, yet vital, acts of kindness. For some of the marginally aged poor, this would have been just enough support to allow them to maintain their independence.

An independent old age seems to have been the goal of the elderly everywhere, and in every station of life. This is not to say that they sought an isolated old age, removed from neighbours, family and community, but rather it was one in which their care and maintenance were ultimately derived from their own efforts. For the middling sort, old age arrangements were set out in wills or recorded in the manorial courts, as land was converted into old age support. These private arrangements spanned the traditional bed and board arrangements so common in the late Middle Ages and the early years of the sixteenth century to old age provisions based on cash annuities which were becoming popular at the end of the seventeenth century as England increased

---

[33] *Tales and Quicke Answeres*, in *A Hundred Merry Tales*, p. 316.

[34] In Norwich, these arrangements were also made between unrelated parties. In either case, the gender of the child was immaterial to the success of the arrangement. Pelling, *Common Lot*, pp. 145–65.

its reliance on cash and credit.[35] This segment of the marginally poor, those who neither paid the rate nor collected relief, were in many ways simply less successful versions of the middling sort, small husbandmen as opposed to prosperous yeomen. It seems probable, therefore, that their old age provisions echoed those private contracts of the middling sort, except that the budgets of the marginally poor undoubtedly called for a larger degree of self-help and continued labour, a time-honoured trait of the labouring poor.[36] There was also one more ingredient in the personal economy of those such as Henry Worlich: good luck.

Poslingford also had its own group of elderly who neither paid the rate nor received miscellaneous relief, but in this village the difficult task of teasing out their names and numbers is compounded by the limited information available about ratepayers. Indeed, we can learn very little about such individuals. Apart from those collecting miscellaneous relief (discussed below), we cannot identify the others with precision. We are obstructed by the lack of records prior to 1663, as well as missing documents afterwards. At the close of the seventeenth century, and basing our calculations on the 1696 and 1700 rate, we calculate that about 55 per cent of the elderly were marginally poor. Simple, and admittedly rudimentary, calculations using 55 per cent as a guide, and Poslingford's 105 known aged inhabitants, places the cumulative number of marginally poor at fifty-eight, including the sixteen receiving sporadic assistance. The best this study can do is eliminate the sixteen known recipients of miscellaneous relief and estimate that forty-two elderly individuals spread over approximately 150 years found themselves too poor to pay the rate, though not poor enough to receive relief. Admittedly, this is far from satisfactory.

We may extrapolate from the Cratfield evidence, and draw from our general knowledge of Poslingford, to suggest that in Poslingford this group was better off than pensioners, yet not securely provided for with certain accommodation, ample income and a trouble-free old age. In their younger days these individuals were probably very similar to the 'poorer sort' in the parish of Strood, Kent, whose overseers in 1598 described them as 'which are yet able to work and doth neither give nor take, but if the husband should die are likely to be a parish charge'.[37] In Poslingford, with its closely guarded parish purse, very real economic problems, and very limited numbers even able to collect an annual charitable disbursement, many of this group were probably closer to the brink of destitution than were the marginally poor in Cratfield. We

---

[35] L. A. Botelho, '"The Old Woman's Wish": Widows by the Family Fire? Widows' Old Age Provision in Rural England, 1500–1700', *Journal of Family History* 7 (2002), pp. 59–78.
[36] T. Sokoll, 'Old Age in Poverty: The Record of Essex Pauper Letters, 1782–1834' in T. Hitchcock, P. King and P. Sharpe, eds, *Chronicling Poverty: The Voices and Strategies of the English Poor, 1640–1840* (Basingstoke, 1997), p. 145.
[37] As quoted in K. Wrightson, '"Sorts of People" in Tudor and Stuart England' in Barry and Brooks, *The Middling Sort of People*, p. 34.

cannot reconstruct the family structure of these aged individuals, nor guess at the role of support the presence of an adult child might provide. We can summarize from what we know of the nature of Poslingford's poverty in general that their lot was not an easy one, and that the key to their survival was unrelenting work and countless informal acts of charity.

Miscellaneous relief

For a small but not insignificant minority of the poor's population, private arrangements and informal charity would simply not be enough. They would be forced to turn to the aid of overseer and churchwarden to weather the moments of crisis when their personal economies faltered or even failed. They did not receive weekly aid, although it is arguable that many people in Poslingford actually needed it, but in Cratfield they collected the odd – or at most seasonal – gift of rent, firewood, medical care and cash, and in Poslingford they probably would have considered themselves lucky to collect one of the annual disbursements of a few pence from a named charity.

Because this group of people left a trail in the records of poor relief, we have been able to learn a great deal about the nature of low-level poverty, about the set of circumstances that typically proved too difficult to handle on one's own, about the times of year that were the toughest for the aged poor and, perhaps most importantly, about how often private arrangements failed. In many ways these aged individuals were simply less successful versions of that earlier group of marginally poor, who neither paid the rate nor benefited from it.

Life-cycle and miscellaneous relief

For most people in Cratfield, an appeal to the overseer for assistance in cash or kind was an ill omen, a harbinger of a poverty-stricken life to come, living on the dole and at the mercy of the vestry. Of those who found themselves seeking this type of assistance, 72 per cent would eventually collect a weekly pension. The remaining 28 per cent would manage to keep destitution at bay and prevent a visit to the parish chest from devolving into regular relief. For fifty-four individuals living into old age, miscellaneous relief remained a temporary solution to a short-term crisis, figuring into their lives under three distinct circumstances: periodic assistance at all stages of life; aid only in their early and struggling years; and for some, aid confined to their old age. There is also a small minority of elderly individuals for whom we do not have enough age information to categorize (Figure 3.3).[38]

---

[38] Of this group of fifty-four, seven received aid only in their younger days; sixteen collected relief only in old age; twenty-two received assistance throughout their adulthood; and nine did not have adequate age information for analysis, most of whom fell outside the limits of the reconstitution.

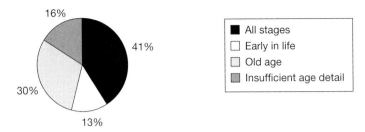

Figure 3.3 Cratfield: timing of casual relief

Most of these individuals spent their lives poised on the brink of full-fledged poverty. Like Joseph Smith, who received casual assistance annually for years on end, they applied to the parish for assistance in their young adulthood, middle age and old age.[39] For the elderly, the least common encounter with parish relief was in their younger years. This relatively small group then continued to live in the village long into old age, without another brush with organized poor relief or a contribution to the rate. At death, some were even able to leave their widows a small estate. Richard Smith, husbandman, received a single relief payment of 12d in 1580.[40] On his death he left his widow a lump sum of £20, the use of a chamber in his house and an assortment of housewifery implements.[41] His widow managed her small estate well and she was able to live out the remainder of her life in Cratfield without recourse to formal relief. Economic stumbles while young did not necessarily condemn a family to poverty or social ruin: some of the village's most prosperous elderly inhabitants had in their past turned to the overseer, without taint, stigma or ill-effect on their subsequent success. The sometime churchwarden and concurrent chief inhabitant, William Aldus, was just one example.[42] The tailor and Commonwealth 'regester of the towne of Cratfield', Thomas Turner, was another. Having received 2s in relief in 1652, Turner finally died in 1678 at 93 years of age, leaving lands to his son, money to his grandson, a £3 annuity to his daughter Alice, and the hope that 'love and peace may be settled

---

[39] Joseph Smith received relief in 1625, 1628, 1631, 1634, and 1648–9. Cratfield CWA, SROI, FC62/A6/149, 154, 159, 161, 167, 200, 203, 211, 215, 217, 220, 235, 239, 240, 242, 246 (1625, 1634, 1650, 1651, 1654, 1655, 1656, 1657, 1658); Cratfield OSA, SROI, FC62/A2/1 (1625, 1628, 1631, 1634, 1649, 1650, 1651, 1652, 1653, 1656, 1657, 1659).
[40] Cratfield CWA, SROI, FC62/A6/66 (1580).
[41] Will of Richard Smith, husbandman, Cratfield, 1586, SROI, R32/242.
[42] William Aldus received £2 10d in 1661 when in 'sickness and distress'. Its exceptionally large size may signify a serious illness or even Aldus' elevated status as chief inhabitant. Cratfield OSA, SROI, FC62/A2/1 (1661); see his signature verifying town accounts for the years 1659–66 (overlapping with his relief payment) and 1668–73; and Cratfield TB, SROI, FC62/E1/3, *passim*.

betweene my children'.[43] Momentary poverty in early life was something from which one could recover. Old age, its burdens and recourse to occasional aid characterized the lives of a significant portion of Cratfield's marginally poor.[44] Physical frailty and decreasing stamina eventually led a number of the elderly to seek short-term aid from the parish. The life of Bridget Spink illustrates the stop-gap nature of miscellaneous relief and suggests a strong will to remain independent. Bridget never married and appears to have been the mistress of her own support for sixty-seven years, at which point she was given 13s 4d 'towards her howse rent and fyerwood'.[45] This was followed only two years later for a payment of 14s 4d in her 'sickness and disstress'.[46] Unfortunately, this parochial intervention was either too little or too late: Bridget Spink died later the same year. For Cratfield's aged, staying above the village's minimum 'standard of living' was achieved through the combined means of self-help, the skill of necessity and the favour of fortune.

Poverty-stricken Poslingford, in the second half of the seventeenth century, contained the same mix of aged marginally poor as did Cratfield. Some elderly received miscellaneous relief, and others were slightly more successful at balancing between poverty and prosperity, but were still never prosperous enough to pay the poor rate. Fifty-eight elderly individuals were identified as marginally poor – eleven of them in receipt of miscellaneous relief – and the strength of our conclusions must bear this in mind. However, the nature of their old age offers important insights into the difference between the two communities. The recourse to miscellaneous relief in Poslingford, for example, was spread evenly over the course of the life-cycle, and not clustered around the final years of life as they were in Cratfield (Figure 3.4).[47]

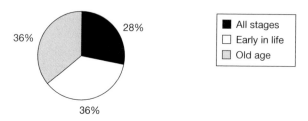

Figure 3.4 Poslingford: timing of casual relief

[43] Cratfield PR, SROI, FC62/D1/ (1653) records his election as register. See also Botelho, *Churchwardens*, p. 143. He was a constable in 1644: Cratfield CWA, SROI, FC62/A6/185 (1644). His relief is recorded in Cratfield CWA, SROI, FC62/A6/215 (1652) and the quote is from the will of Thomas Turner, tailor, Cratfield, 1678, SROI, R73/03.
[44] There were a total of sixteen elderly individuals in this position.
[45] Cratfield CWA, SROI, FC/62/239 (1656).
[46] Cratfield OSA, SROI, FC/62/A2/1 (1658).
[47] The eleven households receiving relief were as follows: four received relief only in old age; three collected aid throughout their adult lives; and four received help in their youth and middle age. Unlike Cratfield, all the elderly members of Poslingford's marginally poor could be assigned ages, or placed within that stage of life.

The ballad *The Poor Folks Complaint: Or, a Hint of the Hard Times* could have been written about Poslingford's Tempest Ranson and other members of the aged marginally poor who dipped into the parish chest only in their younger years, when their children were small and their budgets overstretched:

> Its known provisions are so dear,
> In every place, I need not name em,
> That he that hath a wife and charge,
> Works day and night for to maintain 'em,
> Yet will his labour not suffice,
> His wages are so small and slender;
> So that you scarcely can devise
> The burden that poor men lives under.[48]

Tempest Ranson was married to Sarah White and had two children who were quite young when he found himself receiving 6d from charity and working for Thomas Golding setting up the wood for the poor.[49]

Just as too many young mouths to feed could force a household to seek relief, childbirth and its expense could also force an individual, particularly an unwed mother, to seek relief from the town. Rachel Borley was given 5s 'in sicknesse in childbed' when she gave birth to her illegitimate daughter, Rachel.[50] While no one in Poslingford who received this type of relief early in their lives went on to become a churchwarden or overseer of the poor, men like Tempest Ranson did lead active and productive lives in the parish without obvious social stigma.[51] Things were perhaps more difficult for women. The reputations of Rachel Borley and Joan White fared less well in old age: Rachel was a known bastard bearer and Joan died at age 50, leaving four children on the parish rolls – and at the expense of her unhappy neighbours.

---

[48] *The Poor Folks Complaint: Or, a Hint of the Hard Times* (Pepys, IV: 340). The plight of the labouring poor was a common theme in early modern ballads. See also *The Poor Man Put to a Pinch: Or, A Declaration of these Hard Times* (Pepys, IV: 299); *The Poor Man's Complaint: Or, The Sorrowful Lamentation of the Poor Plain-Dealing, at this Time of Distress and Trouble* (Pepys, IV: 300); and *The Poor Peoples Complaint of the Unconscionable Brokers and Talley-Men* (Pepys, IV: 353).

[49] Poslingford CD, SROB, FL615/7/1 (1677, 1680, 1686); Poslingford OSA, SROB, FL615/7/1 (1679). See Chapter 2, p. 65, for Sarah White and the house of correction. Thomas Bridge was in a similar plight. Bridge is an excellent example of how far the poor rate of 1687 reached down the social structure. In that year, Bridge was assessed at £7 a year and required to pay 3½d, when only the year before he received 1s 6d from the endowed charities. Poslingford CD, SROB, FL615/7/1 (1680, 1686).

[50] Poslingford OSA, SROB, FL615/7/1 (1685).

[51] Tempest Ranson, for example, was employed by the overseers on two occasions. Poslingford OSA, FL615/7/1 (1679, 1680).

A number of Poslingford's elderly suffered continuously at the hands of ill-luck and hard times. An uncomplicated example of chronic, low-grade poverty was Daniel Perry, who collected a few pence from the charities every year from 1663 to 1671, when he died at age 51.[52] His poverty seems to have been bequeathed to his widow, as she resumed these payments immediately, collecting 6d the August after his death.[53] John Collins, meanwhile, called upon the parish at intervals of decades, first seeking assistance from the parish when his young family proved too large for his resources: in 1665, John had three children under the age of 10, including a newborn daughter. In response to familial stress, he collected the sizeable sum of 5s 6d from charity.[54] However, this crisis appears to have been short-lived. Collins neither paid the rate, nor thereafter received assistance from the parish until well into his old age when he received 1s 1½d from the overseer.[55] Collins survived until his death four years later without further charitable assistance. His will identified him as a husbandman and his property was divided between his children and grandchildren.[56] Collins was not destitute, but neither was he rich. The example of his life highlights the weak points of the life-cycle and makes plain the instability of the small landholder, illustrating that economic uncertainty was not confined to waged or landless labourers.

About one-third of Poslingford's relief-receiving marginally poor collected charity only in old age. Philip Metcalfe accepted charity only once in old age, and then lived out the remainder of his life by his own means.[57] Richard Borley, on the other hand, received a steady stream of payments from age 54 to his death at 66.[58] Even with employment in old age, incomes did not always match expenditures.[59] We have already seen Edward Burton, who had just entered

[52] Poslingford CD, SROB, FL615/7/1 (1663, 1664, 1665, 1666, 1667, 1668 missing, 1669, 1670, 1671).

[53] Poslingford CD, SROB, FL615/7/1 (1671). John Green's biography illustrates a similar chronology of charitable doles. Poslingford CD, SROB, FL615/7/1 (1663, 1664, 1665, 1666, 1667, 1668 missing, 1669, 1670, 1671).

[54] Poslingford CD, SROB, FL615/7/1 (1665).

[55] Poslingford OSA, SROB, FL615/7/1 (1682). He was 64 years old when he received this payment.

[56] Will of John Collins, husbandman, Poslingford, 1686, SROB, R2/70/555.

[57] Poslingford CD, SROB, FL615/7/1 (1665).

[58] See also John Siggoe: Poslingford CD, SROB, FL615/7/1 (1663, 1664, 1665, 1666, 1667, 1668, 1669, 1670, 1671, 1672, 1674).

[59] Retirement, many historians argue, is a twentieth-century construct. Regardless of its onset, few elderly poor managed to 'retire' fully in the early modern period, but instead continued to work, albeit with gradually decreasing productivity. See Chapter 1, p. 13, and the following examples: M. Barker-Read, 'The Treatment of the Aged Poor in Five Selected West Kent Parishes from Settlement to Speenhamland (1662–1797)', unpublished Ph.D. thesis (Open University, 1988), pp. 198, 213; J. Boulton, *Neighborhood and Society: A London Suburb in the Seventeenth Century* (Cambridge, 1987), p. 84; T. K. Hareven, 'The Last Stage: Historical Adulthood and Old Age' in D. van Tassel, ed., *Aging, Death, and the Completion of Being* (Philadelphia, PA, 1979), pp. 175–8; M. Pelling, 'Healing

old age, working around the new town house making hooks, hinges and nails.[60] Yet he was also receiving miscellaneous relief from overseers, the local charities, and perhaps the churchwardens.[61] None the less, the sudden death of his widow the year following his own, and her deathbed will, revealed a small estate.[62] Burton's declining productivity in old age was countered by periodic parish assistance to maintain his standard of living. Actively engaged in trade, yet often unable to meet his expenses through its income, Edward Burton's old age undoubtedly contributed to his economic instability.[63] The contents of his widow's will, combined with Edward's earlier relief, illuminate their oftentimes impoverished but not destitute condition.

For the marginally poor, miscellaneous relief in old age represents those points where private arrangements had broken down and self-help was not enough. Such relief payments were not fixed items on the budgets of the elderly poor; they did not belong to the elderly by right, and could not be relied upon year after year. For most people, their own efforts and devices proved adequate – although sometimes only just so – for survival during the bulk of their lives. In Cratfield, the aged marginally poor called upon the parish for help, on average, in only four years of what could be very long lives.[64] In Poslingford, such individuals tended to collect aid over a six-year time span.[65] There was an important difference between the two communities: in Cratfield, the aged villager could and did collect aid several times a year during their period of need; while in Poslingford, with its heavily regulated charitable disbursements, aid was granted to the elderly usually only once a year, and on average only six times in their entire life.[66] In both villages, this help could be scattered anywhere over the life course, from Cratfield's Thomas Turner and his single payment twenty-six years before his death, to Poslingford's Edmund Burton who received aid only in his old age. For the majority of Cratfield's elderly, casual relief was centred on the last two years of life, when the weaknesses of old age were most likely to have overburdened their private provisions and exhausted their strength. Cratfield's response to the ageing process probably reflected the realities of an old age in poverty much better than distribution

the Sick Poor: Social Policy and Disability in Norwich, 1550–1640', *Medical History* 29 (1985), pp. 120–1; and Wales, 'Poverty', pp. 367–9.

[60] Poslingford OSA, SROB, FL615/7/1 (1664). See Chapter 2, this volume, p. 62. His assistant, 'Burton's boy', was paid to help mend the church bell in 1665. Poslingford CWA, SROB, FL615/7/1 (1665).

[61] Poslingford OSA, SROB, FL615/7/1 (1663); Poslingford CD, SROB, FL615/7/1 (1664, 1665, 1669, 1671, 1674, 1675, 1676, 1677); Poslingford CWA, SROB, FL615/7/1 (1673).

[62] Will of Elizabeth Burton, widow, Poslingford, 1677, SROB, R2/66/24.

[63] See Chapter 4, pp. 128–32 below for the nature of male employment and income in old age.

[64] The sixty-four years of recorded actual payments show that the overseers provided such assistance for only 4.3 years in a person's life.

[65] The average was 5.75 years of payments per person.

[66] Such payments averaged 1.3 times per year.

of relief in Poslingford, which, due to its limited nature, appears to have been carefully allotted across the life course in an attempt to spread a little aid a long way. But in either village, the relatively infrequent assistance and the small sums typically involved illustrate extremely well the safety-net role of parish relief and the cultural expectation of self-sufficiency, even in old age.[67]

The forms of miscellaneous relief

The ancillary nature of miscellaneous relief is reinforced further by the source of its funding – in Poslingford by the endowed charities and in Cratfield by both the churchwardens and the overseers. Both villages shared a common structure or framework of parish assistance, but the details differed according to each parish's characteristics. When the personal economies of the marginally poor of Cratfield temporarily disintegrated, both the churchwardens and the overseers distributed small sums of money, helped with urgent medical expenses, and ensured that the marginally poor had roofs over their heads and fuel for their fires. The remedy pursued by Cratfield's leading men took four fundamental forms, the most common of which was a small infusion of cash. Typically for unspecified crises, and noted in the accounts by the ubiquitous 'at her/his want', these payments represent nearly half (48 per cent) of all such parish interventions. The frailties of old age were real, and accounted for the second most common cause of economic hardship. Nearly a quarter of all casual relief to the aged and marginally poor was in response to illness and physical ailments.[68] Amounts paid to the ill and aged could be substantial, such as the pound paid to Thomas Johnson because of his wife's illness.[69] They could also be small, such as the 2s when Thomas 'was lame & cut his hand'.[70] Margaret Pelling's work on Norwich has demonstrated the importance of miscellaneous payments to the poor in times of sickness, where in Norwich it was part of a deliberate social policy directed at the young.[71] If medical care was important for the children, young adults and relatively healthy, it must have been crucial for the aged and frail. For another group of elderly, providing for the daily requirements was within their capabilities, but generating a large sum of money to pay their quarterly rent was sometimes impossible, requiring the parish to intercede on their behalf. The final distinct area for which the budgets of the aged poor were oftentimes inadequate, which still has resonance

[67] Ottaway, 'Providing', passim, and Sokoll, 'Old Age', pp. 144–5.
[68] Newman Brown notes that 'sickness was not usually a cause for regular relief unless it was a permanent disability'. Newman Brown, 'Receipt', p. 411.
[69] Cratfield CWA, SROI, FC62/A6/252 (1660).
[70] Cratfield CWA, SROI, FC62/A6/331 (1679).
[71] M. Pelling, 'Illness Among the Poor in Early Modern English Towns' in her Common Lot, pp. 63–79; 'Healing the Sick Poor: Social Policy and Disability in Norwich, 1550–1640' in her Common Lot, pp. 79–104; and 'Child Health as a Social Value in Early Modern England' in her Common Lot, pp. 105–33.

today, was to economize by not heating their living space. In Cratfield, the parish stepped in with stacks of wood, cut, bundled and delivered to the elderly's door, a task often performed by a younger member of the parish's poor, with both wood and labour paid for by the community. In addition, there were a number of one-off payments made by the parish for exceptional circumstances, such as a non-secured, interest-free loan and parish-provided nursing. Yet most of the time, the aged and marginally poor were able to provide for themselves, and the role of miscellaneous relief was clearly that of a short-term, emergency measure (Figure 3.5).

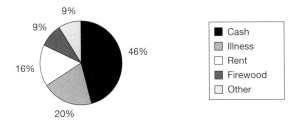

Figure 3.5 Cratfield: type of casual relief

In Poslingford, aid was generally confined to cash payments from locally endowed charities and not divided between cash, medical expenses and a smattering of other needs, as was the case in Cratfield. Surprisingly at first, given contemporary perceptions of an old age 'which not only brings many diseases with it, but is really a disease in itself', there were only four illness-related payments during the seventeenth century.[72] Widow White – at age 50 and on the threshold of old age – collected a substantial range of assistance during the long course of her illness and subsequent death: 'To Mrs Rash for the widow whits rent, 19s; for fetching her from Hevingham where she lay sick 3s 6d and to her in that sickness which was about Sept 1680 8s 6d in all – 12s; more to her in wood, 9s 5d; more to her in her sicknes which was bout the 9th of march 1680 of which sickness she dyed and to her nurses and for laying her forth and for a cophin for her, 14s 6d.'[73] Large sums, despite Widow White's example, were rarely directed towards the sick, whatever their age. The 1670s witnessed the largest general spending to relieve illness, with 10 per cent of expenditure allotted in this way. The relief of ill-health became even less of a priority in the years which followed. The percentage of spending dropped sharply to a mere 1 or 2 per cent throughout the final decades of the century.[74] Medical relief to the poor was simply not a priority of the Poslingford overseers. Cash, and the relief it purchased, was the focus of Poslingford's efforts to ease the burdens of old age (Figure 3.6).

[72] More, *Utopia*, p. 104; and Poslingford OSA, SROB, FL615/7/1 (1671, 1680, 1684, 1685).
[73] Poslingford OSA, SROB, FL615/7/1 (1680).
[74] See Chapter 2, this volume, pp. 57–8.

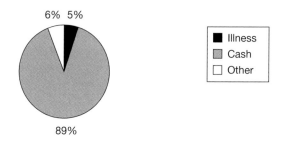

6% 5%

■ Illness
▨ Cash
□ Other

89%

Figure 3.6 Poslingford: type of casual relief

Seasonality of miscellaneous relief

Evidence from the lives of Cratfield's elderly and marginally poor revealed three distinct areas where personal budgets were weak and the elderly's arrangements were potentially inadequate. These were: time of illness; quarterly rent payments; fuel; plus a multitude of small crises in times of distress. Did these personal crises coincide with particular seasons of the year? The records in seventeenth-century Cratfield were particularly well kept and detailed, a reflection of the increased level of literacy and writing in general which corresponded to the years of the vicar, Gabriel Eland.[75] Consequently, a number of miscellaneous relief payments were dated by month of disbursement. Between the years 1625 and 1700, 172 payments were dated from a total of 542 disbursements. Rather than peaking at certain points in the year, a feature that might suggest periods of seasonal hardship, the payment of most temporary assistance was constant and unaffected by climatic changes or economic cycles. The short-term needs of the summer were replaced by the requirements of autumn, and then superseded by the necessities required to survive a cold, damp East Anglian winter. Spring brought with it its own problems for the elderly, only to be replaced once again by summer-time shortfalls to continue the unending demands of the needy.[76] Most of the casual relief to the elderly was in cash, and so too were the majority of dated payments. The elderly's need for money was apparently independent of either harvest or season, and accounts for the constant levels of miscellaneous payments to the marginally aged poor. Gifts of firewood could be dated in only a few instances, telling us little about the seasonality of this sort of help. Rent payments reveal little about seasonal hardship, since they were still tied to traditional reckoning dates, such as Michaelmas and the Feast of the Annunciation. Most of the

---

[75] Botelho, 'Provisions', pp. 69–72, Appendix 1.
[76] The 172 payments were spread throughout the year as follows: January, 20; February, 15; March, 20; April, 17; May, 14; June, 15; July, 13; August, 3; September, 17; October, 16; November, 10; and December, 12.

weak links in the elderly's budgets did not appear to correspond with the weather.

However, the dated payments for illness raise intriguing questions about the morbidity of the aged poor. From this small sample, it appears that the aged suffered two periods of increased illness, a substantial one in early summer and a lesser one in early winter.[77] This pattern of morbidity is somewhat different from that suggested by John Walter and Roger Schofield, who found that illness peaked at midsummer due to heat-spoiled food and in midwinter due to the spread of airborne disease in the 'badly ventilated conditions indoors'.[78] It also differs from the aged's mortality pattern as understood by Wrigley and Schofield, who point to midwinter's 'pneumonia, bronchitis, influenza, and other respiratory tract diseases' as responsible for the national increase of elderly deaths during these months.[79] This village's elderly appear to have been most vulnerable in early summer.[80] The rural nature of Cratfield, with its less crowded conditions and correspondingly lower chance of infection, may well explain why the elderly tended to survive the winter months, in contrast to the more urban dominated national average.[81] Its rural nature may also explain the timing of this morbidity peak. It is possible that the elderly were suffering from illness bred of malnutrition as winter foodstuffs would be running short, and little else was available to supplement them for some months. Their predicament would have been compounded by Cratfield's position in the regional food distribution network. The village's place was to send food out to Norwich and even London, and not, generally, to receive it.[82]

Sadly, even the limited seasonality of miscellaneous relief and its pattern of illness discernible in Cratfield is not found in Poslingford's records, for two reasons. First, casual assistance was typically administered only once a year in this parish and *en masse* as the parish officers discharged their responsibilities and distributed the will bequests of any number of departed souls. For example,

---

[77] There were twenty-two dated payments for illness out of a total of 172. The twenty-two illness payments are divided as follows: January, 1; February, 1; March, 1; April, 0; May, 5; June, 5; July, 3; August, 0; September, 1; October, 1; November, 2; and December, 2.

[78] J. Walter and R. Schofield, 'Famine, Disease and Crisis Mortality in Early Modern Society' in their *Famine, Disease and the Social Order*, p. 54.

[79] E. Wrigley and R. Schofield, *The Population History of England, 1541–1871. A Reconstruction* (1981; repr. Cambridge, 1993), p. 390. See also M. Pelling and R. M. Smith, 'Introduction' in their *Life, Death and the Elderly: Historical Perspectives* (London, 1991), pp. 8–11; and T. R. Forbes, 'By What Disease or Casualty: The Changing Face of Death in London' in C. Webster, ed., *Health, Medicine and Mortality in the Sixteenth Century* (Cambridge, 1979), pp. 117–40. See also O. Hufton for a vivid description of the poor's susceptibility to illness in eighteenth-century France in *The Poor of Eighteenth-Century France, 1750–1789* (Oxford, 1974), pp. 62–7.

[80] See Chapter 2, this volume, pp. 46–7, for a full discussion of elderly morbidity in Cratfield.

[81] Barker-Read, 'Treatment', pp. 114–15.

[82] Botelho, *Churchwardens*, pp. 2–4.

the Frances Golding charity was administered in December 1665, while the charity of John Golding of Lynn's Farm was distributed in different months of different years.[83] Such block disbursements obscure the seasonality of need. Second, few extraordinary relief payments were labelled specifically as being in response to illness, again leaving the historian with little evidence of the pattern of elderly morbidity. Poslingford's records and the structure of their parish relief were fairly reticent about the timing of the elderly's budgetary crises, but common sense suggests that the parish's marginally poor faced the same sorts of problems as did their counterparts elsewhere; the difference is that their neighbours could not afford to address their plight.

Women and miscellaneous relief

In Poslingford the number of women in receipt of miscellaneous relief was negligible, only two in total; while in Cratfield there was only a slight gender bias in the ratio of relief recipients, 1.3 males to every woman. However, there was a significant difference between the sexes in the type of relief received, raising again the possibility that old age was experienced differently by women and men and that, at least with this type of poverty, old age was not a gender-neutral experience. Admittedly, the size of this female population was small, drawn from an already small segment of the poor. None the less, it raises a number of intriguing possibilities about the nature of poverty and the gendering of senescence. In Cratfield, both for women and men, the primary solution to their overtaxed economies was the gift of money. However, women were given money more often than men. They also collected more medical assistance. However, except for one single gift of rent and another of firewood, both to the same woman, Bridget Spink, the range of assistance to females was limited solely to money and medical aid (Figure 3.7).[84]

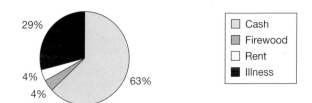

Figure 3.7 Cratfield: casual relief for women

---

[83] Frances Golding's gift, Poslingford CD, SROB, FL615/7/1 (1665). George Golding's gift, for example, was distributed in June 1669; March 1670; and August 1674. Poslingford CD, SROB, FL615/7/1 (1669, 1670, 1674).
[84] Cratfield CWA, SROI, FC62/A6/239 (1656).

Since women and men were forced to call upon Cratfield's generosity at about the same rate and to the same degree, the restricted range of gifts to women suggests that factors were at play in their lives that were missing, or different, for those of men. Given the emphasis on self-help among the poor, the possibility that women were better able to stay employed is immediately raised. Female occupations, such as dairying in Cratfield or spinning in Poslingford, were ageless in the sense that they were carried on by women, young and old, and thus women did not suffer an abrupt curtailment of their employments – such as that oftentimes experienced by men – on account of their declining strength.[85] While this may indeed be true, the employment of this group of elderly women was not facilitated by Cratfield's churchwardens, who would be the source of a great number of jobs for elderly pensioners. Only one-third of the old and marginally poor were given odd jobs by the parish, and those were neatly divided between the sexes.[86] A probable explanation for the narrower range of female temporary assistance is that those 'missing' gifts – rent, firewood, clothing, loans – may have been provided for under previous arrangements, specifically those set forth in wills and manorial courts. A key component of many of the old age arrangements for relatively wealthy, rural widows was the stipulation of annual provisions of firewood or access to accommodation. It may be that for some of these marginally poor women, such items were already provided and when their personal budgets faltered it was not at these points.

In Poslingford, there were only two women during this entire period who collected miscellaneous relief. Their nearly complete absence from the charity pools attests to the ability of elderly women to subsist more successfully than men in Poslingford's 'half agricultural, half industrial' economy. Women of every age spun wool for wages, either locally for the Goldings or for merchants in nearby Clare, and the physical restrictions of old age did not require that

[85] Richard Wall has found that women's income in eighteenth-century Corfe Castle, Dorset, was 'much less likely to vary with age than is the income of men'. The ageless and age-blind nature of women's work may well explain their low but steady incomes. R. Wall, 'Some Implications of the Earnings, Income and Expenditure Patterns of Married Women in Populations in the Past' in J. Henderson and R. Wall, eds, *Poor Women and Children in the European Past* (London, 1994), p. 323. See also Pelling, *Common Lot*, pp. 141–4. In the nineteenth century, elderly men of the working class either worked fewer days at an occupation or shifted to less physically demanding tasks, with correspondingly lower wages. In the early modern period this appears to have placed labouring men in a 'vicious economic squeeze'. R. L. Ransom and R. Sutch, 'The Impact of Ageing on the Employments of Men in American Working-Class Communities at the End of the Nineteenth Century' in D. I. Kertzer and P. Laslett, eds, *Aging in the Past: Demography, Society, and Old Age* (Berkeley, LA, 1995), p. 320.
[86] Rose Mingay, Margaret Aldus, Mother Kemp, William Cross, William Aldus and John Green. Cratfield CWA, SROI, FC62/A6/37, 76, 80, 84, 86, 95, 176, 177, 178, 185, 240, 255, 268, 269, 271, 275, 286, 295, 296, 298 (1562, 1587–8, 1589, 1590, 1591, 1596, 1639, 1640, 1644, 1656, 1661, 1663, 1664, 1665, 1666, 1667, 1668).

they change employment, as was often the case with men. Women, therefore, had a limited but steady source of paid labour that lasted them from youth to old age. The importance of women in the household economy of the aged poor, and their vital role in self-sufficiency, is undeniable when the composition of Poslingford's marginally poor is explored further.

The role of resident kin

Our understanding of the old age experience in marginal poverty is both further complicated and illuminated by the role of kin and family in the personal economies of the poor. This was perhaps the first question raised by the earliest students of old age, especially so in the pioneering work of Peter Laslett. His intellectual heirs have followed his investigatory lead, but have used the changing nature of computers and statistics to shed important light on the multi-faceted relationship between the elderly and their kin. James Smith, employing computer simulation exercises regarding the sixteenth and seventeenth centuries, reckons that approximately one-third of all women over the age of 65 would no longer have any children living. By the late eighteenth century, the chances of women with surviving offspring decreased to a mere 20 per cent. In areas with out-migration, such as the regions surrounding London, the overall outlook for an aged individual having access to their children, and the assistance of such children, was very grim. For those with family, particularly children nearby, their life prospects were markedly improved over those without kin.[87] It appears that resident kin played a positive role in the lives of the elderly and marginally poor of Cratfield, and an essential one in Poslingford.[88] Of those who neither paid the rate nor collected relief in Cratfield, approximately half had adult children still living in the parish, and who probably provided some assistance, even if not always in cash. Among the elderly who collected miscellaneous relief, there were considerably fewer adult children resident in the village. Only one-third, or fourteen of the thirty-eight aged collectors of miscellaneous relief, would have been living near an adult child.[89] In either case, the adult children were evenly divided between the aged men and women. Two possibilities are immediately raised by the differences in the familial circumstances of these two groups of

[87] J. E. Smith, 'The Computer Simulation of Kin Sets and Kin Counts' in J. Bongaarts, T. Birch and K. J. Wachter, eds, *Family Demography, Methods and their Applications* (Oxford, 1987), pp. 249–66.

[88] For a contrary view see S. Klassen, 'Old and Cared For: Places of Residence for Elderly Women in Eighteenth-Century Toulouse', *Journal of Family History* 24 (1999), pp. 35–52 on eighteenth-century Toulouse.

[89] Ten aged individuals had offspring with young families; three had single adult children, and one had a single adult son and a single adult daughter, the latter presumably still living at home.

aged and marginally poor villagers. The first is that having fewer family members present in the community could very easily mean a greater depth of poverty: the group with more family present managed to avoid public charity, while those with significantly fewer immediate kin were forced to turn to public aid as a measure of their increased poverty. The second potential explanation, and one that may well have worked in conjunction with the first, was that these families, both generations, were generally less financially secure than the other group of miscellaneous poor. In other words, most of the adult children had migrated in search of better prospects because their families were poor, and those who stayed in the village remained relatively poor and unable to aid their aged parents.

The poorer nature of these families is borne out when we compare the economic status of Cratfield's marginally poor's adult children. Children of the less destitute marginally poor, those who neither paid the rate nor collected relief, tended to be more economically sound than those whose parents collected miscellaneous relief. In this group of adult children, they tended to share the same economic bracket as their aged parents: no one collected formal relief of any kind. Furthermore, there were three adult children who were ratepayers during the years of their parents' old age. The children of those who collected miscellaneous relief were of a correspondingly lower economic position, again mirroring the status of their aged parents. Two children collected a weekly pension; two more collected miscellaneous relief; six did not receive aid or pay the rate; while two paid the poor rate. However, one of the ratepayers, Robert Milles, may have been stretched to his charitable limit by not only both his aged parents' marginal poverty, but his brother Samuel's similar condition on account of his 'daughter being lame' and his other brother Edmund's collection of a weekly pension.[90] For the most part, the adult children of Cratfield's aged marginally poor were simply not wealthy, or even marginally prosperous, and therefore appear to have been unable to prevent their parents' occasional recourse to public charity.

In Poslingford, the role of children in the parish may be the most fundamental component of the survival strategies of the marginally poor. Unlike Cratfield, where family contributions could have been expected by at most 38 per cent of the elderly, offspring played a much more vital part in poverty-ridden Poslingford. Ninety-one per cent of this group of aged poor had adult children in the parish, and there is every indication that a deliberate strategy was employed by which elderly parents were supported by their offspring.[91] The burden of care for aged parents seemed to ride heavily upon the shoulders

---

[90] Cratfield OSA, SROI, FC62/A2/1 (1654).
[91] Ten out of a sample of eleven households. If this group of elderly parents were co-resident with their adult children, it would run counter to Michael Anderson's understanding that co-residence existed only when poverty was not too severe. M. Anderson, 'Household Structure and the Industrial Revolution: Mid-Nineteenth-Century Preston in Comparative

of daughters, one of whom typically remained unmarried and presumably resident with her parents. Seven aged individuals appear to have lived with their adult children, six of whom were daughters.[92] This suggests that children were an important factor in the survival of this group of elderly.[93] It further suggests that unmarried children were a critical supplement to the elderly's efforts at self-sufficiency, and that cases of miscellaneous relief represent instances where their strategies failed.[94] The remarkable presence of unmarried children underlines the profound differences in wealth between these two communities. It was Cratfield's greater affluence that allowed more children to marry, and still be potential contributors to their parents' old age needs. In Poslingford, on the other hand, economic well-being was less universal, forcing families to adopt particular marriage strategies for their offspring, such as a late age at first marriage, and to 'sacrifice' a female child to help with the long-term care of her parents.[95]

Marriage and self-sufficiency in old age

Lacking household listings, we can only guess at the exact nature of the aged marginally poor's family structure, and surmise a degree of familial assistance from the correlation between the presence of adult children and the degree of the parents' poverty; however, we can speak with confidence about the survival of married couples in old age.[96] Cohabitation would have been an important

Perspective' in P. Laslett and R. Wall, eds, *Household and Family in Past Times* (Cambridge, 1972), pp. 215–35, esp. p. 230. Also cited in R. Wall, 'Elderly Persons and Members of their Households in England and Wales from Pre-Industrial Times to the Present' in Kertzer and Laslett, *Aging in the Past*, p. 82.

[92] Of the remaining four aged individuals, one was childless and three had small grandchildren.

[93] However, such norms may have been internalized and not embodied in a written code, and were probably 'perceived as a matter of choice by the parties immediately concerned even though their neighbors would have reacted in the same way if faced with the same situation'. Wall, 'Elderly Persons', p. 103.

[94] Similarly, James E. Smith writes, 'thus the presence of children in about half of elderly widows' households probably indicates either that adult children were "staying behind" to care for a widowed mother, or that widowed mothers were actually living in a household effectively belonging to one of their children but of which the widowed mother was considered the titular head'. J. E. Smith, 'Widowhood and Ageing in Traditional English Society', *Ageing and Society* 4 (1984), p. 441.

[95] The average age of first marriage in Cratfield (between 1539 and 1700) was 27.3 for men and 26.2 for women. The total sample was 797. In Poslingford (between 1559 and 1700), it was markedly later: 30.7 for men and 27.8 for women. The total sample was 237.

[96] For the household structure of the elderly through household listings, see R. Wall, 'The Residence Patterns of Elderly English Women in Comparative Perspective' in L. Botelho and P. Thane, eds, *Women and Ageing in British Society since 1500* (London, 2001), pp. 139–65; Wall, 'Elderly Persons', pp. 81–106; and Ottaway, 'Old Woman's Home in Eighteenth Century England', pp. 111–38.

factor in the well-being of the married couple; it may also have kept them from pauperdom. The role of cohabitation in the survival of the elderly was complex, and different from the help of kin, as it allowed the elderly couple to remain independent from both family and parish.[97] Among the better-off marginally poor in Cratfield, there appears to have been enough economic stability to allow the survival of single individuals, since in this group only 22 per cent were married and cohabitating with their spouse. However, when the question narrowed to that of self-sufficiency or public support, the presence of an aged spouse seems to have played a decisive role. In this group of Cratfield's marginally poor, those who collected miscellaneous relief, 47 per cent living in Cratfield were still married. At first glance, it might appear that the presence of one's aged partner increased the depth of the couple's poverty. Yet Cratfield's pensioners, who were living at a greater depth of poverty, were overwhelmingly single. Furthermore, from this group of forty-two pensioners, only four were part of a matrimonial union that lasted into the old age of both partners, and in three of the four cases, the male householder entered into regular relief only *after* his wife's death. In the fourth case, the widower did not begin his pension for five years. In other words, when cohabitation ceased, outright poverty began. The couple's self-sufficiency appears to have hinged on the presence of a wife and the continuous, non-age-specific forms of female employment. In Poslingford, 64 per cent of those collecting miscellaneous relief were still married and effectively keeping their husbands and households from full-time support. According to Pelling, 'older women seem to have returned as far as possible to the labour market, rather than becoming home- and childminders for younger families'.[98] She continues: 'in such contexts post-menopausal women appear to have been seen as having a positive value in society which men over 50 would have lacked.'[99] The importance of her presence, and consequently of marriage in old age, is reflected in the household structures of the very poor, which in cities such as Norwich led to a series of 'unequal marriages'.[100] In other words, these were unions whose spouses (of either sex) could be upwards of forty years apart in age, and which were overwhelmingly employed by the aged poor as a means of survival. While neither Cratfield's nor Poslingford's aged poor resorted to such survival expedients, the importance of a married old age was still clear.

In both villages, the poorest of the marginally poor struggled hard to be self-sufficient, to keep their independence, and to stay off parish relief. For the bulk

---

[97] Ottaway found that 55 per cent of all old individuals living in eighteenth-century Puddleton, Dorest, and Terling, Essex, were cohabiting with their spouses. She concludes that it was probably the deciding factor in the ability to survive. Ottaway, 'Providing', p. 395. See also Gordon, 'Working-Class', p. 307, for London's working poor in the 1930s.

[98] Pelling, *Common Lot*, p. 142.

[99] Pelling, *Common Lot*, p. 143.

[100] Pelling, *Common Lot*, *passim*, esp. pp. 147–53.

of their lives, they were successful. Yet there were times, especially during their final years, or when their winter rations were running short, or when the cloth trade once again crumbled, that the arrangements of the aged poor proved inadequate, forcing them to turn to public charity and occasional relief. Ultimately, miscellaneous relief was but a safety-net of dubious strength for the elderly to call upon only when all else failed.

Conclusion

The aim of the elderly was self-sufficiency, even at the expense of their own longevity; the marginally poor had much shorter average life spans than those on weekly assistance. In Cratfield those who managed on their own, without steady outside assistance, lived for an average of sixty-eight years. Yet, with a regular and dependable infusion of aid, life expectancy for aged pensioners was an average of seventy-two years. Similarly, but less dramatically, Poslingford's elderly also found that the struggle for self-sufficiency was typically life shortening. Those who battled to remain financially independent of their neighbours lived for approximately sixty-three years and those who collected weekly relief lived for an average of two more years, typically dying at age 65. The constant battle against poverty, and the frequent lost skirmishes against the same, clearly took their toll on the lives of the marginally poor.

Financial independence during this period was certainly dependent upon one's labours, but it also included help from friends and family, even if we cannot reconstruct the exact nature of it or its size. A crucial component in this calculus of survival was the presence of adult children in the community, especially the availability of daughters in Poslingford. The elderly's reliance on their offspring appears to have been less crucial in Cratfield due to the greater wealth of the parish. In that village, the community functioned in the role of kin, providing a wide range of assistance and keeping the aged individual off the parish pension. In both parishes, but especially so in the poor village of Poslingford, if the elderly could spend their old age years living with their spouse, there was a greater likelihood of the couple remaining independent. This may have been especially true for men, as once they lost the companionship of their wife – and in the process the proceeds of her employments – they tended to quickly move into the ranks of the dependent poor. Still, the key to the aged marginally poor's survival was their own labours, supplemented by private arrangements. Temporary relief from the parish was exactly that: short term, periodic and clearly inadequate for survival. It was a safety-net when all else failed.[101]

The study of the aged marginally poor sheds important light on the nature of poverty in early modern England. As long as the elderly struggled to retain

---

[101] For the eighteenth century, see Ottaway, 'Providing', p. 411.

their financial independence, the grinding effects of poverty would prove to be detrimental to life, since life expectancy for both sexes declined as poverty grew. The steadiness and relative security of a weekly pension had its own distinctive influence on the elderly's longevity and health, but by then the struggle for financial independence had already been lost. This study of the aged and marginally poor also highlights the importance of the local context and personal circumstances in attempting to understand why and how the elderly turned to the parish for assistance. Finally, this investigation into the historically elusive marginally poor reveals that life-cycle poverty, especially in one's younger years, was an understandable setback that need not carry a stigma and could be successfully overcome, as a number of villagers did in Poslingford and Cratfield.

By looking at marginal poverty we have also gained an insight into old age. An important observation is that it was composed of stages or phases: one did not suddenly become feeble upon entering its domain. The first stage, called 'green' old age, was characterized by the elderly's continued ability to work hard and perform well. Only later, in mature old age, were the physical demands of labour too taxing.[102] We can see this gradual decline of capabilities in Cratfield, where the disbursement of miscellaneous relief was *ad hoc* and not tied to set days as it was in Poslingford. These people may have been old, but they kept themselves housed, fed and cared for until the end when the parish began to step in and ease their burdens.

The experience of old age in poverty was immensely complex, consisting not only of gender distinctions and distortions, but also of the changes wrought by poverty itself. The matrix for understanding this experience is greater than a simple two-by-one, poverty and sex, framework. Indeed, it is greater than a three-by-two paradigm where the experience of old age must be examined across three levels of poverty (two types of marginal poverty and pauperdom) and between two genders. It must take into consideration the presence or absence of adult kin, one's marital status, the reputation of the elderly individual and how it may have influenced his or her receipt of relief, as well as the many stages that make up old age itself – as one most certainly did not immediately become frail and debilitated.

---

[102] L. A. Botelho, 'Old Age and Menopause in Rural Women of Early Modern Suffolk' in Botelho and Thane, *Women and Ageing*, p. 47.

4

The aged parish pensioner

Parish paupers, that 'multitude of poor and needy folks', hovered near the bottom of early modern England's social hierarchy.[1] Constituting the final rung of respectable society, they were only a mis-step away from the world of the idle and the vagrant.[2] The elderly members of this group, however, held the place of highest honour, and were considered by many to be the quint-essential worthy poor. Key to their rank was their position at the conjunction of two themes of contemporary thought: discriminatory poor relief and respect for the elderly. Throughout the period, society was obsessed with separating out the truly poor from the merely lazy and was equally concerned to direct all charitable efforts into the hands of the deserving. The aged poor fulfilled this brief with distinction. No one could blame them for their failing physical abilities, for their loss of labour, or their eventual need of aid: they were poor through no fault of their own. The elderly formed, along with widows and orphans, a trinity of worthy poor. Statutes ordered their relief, and sermons, treatises and pamphlets joined together to form a chorus calling for charitable aid to be given to these 'aged decayed and ympotent poor people'.[3]

Despite their poverty, aged paupers were still to be accorded the respect due their years. As William Gouge wrote in his 'Epistle to the Reader' of Thomas Sheafe's *Vindiciae Senectutis, or, A Plea for Old-Age*:

> Old Age hath in all ages beene much honoured. So it is among the Heathen: so much more ought it be among Gods people. The Lord himselfe giveth his charge (Lev. 19. 22) *Thou shalt rise up before the hoary-head, and honour the face of the Old-Man, and feare thy God* ... our feare of God, who is invisible, is testified by our reverence to those that visibly beare his Image, as Old-Men doe. For God himselfe is stiled [styled] (Dan. 7.9) *the Ancient of daies, and the haire of his head* is said to be

---

[1] Quoting W. Marshal, *The Forme and Maner of Subvention of Helping for Pore People* in F. R. Salter, ed., *Some Early Tracts on Poor Relief* (London, 1926), p. 37.
[2] While contemporaries may have considered the vagrant as being 'vile, wretched and [of] filthy purposes', A. L. Beier has demonstrated that most of those arrested for vagrancy were in fact simply unemployed and travelling in search of work; the line between respectable poverty and punishable idleness was in fact faint and uncertain. A. L. Beier, 'Vagrants and the Social Order in Elizabethan England', *Past and Present* 64 (1974), esp. p. 21. Quoting P. L. Hughes and J. F. Larkin, eds, *Tudor Royal Proclamations*, Vol. I (New Haven, CT, 1964–69), No. 250.
[3] Quoting 13 Eliz. I. C. 25.

like pure wooll, that is white, not spotted, not stained, not soiled: such as the haire of Old-men useth to be.[4]

As scripture required people to honour and respect old age, God also punished those, especially youth, who mocked it. According to John Strype, 'and God did most signally once punish a parcel of loose youths, for despising an aged, holy man, and crying to him in derision, *Go up, thou bald pate, Go up, thou bald Pate,* 2 King.ii.23. They were torn in pieces, forty-two of them at once by bears out of the wood.'[5] Given their divine backing, the aged poor should have been awarded a position of privilege in early modern society.

Elderly men, moreover, were blessed with the 'graces and vertues of Old-Age': knowledge, faith, wisdom, patience, steadfastness, temperance and love, themes echoed in any number of tracts and sermons.[6] The venerable status of the aged was reinforced by the continuation of the traditional Christian teachings of charity to the poor, including this mid-seventeenth-century interpretation of 'Proverbs or Sentences of the Old-Age to the Child-hood or Youth': 'Turn not right into wrong, nor take from the poor his bread: help to deliver the Captive, and distribute thy bread to the poor: then shall the Lord cause his light to rise upon thee, like the Sun of Heaven.'[7]

On the surface, the aged gave every indication of being able to receive relief upon demand: their failing bodies were not their fault and society was inundated with commandments to 'stand, and honour thy hoary head'. Yet there is often a world of difference between theory and fact. Not all aged individuals were honourable, nor was every knee bent before the ancient members of the parish. While their advanced age undoubtedly gave them an important negotiating platform when approaching the overseer for a pension, the aged poor were still members of the politicized parish and still under the scrutiny of the vestry. Widow Margaret Doughty of Salford, Warwickshire, for example, temporarily had her pension cancelled until her behaviour fell into line with the vestry's expectations. In 1633, fourteen years after her

---

[4] T. Sheafe, *Vindiciae Senectutis, or, A Plea for Old-Age* (London, 1639), B2.
[5] J. Strype, *Lessons Moral and Christian for Youth and Old Age; In Two Sermons Preach'd at Guildhall Chappel,* London (London, 1699), p. 96.
[6] R. Steele, *A Discourse Concerning Old-Age* (London, 1688), pp. 79–128. Examples are many, but see *A Spiritual Journey of a Young Man* (London, 1659), which is a dialogue between 'old-age' and a 'young man'; and the printed funeral sermon by Fulk Bellers, *Abrahams Interment: Or, The Good Old-Mans Buriall in a Good Old Age* (London, 1656); but esp. George Estey, *A Most Sweete and Comfortable Exposition, upon the Tenne Commaundements, and upon the 51. Psalme* (London, 1602), N7v, O1–O1v, who presents an entire section on honour due to parents, magistrates and schoolmasters, 'who signifie all supervisours whatsoever', and the elderly in general: 'Out of the house in civill life the elder for yeares, especially he or shee who is so many yeares before us as they might be our father or mother: for so they did adore such as for yeares might have been their children.' Estey was rare in his explicit reference to the honour owed to aged women.
[7] Quotes from *Spiritual Journey of a Young Man,* pp. 80, 92.

first pension, Widow Doughty had 'grown clamorous' and acted 'in a very peremptory manner as if she were careless of the benefit of the said collection or at least altogether unthankful' for it. The magistrates then ordered her pension to be stopped until she began to 'behave and demean herself peaceably and orderly', as well as to exhibit herself 'thankful of the same'.[8] There was, as the elderly themselves must have known, no pension by right, no age of entitlement, no tenure to their relief.[9] They may have *expected* to receive relief because of their increasing physical disabilities and society's claims of gerontocratic respect, but the aged poor were wise enough not to *demand* it. The risk of alienating magistrate or vestry was too great and the potential loss of assistance too life-threatening. Even the consequences of having one's assistance reduced, but not cancelled, would probably have threatened one's very survival. While nearly all aged applicants to the parish purse may have received some level of relief, they were not likely to claim it by right.

Sixteenth- and seventeenth-century England experienced the 'birthpangs' of the English welfare state, but not its actual birth.[10] People were not yet paying

---

[8] As quoted in S. Hindle, 'Exhortation and Entitlement: Negotiating Inequality in English Rural Communities, 1550–1650' in M. Braddick and J. Walter, eds, *Negotiating Power in Early Modern Society: Order, Hierarchy and Subordination in Early Modern Britain and Ireland* (Cambridge, 2001).

[9] J. Boulton, 'Going on the Parish: The Parish Pension and its Meanings in the London Suburbs, 1640–1724' in T. Hitchcock, P. King and P. Sharpe, eds, *Chronicling Poverty: The Voices and Strategies of the English Poor, 1640–1840* (Basingstoke, 1997), p. 37; Hindle, 'Exhortation and Entitlement'; and T. Sokoll, 'Old Age in Poverty: The Record of Essex Pauper Letters, 1782–1834' in *Chronicling Poverty*, pp. 145–6. However, Mary Barker-Read, in her pioneering work on the aged poor, argued for an informal age requirement for a parish pension. In support, she cites instances where younger people received miscellaneous relief every month and at the same level as old age pensions. Thus she concluded that 'pensions' were confined to the elderly. M. Barker-Read, 'The Treatment of the Aged Poor in Five Selected West Kent Parishes from Settlement to Speenhamland (1662–1797)', unpublished Ph.D. thesis (Open University, 1988), pp. 163–4. Others who argue for a right to relief include: W. Apfel and P. Dunkley, 'English Rural Society and the New Poor Law: Bedfordshire, 1834–47', *Social History* 10 (1985), pp. 56–60; T. Hitchcock, P. King and P. Sharpe, 'Introduction: Chronicling Poverty – The Voices and Strategies of the English Poor, 1640–1840' in *Chronicling Poverty*, pp. 26–33; L. H. Lees, *The Solidarities of Strangers. The English Poor Laws and the People, 1700–1990* (Cambridge, 1998), pp. 11–12 and her 'The Survival of the Unfit: Welfare Policies and Family Maintenance in Nineteenth-Century London' in P. Mandler, ed., *The Uses of Charity: The Poor on Relief in the Nineteenth-Century Metropolis* (Philadelphia, PA, 1990), pp. 68–91; M. H. D. van Leeuwen, 'Logic of Charity: Poor Relief in Preindustrial Europe', *Journal of Interdisciplinary History* 24 (1994), esp. pp. 607–9; P. Sharpe, '"The Bowels of Compation": A Labouring Family and the Law, c. 1790–1834' in *Chronicling Poverty*, p. 87; E. P. Thompson, 'The Moral Economy of the English Crowd in the Eighteenth-Century', *Past and Present* 50 (1971), p. 136; and S. J. Woolf, *The Poor in Western Europe in the Eighteenth and Nineteenth Centuries* (London, 1986), p. 39.

[10] For the application of this term to the development of the Old Poor Law, see S. Hindle, *The Birthpangs of Welfare: Poor Relief and Parish Governance in Seventeenth-Century Warwickshire* (Dugdale Society Occasional Papers No. 42, 2000).

into the system, in this case through the poor rate, with the expectation of some day drawing upon the system themselves in old age. Historians, such as P. King, who have made such claims have tended to do so by extrapolating their conclusions, based on the eighteenth and nineteenth centuries, into an earlier period. In fact, there were very few individuals whose lives crossed from rate-payer to recipient during the early modern period. Whitchurch, Oxfordshire, was rare in witnessing the 'ultimate convergence', when an overseer became a stipendiary in old age.[11] No one in Poslingford ever found themselves in that position, while in Cratfield, only four individuals crossed the line from taxpayer to collectioner, including the economic free-fall of the former churchwarden William Orford.[12]

Orford is a classic example of how ill-luck and illness could force an otherwise prosperous individual on to parish provisions during old age. Orford served as churchwarden in 1583 and became a parish pauper in 1590. His troubles began only in old age, were compounded by the demands of his family, and were confirmed by the fragility of his own breaking bones. Born around 1519 and married in 1546 to local Cratfield woman Ann Carter, Orford prospered. A child, Ann, was born in 1556, and ten years later William was assessed at £5 in goods for the subsidy. He was active in the parish, serving not only as churchwarden but also boarding a child found in the church porch.[13] Only in his early sixties did Orford require financial assistance, initially in the form of a 20s loan in 1677. Small gifts of money were the order for the next several years, but after an illness in 1582, Orford's financial problems multiplied. In that year he received over 3s 'when he was sicke' and an additional 20s in loans. The following year the churchwardens paid him 40s more, and noted in their accounts that it was for 'when his daughter was to be married'. By 1590 Orford was receiving a weekly pension of 6d, the odd load of firewood and a great deal of clothing. By 1595 his stipend was increased to a shilling a week; his house was in a perpetual state of collapse, followed by an equally perpetual series of parish-funded repairs; he needed shoes; and 10s was spent in 1597 'for setting of Orfers leg', a sure sign of ageing and brittle bones.[14]

Men with Orford's earlier status were uncommon among aged pensioners, who otherwise comprised day labourers, poor husbandmen, and the widows of

[11] This happened three times in Whitchurch between 1665 and 1774. R. Adair, 'Pensioners Under the Poor Law in Early Modern England' (unpublished paper, 1992), p. 20.
[12] The remaining pensioners cum ratepayers were William Stannard, his wife Christian, and Richard Chattin. Cratfield OSA, SROI, FC62/A2/1 (1679, 1680, 1682, 1683, 1684, 1685, 1686, 1687, 1688, 1689, 1694, 1695, 1696, 1697, 1698, 1699, 1700); and Cratfield CWA, SROI, FC62/A6/334 (1680).
[13] Cratfield CWA, SROI, FC62/A6/204 (1650) and L. A. Botelho, *Churchwardens' Accounts of Cratfield, 1640–1660*, Suffolk Records Society, Vol. 42 (Woodbridge, 1999), p. 7.
[14] *Suffolk in 1568, Being the Return for a Subsidy Granted in 1566*, Suffolk Green Books (Bury St Edmunds, 1909); Cratfield CWA, SROI, FC62/A6/49, 52, 63, 66, 69, 85, 86, 87, 90, 93, 94, 98, 99, 104 (1569, 1572, 1577, 1580, 1583, 1590, 1591, 1595, 1597, 1598, 1599).

soldiers and sextons.[15] In Cratfield, aged pensions included two former tailors, a thatcher, a sexton and one husbandman. The depths of Poslingford's poverty are again stressed by the even lower overall status of its pensioners. No stipendiary, it appears, had ever followed a specific trade, but were instead lifelong wage labourers existing on a series of temporary contracts. For the most part, the parish stipend was not an early pensioning scheme for the hard-working ratepayer, so that he might cease his labours in old age. Instead it was the last stop for the marginally poor and humble, and only occasionally for the very unlucky ratepayer, on a long slide into dependent poverty.

The outline of relief

The elderly who eventually found themselves at the rural overseer's door asking for relief, or having a letter written to the local magistrate, would not have suddenly ended up in this unenviable position, but would have arrived at this point after a long, hard-fought battle with poverty. Furthermore, each community developed its own patterns of poverty and poor relief. In the rural villages of Cratfield and Poslingford, only 1 per cent of the elderly population would seek public support, despite Poslingford's exponentially greater poverty.[16] Put another way, by the end of the seventeenth century the elderly made up 7 per cent of Poslingford's pensioners, and 20 per cent in Cratfield. Clearly, given its relatively low occurrence, public support was not the first line of defence against the problems of old age.

Despite the public's stated commitment to care for the aged and impotent, the level and nature of that care was not consistent across the breadth of England. Susannah Ottaway has outlined the contours of the regional variation in the relief of the aged poor, divisions that remained fundamentally in place until the nineteenth century. The South/East region was relatively gener-ous in its provision for the aged poor, especially when compared to the more parsimonious North/Northwest, and the relatively moderate Midlands region. Ottaway suggests four possible explanations for these regional variations: cost of living, patterns of migration, 'socio-cultural assumptions about the role of poor relief', and economic structures. The shape of eighteenth-century relief, Ottaway argues, actually pivoted on the economies of each village, more

[15] See T. Arkell, 'The Incidence of Poverty in England in the Later Seventeenth Century', *Social History* 12 (1987), p. 36; and P. Slack, 'Poverty and Politics in Salisbury, 1597–1666' in P. Clark and P. Slack, eds, *Crisis and Order in English Towns, 1500–1700* (London, 1972), Table 13, p. 182.
[16] Susannah Ottaway's work on eighteenth-century Terling, Essex, and Puddletown, Dorset, indicates that this is an unusually low percentage of elderly people on regular relief. In her case studies, the percentage of the elderly on relief ranges between 4 and 33 per cent, with a strong trend towards more elderly on relief as the eighteen century develops. S. R. Ottaway, *'The Decline of Life': Old Age in Eighteenth-Century England* (Cambridge, 2004), Table 6.5.

so than on any other influencing factor.[17] It appears that the importance of local economic structures was as true for the sixteenth and seventeenth centuries as it was for the eighteenth. Cratfield and Poslingford are located firmly in the more generous South/East region; yet the role of economics continues to operate *within* these broader regions and in ways similar to those post-figured by Ottaway's eighteenth-century scheme. Villages tied to the wobbly economies of proto-industrialization, such as Poslingford, may well have pensioned fewer people and at lower levels of relief for several reasons: the overall poverty associated with an unstable market and the availability of short-term, part-time employment that characterized the proto- and early industrial revolution.[18]

In Cratfield, there would seldom be more than three or four aged pensioners in any year, while in the financially overburdened parish of Poslingford, enough money for only one or two aged people a year was collected. Cratfield's elderly poor would first turn to their parish officers for occasional assistance, small sums of cash, the annulment of their rates, or the payment of their rents. This *ad hoc* relief typically began in the individual's late forties and would continue at relatively low levels of aid for fourteen years. As the poor aged, their aid grew slowly in size and frequency, until their early sixties when casual assistance rolled into regular relief at about 1s a week. The typical pattern of relief for the aged poor of Poslingford shared many of the same outward characteristics with Cratfield, yet there were important differences in the details. Poslingford's indigent elderly did not suddenly receive a parish pension and the security of regular relief; they too spent many years managing on less formal relief and the disbursements of the endowed charities. However, Poslingford's range of aid was restricted to gifts of money and distributed only during limited periods. Most important to the elderly themselves, the amount of money they collected from such agencies was small, seldom more than a single shilling in a year. Those who qualified for such hand-outs, somewhere near their forty-fifth birthday, were carefully monitored so that very few individuals ever managed to collect from more than one municipal fund in the same year. Many were condemned to this low level of relief for their entire lives. For a small, fortunate number of petitioning elderly, a decade of miscellaneous relief would eventually give way to a parsimonious 8d a week pension. For the rural poor, the road to public support and a weekly pension was a long one.

[17] Ottaway, '*Decline of Life*', ch. 5.
[18] Other similarities between Poslingford and typical northern villages include a relatively large number of charitable foundations aimed at the relief of the poor and a greater reliance on co-residence in old age. Ottaway, '*Decline of Life*', ch. 5.

The parts of a pension: age, size, length and ending

The early modern pension was a remarkably flexible device. It did not necessary run the length of an entire year, and if it did, the amount did not necessarily remain constant.[19] Rather, it rose with an individual's need, and receded, sometimes to the point of momentarily stopping, as the individual regained his or her financial feet. Widow Olive Eade is a typical example of the flexibility and individuality of parish relief. In 1619, she was paid 'for 18 weeks at 8d the weeke', and then 'for xxxiiij weeks at vjd the weeke' from the Cratfield churchwardens in an effort to match aid with need.[20] Similar sensitivity was displayed in Poslingford: 'To John Deekes [the third-party overseer] for old Thomas Plume for 54 weekes ending the 22 of Apprill [16]77, 26 of them at 6d per weeke and 28 at 8d per week, £1 11s 8d' or Martha Bastard who collected a pension for forty-nine weeks in 1677 and again in 1686 for '50 weeks and 3 daies'.[21] Just as pensions did not have a predetermined length, neither did they have an official age of entry, as do modern annuity schemes. Rather, these were tailored to the needs of the individual, and only later, in the latter part of the eighteenth century, did pension levels become standardized. Because of the pension's *ad hoc* nature, and its response to personal circumstance, we can learn a great deal about the individual aged poor, such as when one's physical abilities declined past the point of self-sufficiency. By analysing groups of aged pensioners, the contours of an old age spent in penury emerge, as well as the community's preoccupations and priorities as they attempted to come to their aid.

We have already seen Poslingford's growing preoccupation with the problems of the labouring poor, as they increasingly directed their limited resources towards the younger members of the parish.[22] Consequently, at the end of the seventeenth century, the village pensioned only a few elderly individuals, who entered full-time relief in their mid-fifties. This also happened in Cratfield during the same period. Like Poslingford, Cratfield became more concerned with the working poor over the course of the seventeenth century, and consequently the average age at first pension fell steadily in this parish, from 69.3 years in the mid-sixteenth century to 52.1 years of age at the close of the seventeenth century. The emphasis on helping working-age men, presumably with families to support, is reflected in the seventeenth-century move towards lower pensioning ages for men. Women too experienced a growing youthfulness at the age at first pension, although at comparatively elevated ages, reflecting a widow's entry on to the rolls after the death of her husband. As the seventeenth century drew to a close, it was the problems of the younger

---

[19] See also Hindle, *Birthpangs*, p. 17.
[20] Cratfield CWA, SROI, FC62/A6/141 (1619).
[21] Poslingford OSA, SROB, FL615/7/1 (1677, 1686).
[22] See Chapter 2, this volume, p. 59.

set, as opposed to the elderly, that became the focus and chief concern of the overseers and vestry, since they were viewed as a potentially disruptive element in an ordered society.

England's society of hierarchy was arranged in ascending order, from the poor to the prosperous. Its categories were subdivided in terms of age, with the elderly to be granted more respect and honour than the young. Yet this seemingly simple hierarchy could be transformed in instances where old age overrode status and wealth. Given the literary dictates enshrined in the Ten Commandments and posted in every church, to honour thy Father and Mother, that

> Honour belongs to the very age of an Old-Man: for it is certaine, and will not be denied, that men in yeeres, even for their yeeres, are to be ranked among the Fathers meant in the fift Commandement. Now to all Fathers is Honour there allotted, asto [sic] Fathers.[23]

one would expect to find age preferencing in the size of pension received, with the elderly collecting the largest payments, out of respect for their age and in recognition of their declining strength.

Age did matter in the allocation of pensions, but not in the manner advocated by Thomas Sheafe, Richard Steele and other panegyrists of the elderly: old age discrimination was rural Suffolk's response to the demands of the poor. The elderly pensioners of Poslingford had to manage with under a shilling a week in parish relief, while their younger counterparts typically received 19d. The teachings of Leviticus were honoured more in the breach than in the observance by Poslingford's overseers.[24]

In Cratfield, the 1630s were a turning point in the priorities of Cratfield's overseers, affecting both the age and gender composition of the pension.[25] Previously, the elderly received both the largest entry-level pensions and the largest pensions overall. After 1640, the size of the elderly's pension decreased in relative terms, and eventually equalled or was less than that of the labouring poor, reflecting a changed community concern and concentration on this 'new'

---

[23] Sheafe, *Vindiciae Senectutis*, p. 181.

[24] 'You shall rise up before the hoary head, and honour the face of an old man.' Leviticus 20: 32. See also Proverbs 16: 31: 'The hoary head is a crown of glory.'

[25] If only one apparent 'shift' occurred during the 1630s, the phenomenon might well be explained as a problem associated with the manipulation of small numbers. However, two such changes, in age and gender, occurred during this decade, lending rather more weight to the idea of a deliberate change in pensioning policy. Although there was neither a new vicar nor new parish leaders, a change in the community's priorities probably occurred in the early seventeenth century. For a slightly later turning point in parish relief, see T. Wales, 'Poverty, Poor Relief and the Life-Cycle: Some Evidence from Seventeenth-Century Norfolk' in R. M. Smith, ed., *Land, Kinship and Life-Cycle* (Cambridge, 1984), pp. 354, 387, and Ottaway, *'Decline of Life'*, ch. 5.

type of poverty.[26] While the elderly no longer received the largest pensions, they did not experience the overt age discrimination foisted on to their counterparts in Poslingford. None the less, even the prosperous village of Cratfield experienced the changing nature of seventeenth-century poverty, with increased numbers of young and middle-aged paupers. The redefined priorities of parish officers in the 1630s manifested themselves in another aspect of the aged poor's pensions. Unlike Poslingford, whose pensions remained relatively low regardless of the person's tenure, the size of Cratfield's pensions grew over time, especially those assigned to the elderly. Consequently, the largest pensions, those over 2s a week, were not granted to the newly poor but to the elderly, and were a direct result of their long association with the parish purse. This remained true on either side of the 1630s divide, but what shifted between these periods was the type of elderly person to collect large pensions. In the early years it was the elderly woman who benefited from enhanced stipends, but after the 1630s only old and sick men would collect the largest weekly sums. In neither parish did a weekly pension, either great or small, stretch out across the decades.

Women experienced poverty in old age in ways fundamentally different from men. Women in Cratfield turned to the parish at a later age than did men.[27] At first glance this appears to be a function of their subordinate status, with the existence of pension-dependent women being obscured by their husbands' stipends, but this was not the case. A gap on average of five years existed between widowhood and a woman's enrolment on regular relief.[28] Instead of 'becoming visible' only upon widowhood, the elderly woman's later age at first pension illustrates her greater ability to be self-sufficient in old age.[29] Unlike in Cratfield, women entered Poslingford's pensioning scheme at approximately 54.8 years, eleven years earlier than men.[30] They also became

---

[26] Before 1630 all entry-level pensions over 6d were given to the elderly. Entry levels do not include payments to orphaned children who may have become pensioners later in life.

[27] Women in Cratfield began receiving pensions 6.5 years later than men. Barker-Read found the converse to be true in her Kent case studies. In all Cratfield cases men entered regular relief at a later age than women, though typically the sexes were quite close together in age with age differences as low as 1.4 years and as high as 5.4. Barker-Read, 'Treatment', p. 192. Adair's work in Whitchurch, Oxfordshire, and Terling, Essex, suggests that women and men had a more uniform experience in this regard, with the mean age of first pension at 54.6 and 54.0, respectively. R. Adair, 'Pensioners in Terling: Some Preliminary Results' (unpublished paper, 1994), p. 5.

[28] Like the generally lower age of first pension, the gap between widowhood and pension fell throughout the sixteenth and seventeenth centuries from 6.4 years to 2.25 years.

[29] For the invisibility of poor women, see R. Jutte, *Poverty and Deviance in Early Modern Europe* (Cambridge, 1994), pp. 42–4.

[30] Women entered relief in Poslingford at approximately 43.5 years of age, as compared to 54.8 years for men. For similar findings, see R. Wall, 'Some Implications of the Earnings, Income and Expenditure Patterns of Married Women in Populations in the Past' in J. Henderson and R. Wall, eds, *Poor Women and Children in the European Past* (London, 1994), p. 331.

pensioners thirteen years earlier than women in Cratfield. Significantly, they were all single women or widows when they entered full-time relief. Their situation illustrates the paradox of female employment: they may well have found some task to generate income, but with low pay befitting, as contemporaries thought, the labours of a woman. Some women who were dependent upon the unstable and ever-shifting cloth trade may have been working hard, yet would none the less have starved without the aid of the parish.

For the general parish pauper, the pension offered security and sometimes a chance to rebuild a malfunctioning personal economy. Consequently, weekly stipends did not usually last for decades at a time. Even in the generous village of Cratfield, the young householder overburdened by his children might collect relief for 8.8 years, the parish average. The typical pension in Poslingford was much shorter, 4.6 years, reflecting the set of constraints at play there.

Yet the situation was fundamentally different for the few aged women in Poslingford who received a stipend. These single women were supported by the parish for startlingly long periods. Susan Borley had a ten-year pension. Martha Bastard was maintained at the village's expense for her entire old age, and a good portion of her middle age, too. In all, she collected weekly relief for twenty-four years. The record for the length of tenure, however, was held by the never-married Susan Green, who collected 4d a week for thirty-five years.[31] In part, the longevity of these pensions can be explained by their relatively young starting age. It also speaks to the ability of single women to 'manage' in a state of dependency and on relatively little income. While the village's aged women collected relief for decades on end, Poslingford's elderly men lived on public relief for just three years before they died. The evidence from Poslingford's aged males, with their short pension periods in the seventeenth century, is joined by research for the eighteenth century to lend weight to the idea that men tended to die shortly after the loss of their independence.[32]

Death seemed the only sure way of leaving a life of public support.[33] In Cratfield, only three of the fifty-one elderly collectioners stopped receiving weekly aid before their last year of life. One was Rubin Tallant's son Thomas, who suddenly left public assistance a full twenty-six years before his death.[34] He found work in the village, following his father's footsteps as sexton, but it barely kept him off relief and certainly was not enough for him to pay the

---

[31] Poslingford OSA, SROB, FL615/7/1, *passim*. Cf. S. R. Ottaway, 'Providing for the Elderly in Eighteenth-Century England', *Continuity and Change* 13 (1998), p. 404.

[32] Ottaway, 'Providing', p. 404; Barker-Read, 'Treatment', p. 197; Chapter 3, this volume, pp. 98–101.

[33] See also Wales, 'Poverty', p. 360.

[34] There were other long and unexplained absences from the records. William Mills paid the rate in the 1650s, and received a one-off, year-long pension in 1687 before disappearing from recorded parish life until his burial in 1705. Cratfield OSA, SROI, FC62/A2/1 (1653, 1654, 1655, 1656, 1687). Less mysterious was Thomas Fiske, who ceased receiving a weekly

rate. Poslingford, with its shorter pensions, also had more people who left the relief rolls for reasons other than their demise. Those who left the parish's assistance before death had all been distinctly short-term sojourners among the poor. For example, Thomas Chapman's son and daughter were placed in care during the early 1680s, after their mother's death in childbed in 1679. The family then seemingly regained its feet and nothing more was heard of them, except for one small payment when daughter Grace was ill.[35] Similarly after the death of John Smith's wife in 1686, his son John and daughter Sarah lived for several years at the parish's expense. They, too, seem to have re-established their financial equilibrium in 1700 with John's remarriage, and the addition of a woman's work and wages.[36] As these examples show, financial rehabilitation was possible for Poslingford's younger male pensioners whose households had been shattered by the death of the wife and mother. For the elderly, with little chance of remarriage or improved employment, death was the only certain end to dependent poverty.[37]

While death may have been the surest escape from parish support, it did not necessarily come early (Table 4.1). In Poslingford, old age pensioners lived on average until age 65. In Poslingford, old women outlived old men. In Cratfield, again, the pensioned elderly lived the longest, not dying until the average age of 72. Here, old men outlived old women.

Table 4.1 Average age of death of persons over the age of 50 in Cratfield and Poslingford

Village	Total population	Elderly pensioners	Female elderly pensioners	Male elderly pensioners
Cratfield	68.3	72.6	66.3	73.7
Poslingford	64.3	65.3	68.5	62.0

Source: Family Reconstitution

stipend (at the age of 84). He died eighteen months later. Given Fiske's extreme old age, it was not inconceivable that he could no longer care for himself, and entered some form of sheltered accommodation, perhaps with family. For examples of his relief, see Cratfield CWA, SROI, FC62/A6/123, 127 (1609, 1611).

[35] Poslingford CWA, SROB, FL615/7/1 (1679) and Poslingford OSA, SROB, FL615/7/1 (1680, 1682, 1684).

[36] Poslingford CD, SROB, FL615/7/1 (1680, 1686); Poslingford OSA, SROB, FL615/7/1 (1684, 1685, 1688, 1689, 1690, 1692, 1693, 1694, 1695); Poslingford CWA, SROB, FL615/7/1 (1687). Sarah, the daughter, would later give birth to a son, John, out of wedlock with John Hodskins in 1698. She would later marry Hodskins and have several more children before dying in 1740 at the age of 65.

[37] Death was still the most common end to a parish pension in the eighteenth century. Ottaway, '*Decline of Life*', ch. 5, and her 'Providing', p. 404.

There are two possible explanations for why aged pensioners had the longest collective life spans in these rural villages. First, the act of living long – their very longevity – meant that their bodies would wear out and they would end up on relief, but only late in life. This was most certainly true of some aged pensioners, such as Cratfield's Besse Green, who only collected aid after growing frail, ill and dependent before she died at the age of 94. In cases where old age was the instigator of relief they entered relief during very old age, as did Besse Green, who collected her first pension at the age of 86. In other words, the pension was a product of her longevity, and not her longevity a product of her pension.

Yet for most of Cratfield's aged pensioners, it appears that the security of a weekly pension did contribute to their long lives. Most people came into the relief system in their late forties as collectors of miscellaneous relief. They were members of the marginally poor who had lost the battle for independence. Clearly, they were not yet old (still in their forties) and thus it was economic hardship and not old age that led to their final years on public assistance. A regular pension and the opportunity to perhaps ease (but not stop) their labours could be an invaluable asset in the unstable world of the elderly.

A feminization of poverty?

The standard interpretation of the old poor law, be it in the sixteenth or eighteenth centuries, is that pension rolls were the safe haven of women who could not manage on their own. Indeed, it has been suggested that once on relief, women were treated in manifestly unfair and unresponsive ways.[38] Yet most of what we know about early modern poverty is based on the conditions in cities and towns, areas certainly more urban than rural Cratfield and Poslingford. In those areas of concentrated population, most of the poor were women. In number, they were at least double that of men, and oftentimes even greater than that. In these Suffolk parishes during the second half of the seventeenth century, the sex ratio was more neatly balanced, at approximately 1.5 poor women to every poor man. This ratio was similar to that of Elizabethan Hadleigh, Essex, which had a larger but still rural population. The period between 1625 and 1649 was a particularly difficult time for women in Cratfield, as they came to dominate the village's poor relief. The exact reasons behind their crises are unknown, but it may well have been connected to Cratfield's involvement in the early years of the civil wars, when the village sent both regular soldiers and volunteers for 'Parlement's service'.[39] While these

[38] R. M. Smith, 'Ageing and Well-Being in Early Modern England: Pension Trends and Gender Preferences Under the English Old Poor Law, c. 1650–1800' in P. Johnson and P. Thane, eds, *Old Age from Antiquity to Post-Modernity* (London, 1998), p. 91, and Ottaway, *'Decline of Life'*, ch. 5.
[39] Cratfield CWA, SROI, FC62/A6/185 (1644) and Botelho, *Churchwardens*, pp. 16, 18–19.

men were away, the parish stepped into their household economies by paying relief to their wives and families, and momentarily inflating the presence of women among the poor. If the disproportionate number of women on weekly relief was a war-related anomaly, and the relative gender parity among the poor was a typical situation, then the evidence from Cratfield and Poslingford suggests that significant differences may have existed between urban and rural poverty (Table 4.2).

Table 4.2 Sex ratio. Old age pensions in Cratfield and Poslingford (female: male)

Period	N	Cratfield	N	Poslingford
1550–99	18	0.9: 1.0	n/a	n/a
1600–49	37	1.5: 1.0	n/a	n/a
1650–1700	31	0.9: 1.0	7	0.6: 1.0

Note: Poslingford is calculated for the years between 1663 and 1700.

Source: Cratfield CWA, SROI, FC62/A6/1–363 and OSA, SROI, FC62/A2/1, *passim*; Poslingford OSA, SROB, FL615/7/1, *passim*

Looking specifically at elderly collectioners, the axiom that early modern poverty was a society of women is again challenged. In Poslingford, aged poor males were nearly twice as likely to receive a weekly pension than were women at the close of the seventeenth century. Old age poverty in Poslingford was anything but feminized. In fact the overwhelming presence of men is extremely suggestive of the ability of women to survive in old age due to the high demand for female spinners in Poslingford's cloth industry. An analysis of Cratfield's larger number of pensioners, coupled with its longer run of records, reinforces the impression that rural poverty, even among the old, was not characterized by women. Between 1500 and 1700, fifty-one individuals collected a weekly stipend, divided almost equally between men and women. A masculization of poverty did not exist, as it did in Poslingford, or as it would come to exist in eighteenth-century England more generally, but instead a rough parity existed between the sexes.[40] It is also apparent that Cratfield's aged poor did experience the effects of the civil wars.

The historical commonplace that early modern poverty was a world of women, and old ones at that, appears to be an illusion of the historiography.[41] Much of the existing scholarship on poverty has focused on large villages, cities,

[40] For the decreasing proportion of female pensioners in the eighteenth century, see Smith, 'Ageing and Well-Being' in *Old Age from Antiquity to Post-Modernity*, p. 85. For the general decline in the quality of female poor relief during the eighteenth century, see Ottaway, '*Decline of Life*', ch. 6, and Smith, 'Ageing and Well-Being', p. 91.

[41] A. L. Beier, 'The Social Problems of an Elizabethan Country Town: Warwick, 1580–90' in P. Clark, ed., *Country Towns in Pre-Industrial England* (Leicester, 1981), p. 6; W. Newman Brown, 'The Receipt of Poor Relief and Family Situation: Aldenham, Hertfordshire

towns and urban centres, features of the early modern geography that were in fact unusual in England. Not only were women in the majority in early modern England, but also the majority of individuals who lived in towns, further underlining that our perception of a feminization of poverty may well be more a product of historical enquiry than history itself.[42] Perhaps as high as 80 per cent of the population lived in small, rural villages, very much like Cratfield and Poslingford. Rural poverty and not urban penury was most characteristic of seventeenth-century England, and consequently, gender parity may likewise prove more typical than the current feminization-of-poverty model.

Supplementary aid

As we know, the parish pension was not the sum total of the assistance received by the poor in old age. Cratfield, in particular, offered a wide range of supplemental aid and charity to its needy villagers. Many studies of early modern poverty fail to understand how the pension interacted with other forms of relief. Typically, they look only to the weekly pension when pronouncing upon the effectiveness of poor relief.[43] A notable exception is John Walter's work on the social economy of dearth, in which he stresses the importance of the 'interrelationship between formal and informal crisis relief' in the survival of the poor.[44] The historiographical emphasis solely on the pension has produced two sets of problems. The first, as noted above, is that simple comparisons between communities, based only on the proportion of the population collecting a stipend, raises the possibility of obscuring the true degree of poverty. This would happen if Cratfield and Poslingford were compared in this manner. The second problem is that a large and vital aspect of poor relief, supplemental aid, is

1630–90' in *Land, Kinship and Life-Cycle*, pp. 412–13; and R. M. Smith, 'Some Issues Concerning Families and their Property in Rural England 1250–1800' in *Land, Kinship and Life-Cycle*, p. 78.

[42] Margaret Pelling's observation that poor women typically moved to towns, seeking employment and not hand-outs, in greater number than men may help to explain this demographic imbalance, and why conclusions drawn from towns would be particularly problematic. M. Pelling, 'Who Most Needs to Marry? Ageing and Inequality among Women and Men in Early Modern Norwich' in L. Botelho and P. Thane, eds, *Women and Ageing in British Society since 1500* (London, 2001), pp. 21–42.

[43] Examples include: Arkell, 'Incidence of Poverty', pp. 23–48; A. L. Beier, 'Poor Relief in Warwickshire, 1630–1660', *Past and Present* 35 (1966), pp. 77–100; E. M. Hampson, *The Treatment of Poverty in Cambridgeshire, 1601–1834* (Cambridge, 1934); E. M. Leonard, *The Early History of English Poor Relief* (London, 1900); and M. K. McIntosh, 'Local Responses to the Poor in Late Medieval and Tudor England', *Continuity and Change* 3 (1988), pp. 209–45.

[44] See Chapter 2, this volume, pp. 43–5. J. Walter, 'The Social Economy of Dearth in Early Modern England' in J. Walter and R. Schofield, eds, *Famine, Disease, and the Social Order in Early Modern Society* (Cambridge, 1989), p. 122; and I. Archer, *The Pursuit of Stability: Social Relations in Elizabethan London* (Cambridge, 1991), p. 182.

overlooked. Consequently, the picture thus formed is far from complete, and significant differences between communities obscured.

The differences between Poslingford and Cratfield are nowhere greater, nor of deeper significance, than in the area of supplemental relief. Once pensioned in Poslingford, the aged poor could expect little else from their parish chest (Table 4.3). Wood for fuel, clothing for one's back and special care when sick were provided regularly for others, but seldom for the dependent elderly. Supplementary payments to the aged were strikingly disproportionate. The elderly comprised a minimum of 30 per cent of all annual pensioners, but typically received far less than 'their share' of supplemental aid. For example, of the seventy-four different clothing payments, fewer than 20 per cent went to those over age 50. Likewise, the Poslingford overseers made forty-eight payments in times of sickness, of which only eight went to elderly pensioners. As old age and illness travelled hand-in-hand, it is at first surprising not to find more payments to the elderly.[45] Indeed, Pelling has drawn attention to the importance of 'extra or temporary payments made to the poor in time of sickness'. In Pelling's Norwich, there was a similar tendency to treat or cure the young in preference to the old, which she associates rightly with a deliberate social policy. Poslingford's overseers likewise appear to distribute their scant resources according to a similar philosophy.[46] The infrequent and low-level parish supplements to the elderly confirm our understanding of Poslingford's pensions; money was paid to third-party overseers with the intention that they were then responsible for necessities in all but the most extreme situations.[47]

This system of third-party overseers was an unusual one. Most vestries that paid another to support the elderly did so by paying an adult child or sibling of the aged pensioner, and not by placing the elderly into the household of non-kin.[48] In Poslingford, the quality of the aged's care was in the hands of a non-relative, probably someone without an emotional tie to the aged, and who may have been tempted (perhaps by their own pressing poverty) to economize on the care of the elderly tenant in order to bolster his or her own resources. Therefore, even if the aged pauper might have expected relief by right, that aid could come at the cost of one's personal freedom, just as it did with a place in the local almshouse. It could also come at the loss of one's

---

[45] For a discussion of long-term care-giving for the elderly in medieval England, see E. Clark, 'The Quest for Security in Medieval England', in M. Sheehan, ed., *Aging and the Aged in Medieval Europe* (Toronto, 1990), pp. 189–200. For a discussion of the responsibility of religious guilds towards their sick members in late medieval England, see H. F. Westlake, 'The Origin, Purposes and Development of Parish Gilds in England', *Suffolk Institute of Archaeology and Natural History* 17 (1921), p. 164.

[46] M. Pelling, 'Healing the Sick Poor: Social Policy and Disability in Norwich, 1550–1640', *Medical History* 29 (1985), p. 121, also fn. 18.

[47] See Chapter 2, this volume, pp. 67–8.

[48] In one instance, Poslingford's overseers paid a sibling to provide care: 'to Anne Bastard for the Maintanaus of Martha Bastard hur sister to the 22 of Apprill [1666], £8 10s 10d.' Poslingford OS, SROB, FL615/7/1 (1666).

Table 4.3 Numbers and percentages of pensioners receiving miscellaneous relief in Cratfield and Poslingford

Relief type		Cratfield (1625–1700)	Poslingford (1663–1700)
Fuel	No. of payments	80	93
	No. of times to aged pensioners	26	19
	Percentage of total	33	20
Rent	No. of payments	47	47
	No. of times to aged pensioners	11	1
	Percentage of total	23	2
Sickness	No. of payments	277	48
	No. of times to aged pensioners	66	8
	Percentage of total	24	17
Nursing	No. of payments	52	9
	No. of times to aged pensioners	7	1
	Percentage of total	14	11
Caretaking	No. of payments	0	3
	No. of times to aged pensioners	0	0
	Percentage of total	0	0
Cash	No. of payments	689	13
	No. of times to aged pensioners	196	3
	Percentage of total	28	23
Pauper burial	No. of payments	30	14
	No. of times to aged pensioners	9	2
	Percentage of total	30	14
Food	No. of payments	15	1
	No. of times to aged pensioners	11	0
	Percentage of total	73	0
Clothing	No. of payments	78	74
	No. of times to aged pensioners	4	14
	Percentage of total	5	19

Source: Cratfield CWA, SROI, FC62/A6/1–363; Cratfield OSA, FC62/A2/1, *passim*; Poslingford OSA, SROB, FL615/7/1

personal possessions as well, since pauper inventories were increasingly made as a condition of their relief, with their property reverting to the parish upon their death.[49] The revenue generated by the sale of pauper possessions was added to the income from Poslingford's rate, despite their small amounts.[50] In 1700, the parish 'sold the Wedowe Matcalfs things'. In their entirety they fetched only 9s, which was duly recorded by the overseers.[51]

The third-party system was an extremely important component of Poslingford's scheme. It served to regulate the behaviour of their pensioners, as well as clearly identifying those who, within this heavily travelled area, were the certified worthy poor. In this way, the third-party overseer system functioned in a similar manner as badging of the poor, which the parish did in 1699.[52] Both personal overseers and badges helped to ensure that charitable alms were directed into approved hands: 'Repulse not the poor: but give Almes unto him of thy goods: but before thou givest them, learn to know the true godly poor, least thou bestow the upon the wicked.'[53] They, both badges and overseers, were also 'symbol[s] of social identification, differentiation and perhaps humiliation'.[54] But the personal overseers' most important con-tribution to Poslingford's poor relief scheme was financial. They themselves were overwhelmingly drawn from the marginally poor. Thus, by paying a third party to care for the elderly, the vestry also kept the personal overseer off regular relief. The parish's use of what some might consider Machiavellian measures was, in fact, much less sinister. While certainly self-serving it was a result of its poverty. It also kept the parish's obligation to provide miscellaneous forms of assistance to the barest minimum, since it placed that burden upon the shoulders of the personal overseer.

Cratfield, with its prosperous ratepayers and healthy coffers, took a different tack with its old age collectioners. Rent, fuel, cash and care-givers were not uncommon additions to the parish stipend. Jobs such as running errands, 'stowinge and brattlinge the woode for the poore', 'mending the guidhall', tending the sick and washing the dead were also dispensed by Cratfield's churchwardens.[55] As one became older, rent and fuel allowances were added

---

[49] Boulton, 'Going on the Parish', p. 35. See M. K. McIntosh's *A Community Transformed. The Manor and Liberty of Havering, 1500–1620* (Cambridge, 1991), p. 282, for a discussion of how 'their [the almspeople's] conduct and deference were closely supervised by the almshouse bailiff'.

[50] Chapter 2, this volume, p. 54.

[51] Poslingford OSA, SROB, FL615/7/1 (1700).

[52] Poslingford OSA, SROB, FL615/7/1 (1699?). See Chapter 2, this volume, p. 67, for the place and role of badges in Poslingford's relief of the poor.

[53] *Spiritual Journey*, p. 92.

[54] Boulton, 'Going on the Parish', p. 34.

[55] Running errands, Cratfield CWA, SROI, FC62/A6/17 (c. 1550); stowing wood for the poor, Cratfield CWA, SROI, FC62/A6/*passim*; mending the guildhall, Cratfield CWA, SROI, FC62/A6/117 (1607); tending the sick, Cratfield CWA, SROI, FC62/A6/154 (1628); and washing the dead, Cratfield CWA, SROI, FC62/A6/334 (1680).

to the relief package, replacing what had been derived from other employments. Over 50 per cent of aged pensioners received such gifts at various points during their old age, though never for extended periods of time. The aged pauper of Cratfield could also expect additional relief when frail or ill. In December 1628, the churchwardens paid 14s 'to John Alldus wife for lokeing to the Widow Eade & wachinge [watching] with hur in sikness'.[56] Likewise, decrepitude and helplessness were softened by parish-provided care-givers who often served for several years in this role. Even the poorest did not die alone. Often other poor people were paid to watch and comfort the dying, generally staying on after death to wash and properly lay out the body. Elisabeth Stannard was far from unique in receiving 2s 4d 'for laying of him [Phinias Smith?] forth and watching with him that night he dyed'.[57]

In Cratfield, there were a few things which the aged pensioner could *not* expect in addition to their pensions, such as clothing and food. Only eleven old people received gifts of clothing, usually in the form of a complete suit, suggesting that clothes were ragged before they were replaced at the parish's expense.[58] There was also an active market in used clothing, with local widows often at its nexus, and certainly at the helm of the local pawnshop.[59] Clothing the poor may well have been accomplished in ways much less costly than the commissioning of a new suit. Furthermore, the pension was intended to meet ordinary food consumption. Ale in the sixteenth, and beer by the seventeenth century, could probably be purchased locally from Widow Aldus who ran the mid-seventeenth-century public house and hosted the annual parish dinner on the Reckoning Day, as well as entertaining official visitors to the village.[60] Bread for daily consumption may well have been baked at the town house, but it could certainly be purchased from neighbouring Laxfield, where the mid-seventeenth-century churchwardens bought the bread for communion. However, the diet of the poor and labouring was limited in its amount of animal fat and protein, and it was these items that the parish purchased when the aged poor fell ill. Everyday foodstuffs were the responsibility of the pensioner, but gifts such as Widow Butcher's 'rack of veall' in 1632 or Phinias Smith's

[56] Cratfield CWA, SROI, FC62/A6/154 (1628).
[57] Cratfield CWA, SROI, FC62/A6/334 (1680). See also C. Gittings, *Death, Burial and the Individual in Early Modern England* (London, 1984).
[58] Barker-Read, 'Treatment', pp. 95–8.
[59] See the work of Beverly Lemire, especially 'Consumerism in Preindustrial and Early Industrial England: The Trade in Secondhand Clothes', *Journal of British Studies* 27 (1988), pp. 1–24; her 'The Theft of Clothes and Popular Consumerism in Early Modern England', *Journal of Social History* 24 (1990), pp. 245–76; and her *Dress, Culture and Commerce: The English Clothing Trade before the Factory 1660–1800* (Basingstoke, 1997), pp. 104–12, for women and pawnbroking. I would like to thank Dr Anne Laurence for these references.
[60] Cratfield CWA, SROI, GC62/A6/286, 295 (1666, 1667) and J. M. Bennett, *Ale, Beer, and Brewsters in England: Women's Work in a Changing World, 1300–1600* (Oxford, 1996).

'pint of Butter' in 1680 could be expected during times of acute illness, but not as a matter of course.[61]

As Cratfield's poor relief scheme developed over the decades, its parish-provided pension clearly came to be viewed as the centre-piece of the public's support of the aged. Equally clear, however, was the fact that the pension did not stand alone as the sole means of their support. Instead, it was underpinned by secondary levels of assistance provided by both the vestry and the church-wardens in a remarkably flexible manner, one that was for all intents and purposes tailored to the actual needs of a particular elderly person.[62] It was sensitive, humane and understanding of personal circumstance, so much so that it could compensate for domestic strife and provide a 1s payment to the do-nothing sexton Rubin Tallent, who on 'the 5 of June [he] being Throwneout and lyeing abroad'.[63] The full range of non-stipendiary assistance available to the elderly was not limited to those items discussed above (food, medical aid, fuel, nursing and the death watch), but also included accommodation and employment. In these two areas the efforts of the parish overlapped with the self-help endeavours of the old and are treated separately below.

Accommodation

The elderly were not 'left to live and die alone, in their tiny cottages' doling 'out their few pence on food, fuel and other necessities', as Peter Laslett initially thought. Neither did they spend the entirety of their old age perched on stools drawn close to the family fire, surrounded by children, grandchildren, love and good cheer, as Margaret Spufford suggested.[64] The accommodation of the aged poor was creative, complex and much more varied.

The most direct way of learning about early modern household composition is through an analysis of listings of inhabitants, documents which enumerate

---

[61] Cratfield CWA, SROI, FC62/A6/162, 334 (1632, 1680). See also Cratfield CWA, SROI, FC62/A6/141 (1609) and A. Laurence, *Women in England 1500–1760: A Social History* (New York, 1994), p. 149. For diet more generally, see A. B. Appleby, 'Diet in Sixteenth Century England: Sources, Problems, Possibilities' in C. Webster, ed., *Health, Medicine and Mortality in the Sixteenth Century* (Cambridge, 1979), pp. 97–117; J. C. Drummond and A. Wilbraham, *The Englishman's Food. A History of Five Centuries of Diet* (1939; London, rev. edn, 1957); and A. Wear, 'Making Sense of Health and the Environment in Early Modern England' in A. Wear, ed., *Medicine in Society* (Cambridge, 1992), pp. 141–7.

[62] See also V. Pearl, 'Social Policy in Early Modern London' in H. Lloyd-Jones, V. Pearl and B. Worden, eds, *History and Imagination. Essays in Honour of H. R. Trevor-Roper* (London, 1981), p. 123.

[63] Cratfield CWA, SROI, FC62/A6/162 (1632).

[64] P. Laslett, *The World We Have Lost. England Before the Industrial Age* (2nd edn, London, 1971), p. 11. M. Spufford, *Contrasting Communities: English Villagers in the Sixteenth and Seventeenth Centuries* (1974; repr. Cambridge, 1987), pp. 106, 144–51, 159, *passim*.

the household head and all its members. 'The assumption inherent in this approach,' according to Gordon, 'is that co-residence embodies notions of duty, responsibility, care and assistance, and therefore such analyses may perhaps tell us a great deal about the extent of kin support.'[65] Unfortunately, few documents of this nature survive, and none exist for Cratfield and Poslingford.[66] We do know with certainty about the place of residence of most of Poslingford's aged pensioners. They lived with non-kin – their third-party overseers – in complex households, as part of the parish's organized poor relief scheme. Their accommodation was thus ensured, and debates about co-residence with adult children are not applicable to this village.[67] Those who have worked with household listings for the eighteenth century suggest that a significant number of elderly, about 40 per cent, had adult children in the vicinity and that co-residence was common. None the less, not all elderly paupers had children living nearby, nor did all those with accessible offspring form extended households with them. Instead, other household structures were developed, based upon a complex calculation of need, ability and personality.

A close reading of rural Cratfield's exceptional documents, from wills to town accounts, reveals an enormously rich variety of elderly households. One form of elderly accommodation was to 'club together' in combined households, thus providing company and additional resources with which to negotiate the pitfalls of old age. Mary Barker-Read, for example, views such households as a common arrangement. In her work on Tonbridge, she found aged pensioners collecting 'at first a small pension with work; [then] when no longer capable of work, additional items were added. Physical disability was accompanied by removal into shared accommodation.' The relatively able cared for the feeble; the strong helped the weak. This arrangement, according to Barker-Read, was especially prevalent among women, who meanwhile continued to receive separate and individual pensions.[68]

Cratfield's elderly pensioners did not 'cluster' in great numbers. Only four elderly pensioners shared private accommodation, including households of mixed age groups. These trans-generational arrangements appear to be cases of the young tending the old, similar to the short-term care arrangements found

---

[65] C. Gordon, 'Familial Support for the Elderly in the Past: The Case of London's Working Class in the Early 1930s', *Ageing and Society* 8 (1988), p. 291.

[66] Peter Laslett's 'The Study of Social Structure from Listings of Inhabitants' in E. A. Wrigley, ed., *An Introduction to English Historical Demography* (London, 1966), pp. 160–208, demonstrates what may be gleaned for those communities where such documents do exist.

[67] T. Sokoll, 'The Household Position of Elderly Widows in Poverty. Evidence from Two English Communities in the Late Eighteenth and Early Nineteenth Century' in J. Henderson and R. Wall, eds, *Poor Women and Children in the European Past* (London, 1995), pp. 207–24.

[68] Barker-Read, 'Treatment', pp. 70, 201, 203. Elaine Clark has found a similar strategy employed by childless peasants in medieval England. E. Clark, 'Quest', pp. 195–7.

in Elizabethan Hadleigh.[69] However, unlike McIntosh who saw these arrangements as finite, short and for a special purpose, and Barker-Read who viewed such arrangements as a general solution to old age dependency, cases of trans-generational co-residence in Cratfield often involved those who were neither sick, bedridden nor otherwise physically dependent. Nor were these arrangements short-lived.[70]

Mother Green, for example, was not a widow lacking nearby family. Her son lived in the village and likewise was on relief. Mother Green and the younger Elizabeth Kempe received three sequential joint relief payments in 1582 of two, four and three shillings. Mother Green's age is unknown for these years, but she was already referred to and identified by her age-related title of 'mother' in these transactions, and at the very least, Cratfield's churchwardens considered her old.[71] More is known about Elizabeth Kempe. At age 21 she formed a household with Mother Green. Elizabeth also shared accommodation with Ann Kempe between 1557 and 1558 and again in 1580. After her stay with Mother Green she is no longer traceable in the records and no burial is recorded. Elizabeth Kempe probably migrated elsewhere. Old Mother Green continued living in the parish for another fifteen years, before suffering a long, two-year illness and receiving a pauper's burial 'two wekes after midsemer' 1597. In the intervening fifteen years between residency with Elizabeth Kempe and her final illness, Old Mother Green did not receive any relief specifically for sickness and appeared to be an active and fully-functioning, if old, member of the community.[72]

The second and third instances of combined households involved the widow Besse Green.[73] Joint relief payments by the churchwardens show Besse living with Alice Sparham in 1602, the year after Alice was widowed. Besse and Alice received a total of seven joint payments in 1602 and 1603.[74] Neither appears to have been sick or injured, and there is no indication that disability caused their cohabitation. They probably lived together for several more years. In 1607, three loads of wood were delivered to 'the Widow Sparham, the Widow

[69] M. K. McIntosh, 'Networks of Care in Elizabethan English Towns: The Example of Hadleigh, Suffolk' in P. Horden and R. M. Smith, eds, *The Locus of Care: Families, Communities, Institutions, and the Provision of Welfare Since Antiquity* (London, 1998), pp. 13–14; S. Klassen, 'Old and Cared For: Places of Residence for Elderly Women in Eighteenth-Century Toulouse', *Journal of Family History* 24 (1999), p. 45.

[70] Cratfield CWA, SROI, FC62/A6/63, 66 (1577, 1580). For an example of Mother Green's active service in the community see her assistance of Ann Orford: Cratfield CWA, SROI, FC62/A6/71 (1585).

[71] For the use of honorific titles such as 'Mother', 'Father' and 'Old' in the assessment of the onset of old age, see L. A. Botelho, 'Old Age and Menopause in Rural Women of Early Modern Suffolk' in Botelho and Thane, *Women and Ageing*, pp. 43–65.

[72] Cratfield CWA, SROI, FC62/A6/63, 66 (1577, 1580).

[73] Besse Green was not related directly to Mother Green.

[74] Cratfield CWA, SROI, FC62/A6/107, 111 (1602, 1603).

Grene and Anne Wryght'.[75] The younger Anne Wright may indeed have been there to provide support and assistance to these two now quite elderly widows. Both widows were in their nineties, and Besse was in the midst of a long, terminal illness. Significantly, both Anne Wright and Mother Sparham attended and nursed Besse during her final days.[76] It is clear that by this stage of Besse's life – she died at the age of 94 – her cohabitation was both social and dependent.[77] The burden of Besse Green's advanced old age and her reliance on Alice Sparham was confirmed in a churchwarden's entry of the following year. Mother Sparham received 1s 'for her paines and charges which she besowed [sic] abouth bess grene by concent [of the town]'.[78]

It is unlikely that Mother Sparham continued to live with Anne Wright, who dropped briefly from the records at this period and may indeed have been serving one of her regular stints in gaol.[79] Mother Sparham roomed instead with Anne Wright's child, probably the 11-year-old Anne, until Sparham's death.[80] This arrangement was probably one of mutual support and parish economy: it furnished young Anne with a foster-parent; it ensured a pair of steady hands for the very aged Widow Sparham; and it provided accommodation for two indigent parishioners for the price of one.[81]

These examples stretch our previous understanding of the circumstances surrounding such households. They resembled the 'unequal marriages' and mixed-age households used as survival mechanisms by the poor in sixteenth-century Norwich.[82] Their relatively infrequent use here implies that they were not a typical response to poverty in old age, at least in Cratfield. Physical dependency and shared accommodation were not unavoidable steps on the ladder of ageing. Likewise, they were not merely short-term, crisis-driven solutions to the problems of physical well-being. Instead, arrangements

---

[75] The Anne Wright listed here was the village's ne'er-do-well, bastard bearer, excommunicant and administrative headache, already boasting at least one child boarded out upon the town. Cratfield CWA, SROI, FC62/A6/117 (1607).
[76] Cratfield CWA, SROI, FC62/A6/123 (1609).
[77] Cratfield CWA, SROI, FC62/A6/126 (1610).
[78] Cratfield CWA, SROI, FC62/A6/126 (1610).
[79] Anne Wright lived with Margaret Cady in 1611 and received 2s, 'beinge bothe sicke'. Widow Cady has been identified at a later date as living in the local almshouse, though it is uncertain whether she was living there at this time.
[80] 'Paid to Mother Sparham for aprons, hat, smocke and other necessaries for Mother writs gyrle, 5s.' Cratfield CWA, SROI, FC62/A6/26 (1610).
[81] Similar practices were found in West Kent. See Barker-Read, 'Treatment', pp. 204–5. It does not seem to have been a popular strategy in Cratfield.
[82] M. Pelling, 'Old Age, Poverty, and Disability in Early Modern Norwich: Work, Remarriage, and Other Expedients' in M. Pelling and R. M. Smith, eds, *Life, Death and the Elderly: Historical Perspectives* (London, 1991), pp. 87–90, and her *The Common Lot: Sickness, Medical Occupations and the Urban Poor in Early Modern England* (London, 1998), pp. 115, 140, 147–52, 162.

seem to have encompassed both of these and more, including simple co-habitation for the often overlooked, but none the less important, desire for companionship.

One place where elderly pensioners unquestionably 'clustered' was in alms-houses, guaranteeing the occupants a continuing involvement with village life.[83] Cratfield's almshouse, as discussed above, was centrally located, imme-diately to the south of the parish church.[84] Interchangeably called guildhall, town house and almshouse, Cratfield had a structure which served both as the centre of parish activity and business, as well as a home for its needy elderly.[85]

The final place of old age accommodation was in private, independent dwellings. In times of need, the parish paid or waived the aged's annual rents, 'evidence', according to Newman Brown, of 'residential independence'.[86] In other words, the poor rate was used to maintain the elderly poor in their own homes and allow them to retain their positions as household heads. Most overseers did not itemize such payments, but instead recorded annual expenditure under general headings of rent or housefarm. Luckily, Cratfield has six years of extremely detailed payments, offering an intriguing glimpse into the world of pensioner households.[87] Nearly all pensioners would simultaneously have received rent assistance and a pension at least once.[88] Furthermore, those in receipt of dual aid were typically in their sixties and seventies.[89]

Exceptions to this pattern suggest some degree of flexibility in the selection of rent recipients, and the Elizabethan Poor Law overall. The Widow Hayward,

---

[83] McIntosh suggests that almshouses may have also been used as places where some kind of 'informal' care might be given to the more 'fragile' members. McIntosh, 'Networks of Care', p. 11. See also Barker-Read, 'Treatment', pp. 83–8; Newman Brown, 'Receipt', p. 414.

[84] See Chapter 2, this volume, and L. A. Botelho, 'Accommodation for the Aged Poor of Cratfield in the Late Tudor and Early Stuart Period', Suffolk Review n.s. 24 (1995), pp. 19–31, for a fuller discussion of the elderly's accommodation in the Cratfield almshouse.

[85] See Chapter 2, this volume, pp. 33–5. For institutional care of the aged poor in eighteenth-century Toulouse, see Klassen, 'Old and Cared For', pp. 45–7. This article assumes that families provided care for the elderly as the 'normal' old age provision. In those families too poor to provide for their aged parent, the elderly turned to institutional relief.

[86] Barker-Read, 'Treatment', pp. 50, 82; Newman Brown, 'Receipt', p. 414; Pearl, 'Social Policy', pp. 129, 131. In some cases the guild would pay the poor's rents. For an example geographically close to Cratfield, see N. Evans, 'The Holy Ghost Gild and the Beccles Town Land Feoffees in the Sixteenth and Seventeenth Centuries', Suffolk Institute of Archaeology and Natural History 37 (1989), p. 37.

[87] Names are listed for the years 1625–28 and 1633–34.

[88] Eighty per cent of all pensioners collected both rent and pension at least once.

[89] Widow Chettleborough, for example, was 78 and 79 years old when we know she collected dual relief. Cratfield OSA, SROI, FC62/A2/1 (1625, 1626). A fellow pensioner Olive Eade was 74 and 77 when she collected dual payments. Cratfield OSA, SROI, FC62/A2/1 (1625, 1628).

receiving rent in 1625, was probably widowed earlier that year, leaving her at the age of 39 with five children between the ages of 1 and 15. She was a textbook example of a widow overburdened with children. Margaret Smith, meanwhile, presents the opposite side of the same coin: she had no children. Widowed early and childless, the parish paid the widow's rent. The difficulties of widowhood, even without the extra burden of small children, still proved too difficult. Three years later, Margaret received both rent and pension.[90] While rent payments were primarily the domain of the elderly, they were not their sole preserve. Early statutory poor relief was not rigidly codified and systematized, but was flexible and responsive to the needs of individuals.

The ability of the parish officers to cut the suit to fit the cloth is reflected, too, in the case of the elderly William Brown, whose rent was 'forgiven' and allowed to remain unpaid, despite the presence of grown sons in the parish. One son had already moved away by 1625. Another son, John, remained in Cratfield and was unmarried. The third son, Francis, 'was preste for asouldger [sic] and came home maymed' in 1628.[91] Potentially, John could have contributed towards the maintenance of his father and war-wounded brother – indeed, as was mandated by Parliament – and perhaps he did. However, the burden of one, possibly two, dependent family members was conceivably more than John could have managed. At this point the parish overrode statutory directives ordering the adult child to care for an aged parent and underwrote the cost of the elderly William's housing. They provided a safety-net for those aged individuals whose children were simply not able to provide assistance in old age.

In a six-year period, over half of the elderly pensioners received accommodation assistance at some point and by implication headed their own households. It seems clear that Cratfield had a decided policy to maintain the aged poor in independence, and not to force them into subordinate positions and complex household with friends, family, or (as in Poslingford) other poor, even if it meant, as it did in the case of old William Brown, paying his brother-in-law to provide him 'a house to dwell in at Michelmas next'.[92] The role of nearby kin proved to be equally important, as we will see below, for those elderly with adult children in the village, although this assistance took forms other than co-residence. For the majority of the aged poor, there were no immediate family nearby and no chance of a multi-generational household. But neither were the elderly forced to live alone on the margins of village life, isolated from the daily exchanges of neighbourliness. Instead, it appears that the aged poor employed a variety of living arrangements that managed to keep both a roof over their heads and a presence in the community.

---

[90] Cratfield OSA, SROI, FC62/A6/1 (1625–28, 1633–34).
[91] Cratfield OSA, SROI, FC62/A2/1 (1628).
[92] Cratfield OSA, SROI, FC62/A2/1 (1611).

Employment

A parish pension did not allow the elderly to curtail all labour. As with the marginally poor, so with the pensioned: even the aged worked towards their own upkeep, so long as they were physically able to do so, and long past the point modern society finds acceptable. The desire to remain working and their pride in past strength is arguably one of the most consistent character traits of the labouring poor. The words, written in his own hand, of a nineteenth-century Essex man – old, proud of his labours, but whose body was beginning to fail – sums up well the realities of an old age spent in rural poverty, be it in the nineteenth or the seventeenth century:

> for many weeks past, sometimes work, & sometimes none, my Earnings have been but small, not more an Average, than six Shillings or six and sixpence, a week, as near a I can tell – (I may say for some Months this have been my case) with which we cannot procure Necessaries, to support health, nor nature, for the want of which, I find health and strength decaying fast, so that when I have a little work to do, I find myself, through Age, and fatige, incapable to perform it, Walking into the Country five or six Miles in a morning, working the day, and returning home at Night, is a task that I cannot, but without great diff[f]iculty perform several times I have thought, I could not gett home, and it have been the Occasion, of my being Ill, for two or three days, this I attribute in a great degree, to the want, of constant nourishment, to keep up my strength, and of Age ad[d]ed thereto, being now within one Year of Seventy – at this time I am Unwell, and have been several days.[93]

He did not, even in the nineteenth century, turn to the parish for a retirement, but rather for the *easing* of his labours.

The onus to find employment lay squarely on the shoulders of the aged poor themselves, despite – or perhaps because of – the systematic failure of the public works projects designed to set the poor to work. Having established the precedent, it did not mean that parishes were not sympathetic to the plight of the elderly, as they faced fewer job prospects for less wages.[94] Consequently, parishes across England did what they could by providing a series of small jobs, such as care-giving or messenger, to the aged poor. 'There be many aged [who] can worke, and there be some workes require more use than labour, and may easily be done by the olde.'[95] The 4d paid by the Cratfield church-wardens in 1595 to Thomas Chettleborough is an excellent example of the types of employment thought suitable for those of advanced years: 'paid to Father Chetlebur for going to halsworth ffor a surgeon for Orfer [William Orford]'.[96] Old but not decrepit, the aged Thomas was able to walk the ten-mile round trip to Halesworth, and by the effort earn a little money. The

---

[93] As quoted in Sokoll, 'Old Age', p. 144.
[94] Gordon, 'Familial Support'.
[95] *An Ease for Overseers of the Poore* (Cambridge, 1601), p. 23.
[96] Cratfield CWA, SROI, FC62/A6/93 (1595).

availability of such parish-provided employment was far greater in Cratfield than in Poslingford for two primary reasons. First, Cratfield's larger poor relief budget allowed for a greater allocation of funds to this sector. Second, Poslingford's position in the heart of Stour Valley cloth production meant that when there was any life to the industry, by-employment and piece-work abounded, and even when the market retracted it did not die completely, leaving a few jobs in place: jobs which were well suited for elderly hands.[97] Therefore, the role of Poslingford's vestry as a job centre was less developed. In either case, jobs distributed by local officers were part of the village's poor relief scheme, usually a function of their miscellaneous or supplemental relief, and contributed towards (although they did not make up the bulk of) the most important aspect of the elderly's income: waged labour.

Cratfield's was not a one-plank economy, as was Poslingford's. Instead it spanned a fairly full range of traditional agricultural practices, alongside a market-orientated dairying and cheese industry. While certainly providing employment for the village, this type of economy did not result in large numbers of piece-work employment and a high demand for wage labour, as required by the cloth trade. None the less, Cratfield did provide the aged poor with a substantial amount of supplemental assistance, including parish-funded jobs. Just over half of those collecting a stipend were also given small jobs around the parish. Some, like Margaret Cady, the parish 'nurse', found fairly full employment in this way.[98] She first appeared in 1610, earning 13s as the 'keper to olde William Eade'. Between the years 1610 and 1638, Margaret made 59s from tending only the poor. Nursing the better sort, the proceeds of which would not be recorded by the churchwardens, would have increased her earnings considerably. Margaret had, in fact, a thriving trade in caring for others less 'thriving'. Similarly, Ruben Tallant, the sexton, was given considerable additional employment. Weeding the porch, assisting at the 'Reckoning Day', ringing the lecture bell, and assisting various workmen around the church contributed to Ruben's annual income.[99] Most, however, were not as fortunate as Ruben Tallant and Margaret Cady, earning little and irregularly from this source.

To look more closely at the type of odd jobs dispensed by Cratfield's churchwardens, we must first remove three people from further consideration. Two, Margaret Cady and Ruben Tallant, had nearly permanent employment through the patronage of the churchwardens. The sheer volume of their jobs would certainly distort the general picture. The third person is Ruben's son Thomas. His relief history may very well be representative of the parish's efforts

[97] See Ottaway, 'Decline of Life', ch. 5, for the relation between the availability of by-employment and lower pension levels.

[98] Cratfield CWA, SROI, FC62/A6/126, 131, 141, 142, 146, 147, 152 (1610, 1614, 1619, 1620, 1622, 1623, 1627) and Cratfield OSA, SROI, FC62/A2/1 (1628).

[99] Examples include Cratfield CWA, SROI, FC62/A6/179, 185, 189, 215 (1640, 1644, 1652).

to support one of its less capable members. Never married, Thomas started on a parish pension at the age of 26, immediately upon the death of his father. He seemed physically capable, however, since Thomas also immediately assumed his father's position as sexton. The impression one receives is of a young man not entirely able to support himself. He may have been mentally retarded. The protected status of young Thomas Tallant is unique in Cratfield, and would certainly distort our understanding of parish employment.

Cratfield's parish employment was divided into two categories. The first, including the most common odd job, was centred around assisting the community of the poor. 'Stowinge & brattlinge the woode for the poore' employed more men than any other single task and is an excellent example of how Cratfield employed the poor to help themselves.[100] The second group of odd jobs was also for the greater good, but was directed towards the larger community. These men would thatch the town's buildings, mend the lanes,[101] ditch the town 'pygtille',[102] 'daube' at the guildhall,[103] and they were paid for the 'mending of the guildhall and townhouse'.[104] Probably intentional, this scheme closely resembled the great public works envisioned by humanist thinkers such as Vives and Marshall.[105] The scale, however, reflected both Cratfield's more modest needs and its resources.

One is immediately struck by the fact that aged male pensioners were more than twice as likely to receive employment from the churchwardens than were their female counterparts.[106] Their frequency of employment reflects what could be seen as their relative inability to provide for themselves. Employment for Cratfield's elderly women was similar in aim, but different and narrower in scope. Most female employment provided by the parish was centred on the physical body, either in life or death. Women were nurses, watchers, keepers or some other care-giver. Typically, it was an elderly female who was paid to wash and prepare a pauper for burial. The living body was the other focus of female employment. Women were typically paid to provide 'breade and beere' or 'our dinners' during village meetings such as those associated with the casting of accounts or upon the 'vissation [visitation] day'.[107] Such tasks

---

[100] Cratfield CWA, SROI, FC62/A6/1–365.

[101] Cratfield CWA, SROI, FC62/A6/75 (1586).

[102] Cratfield CWA, SROI, FC62/A6/129 (1612).

[103] Cratfield CWA, SROI, FC62/A6/271 (1664–5).

[104] Cratfield CWA, SROI, FC62/A6/117 (1607).

[105] J. Vives, *De Subventione Pauperum* in F. A. Salter, ed., *Some Early Tracts on Poor Relief* (London, 1926), pp. 2–30, and W. Marshall, trans., *The Forme and Maner of Subvention of Poor People* in *Some Early Tracts on Poor Relief*, pp. 36–76.

[106] On average there were 2.5 jobs per elderly woman as compared to 6.2 jobs for their male counterparts.

[107] For example, on 23 March 1637 the churchwardens 'laid out [4s] the same day to the Widow Breisingham for makeing redy of the Chamber and for makeinge us a fire'. Cratfield CWA, SROI, FC62/A6/172 (1637).

required skill and knowledge. The relative infrequency of parish-provided employment for women speaks to issues of the local economy. The dairy industry was 'almost exclusively female', and in areas such as Cratfield this 'could take place on a considerable scale as the provision accounts for cheese for the army reveal'.[108] There were probably more jobs available to the aged female pensioners in Cratfield than there were for old men and they did not need to turn to the parish officers to find them.

Instead of the churchwardens, Poslingford's poor turned to the nearby clothiers in order to support their meagre pensions by spinning wool for the cloth trade. Poslingford's aged poor may have had more opportunity for private employment than their counterparts in Cratfield, but the size of the potential earnings was small. Even the healthy and the young would have been able to earn little from this source. Spinning, the most common by-employment and one easily carried out by the aged and disabled, was a classic example of piece-work, with each individual being paid by the pound or unit. One's strength, dexterity and eyesight could well have a direct influence upon these tasks and thus on one's income.[109] The Suffolk Wage Rate decreed that 'every such servant being a single man and working by the pound to have by the pound 1d'.[110] The aged poor were probably not as healthy, strong and vigorous as a 'single man', and therefore not able to spin as much wool as quickly, nor was there a guarantee that they would receive the same pay for the same work.[111] Women probably did not. Instructions regarding women's work sometimes only gave the barest guidelines, such as 'to pay them such wages as they should deserve'.[112] Even at the top price of 1d per pound, Suffolk spinners would not have earned a great deal. Work shortages and stoppages, competition for employment, and the general decay of the traditional cloth industry decreased further the potential earnings available from Suffolk cloth. None the less, the elderly would have worked, earning what they could, to contribute to their upkeep.

Jobs were available to the elderly poor, and they would have been expected to earn part of their own upkeep for as long as they could turn a hand to a task. The fact remains, however, that the longer they were on a weekly stipend,

---

[108] Laurence, *Women in England*, p. 150.

[109] Pelling's work among poor women in sixteenth-century Norwich suggests that the particulars of female employment shifted with age. Pelling, 'Older Women: Household, Caring and Other Occupations in the Late Sixteenth-Century Town' in *Common Lot*, pp. 155–75, and Laurence, *Women in England*, p. 155.

[110] 'Rates of Wages of Laborores, Articificers, Spinners and Other Working People . . . Rated and Apointed in the County of Suffolk upon Munday 12 Aprilis, . . . 1630', CUL, Add MS 22, fol. 73v.

[111] For gender discrimination among servants in husbandry, see: CUL, Add MS 22, fol. 73v. See also Wales, 'Poverty', p. 378.

[112] R. Dunning, *A Plain and Easie Method: Shewing How the Office of the Poor may be Managed* (London, 1685), p. 8.

the less likely it was that such opportunities would present themselves or that they would have had the strength to fulfil them. Even at the peak of health, parish-provided jobs would not have formed the core of old age earnings. In most cases they were simply too unreliable and too low paid.[113] The aged poor were responsible themselves for locating the bulk of their employment. But the role of work in the poor's economy of makeshifts, either in the form of low-paying jobs arranged by the parish or those found through their own devices, was vital and undeniable.

Surviving children

The survival mechanisms of the aged poor included a great deal more than the receipt of a weekly stipend. It included a range of *ad hoc* relief from the parish officers and formal charity distributed in accordance with the wishes of one of their departed neighbours. Employment too was of fundamental importance, serving as a crucial supplement to the community's relief, as well as being in line with community expectation. Another potentially important component of the poor's old age provision was the contribution of surviving children, which forms a topic of controversy among historians.

Two debates need to be rehearsed before exploring the realities of early modern Suffolk: the legal obligation of children to care for their aged parents, and co-residence among the elderly and their adult children. According to the letter of the law, the families of the aged poor were to assume the cost and responsibility of their parents. Poor parishes were anxious to determine the limits of their obligations and the reach of the statute. The village of Myddle set this question before the magistrates at Quarter Session: did the statute include 'the grand father-in-law, the grand mother-in-law, the father-in-law . . ., the daughter-in-law, though she bee not named in the statute'? Apparently, the answer was 'yes' for the Shropshire bench.[114] Yet, despite the interest of poor villages, this aspect of the law was seldom enforced, including in Poslingford and, as we have already seen, in Cratfield.

The interpretation of this situation as it pertains to the elderly has been a matter of debate between David Thomson and Pat Thane, two modern historians. Thomson argues that because adult children were never taken to court for the upkeep of their parents, family care for the aged was unimportant under the old Poor Law and that the burden of support rested with the community.[115] Thane, however, claims that Thomson argues from the absence

---

[113] For example, many errands were only worth a penny; see Cratfield CWA, SROI, FC62/A6/17 (c. 1550).

[114] R. Gough, *The History of Myddle*, ed. D. Hey (Harmondsworth, 1981), p. 254.

[115] D. Thomson, 'Provisions for the Elderly in England, 1830 to 1908', unpublished Ph.D. thesis (Cambridge, 1980); '"I am not my father's keeper": Families and the Elderly in

of evidence. She offers instead a counterbalancing argument by reinserting the role of kin and family into the care of the aged: 'The Mother bore, the father and she brought up, beare their infirmities, relieve their wants more then others.'[116] Each has valid criticisms of the other, but the realities presented by early modern Cratfield and Poslingford in the seventeenth century, as well as those revealed in recent work on Terling, Essex, and Puddletown, Dorset, in the eighteenth century, are much more complex than previously presented.[117]

The second debate is much less formalized – more a set of conflicting stereotypes – than that between Thomson and Thane, but it flows in large part from it. At stake here is whether the elderly, and not just the poor, maintained independent households or were co-resident with their adult children. Many historians have simply assumed that the elderly were taken into the adult child's family, without considering the high frequency of migration in early modern England and the very real possibility that one's children may no longer be living nearby.[118] Others have likewise assumed a lonely existence of the aged, especially the elderly female, hovering at the edges of the community.[119] Historical demography, however, suggests a much wider range of options.

Nineteenth-Century England', *Law and History Review* 2 (1984), pp. 265–86; 'The Decline of Social Welfare: Falling State Support for the Elderly since Early Victorian Times', *Ageing and Society* 4 (1984), pp. 451–82; and 'Welfare of the Elderly in the Past: A Family or Community Responsibility?' in Pelling and Smith, *Life, Death and the Elderly*, pp. 194–221.

[116] P. Thane, 'Old People and their Families in the English Past', in M. Daunton, ed., *Charity, Self-Interest and Welfare in the English Past* (New York, 1996), pp. 113–38; G. Estey, *A Most Sweete and Comfortable Exposition*; the quote is from O8, but see O6v–P1v for a discussion on honour due to parents. See Ottaway, 'Providing', p. 393, for a useful summary of this debate and criticisms of each position.

[117] For Terling and Puddletown, see Ottaway, 'Providing', *passim*.

[118] This is perhaps the most cited old age provision and one with the greatest number of unsubstantiated claims. Laslett's 'Families, Kinship and Collectivity' is an evaluation of kin vs. collectivity, and is an excellent starting point. Others are less precise; see S. R. Burstein, 'Care of the Aged in England from Mediaeval Times to the End of the Sixteenth Century', *Bulletin of the History of Medicine* 22 (1948), p. 741; Cressy, 'Kinship', pp. 51–2; J. R. Gillis, *Youth and History. Tradition and Change in European Age Relations, 1770–Present* (New York, 1974), p. 11; T. K. Hareven, 'The Last Stage: Historical Adulthood and Old Age' in D. van Tassel, ed., *Aging, Death, and the Completion of Being* (Philadelphia, PA, 1979), pp. 172, 179; Klassen, 'Old and Cared For', pp. 35–45; MacDonald, *Mystical Bedlam*, p. 75; Minois, *History of Old Age*, pp. 218–19; Z. Razi, 'The Myth of the Immutable English Family', *Past and Present* 140 (1993), pp. 26–7; Smith, 'The Structured Dependence of the Elderly', pp. 409–28; and Wales, 'Poverty', pp. 382–4.

[119] Initially suggested by Peter Laslett in *The World We Have Lost*, p. 11, and then echoed in P. Slack, *Poverty and Policy in Tudor and Stuart England* (London, 1988), p. 85. While generally discredited by historical demographers, this view has been repeated as recently as 1998. Lynn Hollen Lees presents alternating images of the place of the aged poor in

The number of aged pensioners with adult children has been traced in Cratfield and Poslingford. On average, only one out of four aged poor in Cratfield still had children residing within the community, a rate strikingly similar to that in Terling, Essex, during the same period.[120] Among the lower orders in early modern Terling, for example, it appears that most householders were 'isolated within the village in terms of kinship, unlinked to other households by either blood or marriage'.[121] Of those with a parent/child or sibling link ('first-order kin') most had only one such connection.[122] 'Extensive kinship networks' appear to be rare, and no household in sixteenth- and seventeenth-century Terling was linked to more than four others.[123] Those over 60 years of age had fewer links still, a consequence of their advanced age and correspondingly decreased likelihood that either parents or siblings would be living. At the same time old age increased the possibility that their own children had relocated.[124] In eighteenth-century Terling, perhaps as high as 40 per cent of the aged who had adult children in the village lived with them.[125] Children living in neighbouring parishes were not necessary unsupportive and may well have been a source of comfort and even financial help, particularly since most early modern migration involved short-distance movement.

In Cratfield, however, most adult children still residing in the community were not in a position to aid their parents. In fact, they were often on relief themselves. For example, Thomas Tallant was not able to help his mother after the death of her husband. He entered regular relief at the same time. His older

---

English society. On one hand she writes that the aged would be 'left alone and unable to care for themselves'. On the other, she claims that many elderly lived with their kin. Lees, *The Solidarities of Strangers*, pp. 52, 53.

[120] Twenty-four per cent of the Terling links were between parents and children. Cratfield registered 25 per cent. While Wrightson is quite clear in his warnings about the dangers of generalizing from the specific, the similarity between the two communities suggests that Cratfield may not have been unusual in the solitary nature of its pensioners. K. Wrightson, 'Kinship in an English Village: Terling, Essex 1550–1700', in *Land, Kinship and Life-Cycle* (Cambridge, 1984), p. 321. Ottaway suggests that in the eighteenth century, about half of the aged men and one-third of the women in the labouring classes had children living in the parish. Ottaway, 'Providing', p. 395.

[121] Wrightson, 'Kinship', p. 316. While many historians acknowledge the importance of kin as a potential source of old age assistance, they seldom provide a sense of how many people could expect to have surviving children. Instead they employ vague language such as 'not necessarily without children married and living in the parish' or 'probably had adult children alive', in an attempt to convey a sense of size and availability. Others simply do not engage with the question, even when focusing directly on old age provisions within the family. For example, see Clark, 'Quest', pp. 189–200; Newman Brown, 'Receipt', p. 414; and Wales, 'Poverty', p. 382.

[122] Wrightson, 'Kinship', p. 317.

[123] Wrightson, 'Kinship', p. 318. See also Gordon, 'Familial Support', p. 293.

[124] Wrightson, 'Kinship', p. 319.

[125] Ottaway, 'Providing', p. 395.

brother, while not on the dole, was encumbered with responsibilities of his own, namely three young children. This may have prevented him from assist-ing either his mother or brother. According to Peter Laslett, this disjunction between generations was fairly typical in western and northwestern Europe: 'The disjuncture between the life-cycle of the parent and offspring generations may have made the elderly peculiarly difficult to support from familial resources.'[126]

Less frequent, however, were cases like that of John and Elizabeth Stannard who lived on John's modest 6d or 9d a week stipend, while at the same time their son was wealthy enough to pay the poor rate at 2s a month.[127] Their son was clearly a fairly prosperous individual, yet his parents received support from the parish coffers. The small size of John and Elizabeth's pension, however, may well reflect some level of contribution from their son towards their main-tenance, and probably represents the joint effort of family and community to support the aged poor.[128] Not all wealthy sons were willing to make such sacrifices on behalf of their aged parents. Popular tradition was steeped in the notion of tight-fisted children and hungry parents. The ballad, *A Most Excellent Ballad of an Old Man and his Wife*, is just one example.[129] In spite of the presence of the Stannards and their potentially helpful son, the overall impression is that the aged poor either lacked nearby family or that such families were poor themselves.[130] In either event, at the level of the dependent poor, adult children were not the main pillar of the elderly's economic support.

Because of early modern England's late age at marriage and relatively uncon-trolled fertility, there were also a number of elderly households with young

[126] Laslett, 'Family, Kinship and Collectivity', p. 169. See also Adair, 'Pensioners Under the Poor Law', p. 21. Sometimes the parish paid children to look after aged parents; for example, see Cratfield CWA, SROI, FC62/A6/327, 331 (1677, 1679). Occasionally, the parish took prosperous children to court to force them to contribute to the upkeep of their aged parent. Barker-Read, 'Treatment', p. 61.

[127] Cratfield OSA, SROI, FC62/A2/1 (1668, 1669). See also: Barker-Read, 'Treatment', p. 60; Smith, 'Some Issues', p. 78, and Wales, 'Poverty', p. 383.

[128] Drawing upon the thinking of Pat Thane, Lynn Hollen Lees writes of the 'multiple close, but voluntary, forms of aid from independent to dependent kin, which poor law officials often supplemented. In her (Thane's) opinion, family support and poor relief complemented one another in varying proportions as part of a larger "'makeshift economy'" of the poor'. Lees, *Solidarities*, p. 170.

[129] *A Most Excellent Ballad, of an Old Man and his Wife, Who in their Great Want and Misery Sought to Children for Succour, by Whom they were Disdained, and Scornefully Sent Away Succourlesse, and God's Vengeance Shewed upon them for the Same* (Pepys, I: 43). See also *A Most Notable and Worthy Example of an Ingratious Sonne* (Pepys, II: 180–1); and *The Ingrateful Son, Or, An Example of Gods Justice upon the Abusefull Disobedence of a Fake Hearted and Cruel Son to his Aged Father* (London, 1672). I would like to thank Dr Alex Walsham for these references.

[130] Wrightson found that most kinship links were within the same social sort. Wrightson, 'Kinship', pp. 322–3.

children.[131] Cratfield alone had ten old age collectioners with children under 21 years. In fact, they accounted for half of the children of the poor.[132] Most of these children had entered some form of employment or were away in service or apprenticeship. In either instance, they were no longer a drain upon their parents. None the less, five elderly pensioners were trying to support very young children on their weekly allowance. Some, like Richard Chattin, had five children under the age of 10, and one just over. As Richard M. Smith has convincingly demonstrated, children were net consumers of household resources until age 16, and not contributors as has been mistakenly assumed.[133] Therefore, too many small children in the households of the elderly could overburden slender economies and declining resources.

The elderly poor of late seventeenth-century Poslingford were as equally isolated from close kin as were those in Cratfield. Only two out of the seven aged collectioners had children living within the community. The first, Henry Parsons, had one adult son with four children of his own. Susan Borley, conversely, had an unmarried daughter. In neither case were these children in situations to help an ageing parent.[134] Not surprisingly given Poslingford's relatively late age at first pension, the village did not have elderly pensioners with minor children. In fact, most of Poslingford's aged pensioners did not have children living in the parish or children at all. Given the absolutely vital role adult children played in the lives of Poslingford's marginally poor, it may be that it was the lack of familial support which pushed some of the elderly on to the public dole. As the parish used a third-party overseer to house, feed and supervise the elderly pensioner, the issue of co-residence is a false one here, but it does not negate the importance of other types of assistance offered by kin.

We do not know how many of the aged pensioners in Poslingford and Cratfield actually lived with their children or whether it was more or less than the 40 per cent suggested for rural communities in the eighteenth century. What may in fact be more important than the formation of multi-generational households was simply the presence of adult children in the vicinity, and the other types of assistance they provided. Looking first at Cratfield, we see a steady drop in the number of available kin as we look further down the social

---

[131] R. M. Smith, 'The Structured Dependency of the Elderly as a Recent Development: Some Sceptical Historical Thoughts', *Ageing and Society* 4 (1984), p. 416.

[132] Sixty-four per cent of these minor children were divided equally between 11 and 21 years of age: eleven children between ages 11 and 15, and ten minor children between 16 and 21 years old.

[133] Smith, 'Some Issues', Table 1.9, p. 70.

[134] In another case, that of Mary and John Metcalfe, the children seemed to have moved away from their home parish; in two cases there were no children (Susan Green, for example, was unmarried); and in the final instance, the case of Henry Collins, no relevant information can be traced.

structure: 50 per cent for those who neither paid the rate nor collected relief; 33 per cent for those who received miscellaneous assistance; and 25 per cent for those who collected a pension. In addition, within the ranks of aged collectioners, the percentage of adult children drops steadily throughout the seventeenth century, from 62.5 in the early years to 14.3 per cent at its close.[135] For the elderly without economic stability and a degree of wealth, there appears to be a strong inverse relationship between the number of resident children and the depth of the aged parent's poverty. The situation was more stark in Poslingford. While virtually all elderly members of the marginally poor had offspring living in the village, only 25 per cent of its pensioners did. Since somewhat less than half – according to the most recent estimates – of the elderly poor who had adult children in the parish actually lived with them, the issue crucial to old age survival may not have been co-residence, but proximity to offspring.[136]

A burden to the community?

The care of the dependent elderly poor was a task carried by many hands: overseers, churchwardens, family and the aged themselves. But was the part borne by the community a heavy or a light burden? Did the aged poor, in spite of their small numbers, cost the parish a great deal of money? Were they the fiscal sore which the statutes and contemporary literature lead us to believe was the case for all poor people? In point of fact, aged collectioners were more the proverbial 'mere flea-bite' on the leg of rural society than literature's open wound.

The average annual cost of maintaining a single dependent elderly person in Cratfield increased over the course of the sixteenth and seventeenth centuries. The cost of supporting an aged pensioner and the country's inflation rate moved in unison, both rising between 1500 and 1650, then stabilizing at about the same level throughout the remainder of the seventeenth century. Similarly, the overall cost of financing Cratfield's poor relief also increased over time. The cost of keeping one elderly individual, including all monies, aid and parish employments, doubled between 1500 and 1650, while the cost of the scheme itself rose from an annual average of £22 16s 3d in the second

---

[135] The number of links and percentage of adult children living in the parish: 1550 to 1574, 1 link, 20 per cent; 1575 to 1599, 0 links, 0 per cent; 1600 to 1624, 5 links, 62.5 per cent; 1625 to 1649, 5 links, 38.5 per cent; 1650 to 1674, 2 links, 15.4 per cent; and 1675 to 1700, 2 links, 14.3 per cent.

[136] Gordon, 'Familial Support', pp. 313–15. Gordon's findings for a later date suggest that 'kin regarded geographical closeness as valuable, that the family have been an important source of informal care for elderly relatives, and further, that support transcended the physical frontiers of residence' (p. 315).

quarter of the seventeenth century to £54 9s 11d a year at the century's close. In other words, the cost of the parish's scheme doubled in the years after England's greatest period of inflation. From this two points emerge: (1) the cost of the *aged* poor did not rise in real terms; its increase over time merely matched the movement of the country's economy, and (2) Cratfield experienced an increase in real terms in the cost of relieving the *general* poor population, as these figures far outstripped any national trends (Table 4.4).[137] The greater cost of poor relief cannot be placed on the shoulders of the aged, as the relative cost of keeping and supporting an elderly person fell dramatically over time. This runs counter to findings elsewhere during the period where, for example, communities in Norfolk and Hertfordshire found the responsibility of supporting the elderly an increasing problem, and that the aged themselves consumed an ever increasing amount of parish provisions. R. M. Smith has also traced a similar trajectory of rising pensions and greater costs from 1650 until the mid eighteenth century.[138] The bulk of the relief here, however, was directed instead into the hands of the labouring poor.

Table 4.4 Average annual cost of maintaining an elderly pensioner

Community	1575–99	1600–24	1625–49	1650–74	1675–1700
Cratfield	£1: 05: 00	£1: 05: 05	£2: 10: 05	£2: 02: 00	£2: 07: 09
Poslingford	n/a	n/a	n/a	n/a	£1: 07: 08

Source: Cratfield CWA, SROI, FC62/A6/1–363 and OSA, SROI, FC62/A2/1, *passim*; Poslingford OSA, SROB, FL615/7/1, *passim*

The aged pensioner accounted for 39 per cent of Cratfield's relief in the years between 1625 and 1649 and only 19 per cent by the late seventeenth century. The level of assistance received by the elderly was disproportionately low compared to their presence among the poor, which never dropped much

[137] Cratfield's annual average expenditure seems generous for its size. Its population was one-third the size of Newman Brown's Aldenham, Hertfordshire, which averaged annual poor relief costs of £74 1s 6d in the 1670s and £78 2s 2d in the 1680s. Newman Brown, 'Receipt', Table 12.3, p. 412.
[138] Wales, 'Poverty', pp. 353–8; Newman Brown, 'Receipt', pp. 409–11; and Smith, 'Ageing and Well-Being', pp. 83–8. Cratfield and Poslingford were considerably smaller villages than those studied by Wales, Newman Brown and Smith, numbering no more than 300 individuals at their peak. This contradiction may be an illusion of the historiography that tends not to discriminate between sizes of rural villages, despite the tendency to delineate by economic underpinning. See pp. 18–19 for a discussion of a deceptive historiography.

below 40 per cent of all pensioners.[139] Clearly, the needs of other types of poor had become more pressing, and their relief was a correspondingly higher priority for the parish officers. The 1630s shift in types of relief provided was, in fact, the vanguard of a much larger shift in priorities away from the worthy poor, traditionally conceived, to the new worthy poor, the labouring pauper and a new understanding of deserving poverty. It reflected the different sets of needs of this younger group of poor. The elderly were never Cratfield's biggest poverty problem, even at 39 per cent of total spending, and certainly by the end of the period they hardly represented a problem at all.[140]

Looking at Poslingford in this light, one is struck again by the differences in the nature of the elderly's parish pension. Cratfield averaged nearly £2 8s annually per elderly person at the close of the seventeenth century. Poslingford averaged a full pound less per person, including whatever they might have received from the endowed charities. Equally contrasting is the small proportion of Poslingford's relief that was spent on the elderly. The aged comprised over 30 per cent of all pensioners; yet they received only 9 per cent of Poslingford's expenditures. Poverty was an undeniably huge problem in terms both of numbers and public funding, but the elderly poor were certainly not the centre of the problem.

The cost of the aged person's pension was small, and while important to historians of old age and poverty, and certainly to the aged themselves, it did not appear to be so to at least these communities in question, and it became less of a concern over the course of the seventeenth century. The aged paupers were always there, in relatively low numbers, with relatively few demands, except perhaps in their final years, with relatively containable costs, and for a relatively short time, as death was soon to claim them. They were a problem easily solved and dispatched by the increasingly harried seventeenth-century civic administrator. Vestries, ratepayers and poor law unions throughout the country struggled with the burden of poor relief, and that struggle would only intensify until the development of the New Poor Law in 1832. It was, however, not motivated by the needs of the elderly.

[139] Until 1675, approximately half of Cratfield's pensioners were elderly, dropping to about 40 per cent during the last quarter of the century. Cf. Ottaway's findings for the eighteenth century that indicate a growing elderly presence on the relief rolls, based on comparisons of percentages of those on relief. But beware my earlier warning of the dangers intrinsic in such comparisons. Ottaway, 'Providing', pp. 393, 402–3.
[140] Ottaway notes the contrary tend in the eighteenth century, with the elderly becoming a greater burden to the community as the century progressed. Ottaway, 'Decline of Life', ch. 6.

Case study biographies

The average old age pension in Cratfield and Poslingford differed by only a few pence a week, yet the availability of additional forms of relief varied significantly between these two communities. The presence or absence of non-stipendiary charity was the pivotal element in determining the elderly's relative comfort levels. By looking in detail at the lives of two representative aged collectioners, we can personalize the statistical averages presented above, and also compare the relative degree of support available to the elderly of both communities, confirming the vital role played by non-stipendiary relief.

Mary Tallant's life and poor relief career were fairly typical among Cratfield's aged pensioners (Figure 4.1). Widow of the ne'er-do-well sexton Ruben Tallant, Mary received her first poor relief payment in her own right in 1654, the year Ruben died. She was then about 56 years old. At the beginning of her widowhood, Mary 'took over' her husband's 12d a week stipend for the remainder of that year.[141] Ruben's death was expensive for Mary, not only in the loss of her husband's wages, but also in the cost of a decent Christian burial, which in Cratfield ran to 3s or more.[142] The churchwardens appear to have responded to this expense by initially maintaining the level of her husband's pension, in spite of the smaller household. The following year her weekly sum dropped to 9d where it remained until 1662 when it was increased again, as Mary turned the age of 65, to 1s a week.[143] Mary Tallant had at least two, but probably three, grown children living in the parish: Elizabeth, already 20 years old at the time of her father's death; Robert, 29, and Thomas, 25 years old. By 1661 Robert was a ratepayer and by 1655 Thomas was on parish relief. The presence of children, including a ratepaying son, did not seem to alter the level of Mary's relief. Her pension remained at 1s a week until her death at age 71.[144]

Mary Tallant received additional assistance at times of acute illness. She was also awarded sizeable cash payments periodically throughout 1663 and 1664, though their causes were not noted.[145] The parish helped her in other ways, including house repairs requiring forty-one 'nayles to use about the Widow Tallen's house' in 1658. It is likely that she may have shared her house with the 64-year-old Rose Brown, for the accounts record 4d 'given to Rose Brown & Widdow Tallowin for a key'.[146] While this key may have been intended for things other than their front door, co-residence was in character

---

[141] Cratfield CWA, SROI, FC62/A2/217 (1654).

[142] See also Cratfield CWA, SROI, FC62/A6/131 (1614).

[143] Cratfield OSA, SROI, FC62/A2/1 (1662).

[144] Cratfield OSA, SROI, FC62/A2/1.

[145] Illness payments: Cratfield OSA, SROI, FC62/A2/1, *passim*. Cash payments: Cratfield CWA, SROI, FC62/A6/268, 270 (1663–64, 1664).

[146] Cratfield CWA, SROI, FC62/A6/246 (1659).

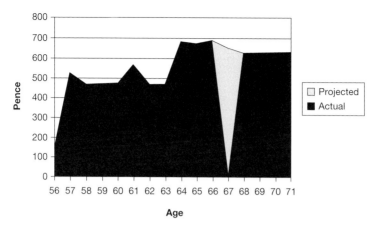

Figure 4.1 Mary Tallant of Cratfield

with what we know about the two women. Rose Brown had a long history of illness, including the 'falling sicknes', and Mary Tallant had a history of caring for others.[147] It was probably a mutually beneficial arrangement for all concerned – Rose Brown, Mary Tallant and the vestry. Widow Tallant did not end her life in the throes of sickness and disease, but seemed to live out her last years on her smallish pension.

Like Cratfield, Poslingford had its own fairly representative aged pensioner. This was 'old' Thomas Plume, born in 1608 and married to the widow Prudence Steven in September 1638 (Figure 4.2). They apparently had no children of their own, nor did the Widow Steven have any from her previous union, at least none traceable within the parish. Thomas entered the arena of organized relief well after the death of his wife, as a recipient of one of Poslingford's endowed charities. He first appeared in the records of May 1662, receiving 4d per year from 'Mistress Ashfield and Mister Strut's gift', which provided 7s annually for the poor of the parish. Thomas was then 54 years old. A few years later he received a small fortune in the sum of 5s 6d, when the will of 'Frances Golding spinster ante to Thomas Golding esquire' was examined, and it appeared that 'she lickwise gave to the poore in monye twenty shillings and as much woode to them as came to six pound tenne shillings'.[148] After a year of relative wealth, Plume resumed his charitable dole on a much less grand

---

[147] Cratfield CWA, SROI, FC62/A6/212, 246, 270 (1651, 1659, 1664). Cratfield OSA, SROI, FC62/A2/1, *passim*. For the employment of the poor, see M. Pelling, 'Illness Among the Poor in an Early Modern English Town: The Norwich Census of 1570', *Continuity and Change* 3 (1988), pp. 273–90, and D. Willen, 'Women in the Public Sphere in Early Modern England: The Case of the Urban Working Poor', *Sixteenth Century Journal* 19 (1988), pp. 559–76.
[148] Poslingford CD, SROB, FL615/7/1 (1665).

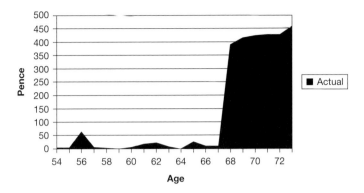

Figure 4.2 Old Thomas Plume of Poslingford

scale. Drawing one at a time upon a number of different endowments, the level of his support remained low, only gradually increasing to a total of 1s a year from the now combined charity of Ashfield, Strut and Golding.[149]

At age 69 'Old Thomas' received his first pension: paid 'to John Deekes for Old Thomas Plume for 54 weekes . . . 26 of them at 6 pence per weeke and 28 at 8 pence per weeke', a fairly traditional amount totalling £1 11s 8d.[150] The fact that this sum was not paid directly to Old Thomas was certainly charac-teristic of Poslingford. Instead of the more typical choice from the marginally poor, it was paid to prominent villager John Deekes. Thomas Plume lived out the remainder of his life receiving a theoretical 8d a week through the hands of John Deekes, with the cost of his burial sheet, 3s 6d, added on at the end.

As pensioners, Mary Tallant and Thomas Plume were similar. Both entered organized poor relief, significantly, after the death of their spouses, and both received similar pensions. They were also representative of the other collec-tioners in their community. Plume and Tallant followed a standard relief pattern and received their village's standard pension. Yet a visual comparison of their poor relief graphs powerfully confirms what a reading of their biographies suggests: the sizeable and sustained availability of non-stipendiary charity in Cratfield's greater poor relief scheme produced strikingly higher levels of old age support.[151] Perhaps there is no more vivid example of the importance of non-pension assistance.

[149] Poslingford CD, SROB, FL615/7/1 (1665–75).
[150] Poslingford CD, SROB, FL615/7/1 (1667).
[151] Both examples are drawn from the late seventeenth century to allow direct comparisons between graphs without having to account for inflation.

The strength of the pension

A question debated hotly among students of the Poor Law is the adequacy of parish pensions. In other words, were they large enough to meet one's needs or were they only supplementary earnings?[152] Popular opinion clearly thought the plight of the aged was the worst of all the poor. 'Poor people are over-charged sore with grief/and the aged sore [sic], alas! they are the chief', expressed the view of at least one ballad writer.[153] Yet social commentators such as William Harrison believed that a well-managed pension *ought* to leave the 'godly and well disposed' 'sufficiently provided for'.[154] Two approaches to this question are pursued below. The first is to compare the value of weekly pensions to contemporary wage rates and estimates of their purchasing power. The second is to construct a hypothetical budget for the aged poor by estimating their expenditures on necessities such as diet, rent, fuel and clothing. A comparison with the daily wages of an agricultural labourer in southern England quickly reveals that pensions in both Cratfield and Poslingford were not intended to replace even the average earnings of a farm worker (Table 4.5). Cratfield's collectioners averaged 1.8d a day in the 1570s compared to 8d available through agricultural employment. Even Richard Dunning, the author of *A Plaine and Easie Method, Shewing How the Office of the Overseer of the Poor may be Managed*, considered 3d a day in the summer and 2d in the winter a reasonable wage.[155] Even when the amount earned by a labourer is deflated to reflect the family it was intended to support, it was still more than what a pensioner typically received. For example, the 8d a day paid to a farm worker might be subdivided as follows: 4d for him, and 2d each for his wife and child. When it is remembered that early modern economies were based on the household, and that the household head, while the greatest contributor, was not the sole one, the gap between what a single male needed to survive and what an aged pensioner was given grew still greater.[156] At all times, in either Cratfield or Poslingford, labourers received between three and ten times more than those on relief.

Looking at purchasing power, we can easily chart the well-documented fall in real wage rates.[157] Interestingly, the drop in the 1610s relative purchasing

---

[152] Questions whirl around the relative generosity of pensions between the old and new poor laws. For a starting point, see Thomson, 'Provision'. See also his 'Decline of Social Welfare', pp. 451–82, and Lees, *Solidarities*, p. 52.

[153] *The Poor Man put to a Pinch: Or, A Declaration of these Hard Times* (Pepys, IV: 299).

[154] W. Harrison, *The Description of England*, ed. G. Edelen (Ithaca, NY, 1968), p. 181.

[155] Dunning, *Plaine and Easie Method*, A3.

[156] This is based on calculations made by Ottaway in 'Providing', pp. 406–7.

[157] For the essential introduction to early modern inflation, see R. B. Outhwaite, *Inflation in Tudor and Early Stuart England* (2nd edn, Basingstoke, 1982).

Table 4.5 Wage rates, price indexes and pensions by decade

Decade	(1)	(2)	(3)	(4)	(5)	(6)
1500s	4.00/d					106
1510s	4.00/d					116
1520s	4.17/d					159
1530s	4.33/d					161
1540s	4.66/d					217
1550s	6.33/d					315
1560s	7.00/d					298
1570s	8.17/d	1.8/d	0.5/d			241
1580s	8.00/d	1.1/d	0.8/d			389
1590s	8.66/d	1.6/d	1.5/d			530
1600s	8.66/d	1.5/d	1.4/d			527
1610s	9.00/d	2.8/d	1.6/d			583
1620s	10.00/d	1.4/d	1.2/d			585
1630s	11.33/d	1.2/d	1.5/d			687
1640s	12.00/d	0.9/d	1.1/d			723
1650s	11.00/d	1.4/d	1.5/d			687
1660s	11.00/d	2.0/d	1.9/d	2.3/d	0.6/d	702
1670s	11.00/d	1.8/d	1.7/d	2.4/d	1.1/d	675
1680s	11.00/d	2.1/d	2.4/d	2.4/d	1.5/d	631
1690s	11.14d	1.8/d	1.9/d	2.9/d	1.8/d	737

Notes: (1) Daily wage rates of agricultural labourers in southern England; (2) Cratfield daily pensions; (3) Cratfield daily aged pensions; (4) Poslingford daily pensions; (5) Poslingford daily aged pensions; and (6) Price of a composite unit of foodstuffs (1451–75 = 100).

power was answered by an increase of the Cratfield pension from 1.5d to 2.8d per day. This mirrors a similar increase in the wages of agricultural labourers, except that the increase in pensions was greater than the rise of prices.[158] Yet a small rural parish could not sustain such efforts indefinitely, and eventually the value of Cratfield's weekly pensions returned to their traditional levels. Prices, however, continued to climb.

Pensioners may have been sheltered by their community from some of the most severe aspects of price inflation through the community distribution of corn and temporarily increased poor relief. The parish subsidized prices in 1623, 1630, 1631 and 1696 of 'wheate which was sould out to the pore'.[159] Yet such parochial means were limited, designed for only short-term alleviation of poverty. The value of the parish stipend fell both in nominal value and real terms between 1570 and 1600. It continued to fall, but less dramatically, until 1650 when prices stabilized and the pension plateaued. Prior to this, pauper

---

[158] Labourers received only a 0.34d a day increase, whereas Cratfield's pensioners collected an additional 1.3d a day.
[159] Cratfield CWA, SROI, FC62/A6/147, 156, 159, 161, 361 (1623, 1630, 1631, 1696).

pensions were certainly no match for the steady grind of rising prices and falling real wages.

Focusing on old age pensions reveals a slightly different situation. Increased pensions between 1570 and 1600 managed to keep the elderly above the overall inflation rate. These favourable conditions did not last and, lacking further substantial increases, the value of the aged poor's stipend faltered and fell. Economic stability and low inflation rates after 1650 slowed, but did not stop, Cratfield's aged poor's descent into further poverty. However, if in the generous Cratfield the weekly pension was not enough to live on, in what position did it the leave the aged poor in Poslingford?[160]

The second approach to gauging the worth of the weekly stipend is to engage in the always dubious exercise of constructing a hypothetical budget, an act fraught with potentially faulty guesses and incorrect assumptions. None the less, historians and economists alike still make the attempt.[161] Using values drawn from contemporary local sources, national figures and Ian Archer's innovative work on London's poor, we can suggest a tentative annual budget for Suffolk's elderly poor during the second half of the seventeenth century.

Food and drink were perhaps the single largest item of expenditure faced by the poor, and their most important outlay. Using the 1630s Suffolk wage rate, we learn that adult male labourers consumed between 8d and 15d a day in food.[162] Clearly, the requirements of an old widow were much smaller. Perhaps more indicative of the poor's needs was the 3d food allowance allotted to 'the woman employed in picking of Hopps weeding or other Husbandry or housewifery'.[163] Arguably, the aged poor could survive on even less. The York authorities in the 1590s felt that 1.5–2d a day was adequate for those who were 'aged, lame and impotente and past their worke', being the minimum 'under which some a poore creator cannot lyve'.[164]

Food costs, however, could be reduced by a diet virtually void of meat and containing only limited dairy products.[165] A subsistence diet of vegetables

---

[160] Others have found the pension inadequate to meet the needs of the poor. See Barker-Read, 'Treatment', p. 139, and Slack, 'Poverty and Politics', p. 175.

[161] Archer, *Pursuit of Stability*, pp. 190–7; Wrightson and Levine, *Poverty and Piety*, pp. 37–40. For France, see O. Hufton, *The Poor of Eighteenth-Century France, 1750–1789* (Oxford, 1974), pp. 38–43, and her 'Begging, Vagrancy, Vagabondage and the Law: An Aspect of the Problem of Poverty in Eighteenth-Century France', *European Studies Review* 2 (1972), pp. 107–8. For criticisms of Archer's budget, see S. Rappaport's review in *History and Computing* 4 (1992), pp. 149–50.

[162] This represents the difference between rates with and without food. CUL, 'Suffolk Wage Rates', fols 72v–73v.

[163] CUL, 'Suffolk Wage Rates', fols 72v–73v, 73v.

[164] Archer, *Pursuit of Stability*, p. 182; *York Civic Records Vol. VIII*, ed. A. Raine (Yorkshire Archaeological Society Record Series, CVIV, York, 1953), pp. 157–8.

[165] Barker-Read, 'Treatment', pp. 120–59, 192, 250–3, and Laurence, *Women in England*, p. 146. For eighteenth-century France, see Hufton, *The Poor of Eighteenth Century France*, pp. 44–8.

and grains, in fact, was a distinguishing characteristic of the poor. William Harrison remarked in his *Description of England* (1587) that to the better sort vegetables 'remained either unknown or supposed as food more meet for hogs and savage beasts to feed upon than mankind'.[166] Further savings could be achieved through a system of 'compromise strategies', such as purchasing poor-quality grain. Ian Archer proposes that another 25 per cent could be saved in this manner. Therefore, 2d a day might be the required minimum for food.

A roof over one's head was arguably less pressing than food for one's stomach. Sleeping rough was as valid an option for the poor in the seventeenth century as it is today. Consequently, rent accounted for a smaller portion of a pauper's budget than food. In the early seventeenth century, Cratfield's overseers paid rents of an average of 15s 7d a year. Wrightson and Levine suggest that a family of five needed 20s a year for accommodation in 1690s Essex.[167] During the same period, Poslingford's overseers paid even higher amounts for single individuals: 6d a week, or 26s a year. Acknowledging the effects of inflation upon Cratfield's earlier rents and recognizing the potential for 'compromise strategies' at work in Poslingford, Wrightson and Levine's annual estimate of 20s is perhaps the best figure for our late seventeenth-century budget.

Fuel, the third item in our hypothetical budget, could vary enormously in price between geographical locations. A London pauper in the 1590s could expect an annual fuel cost of 12s a year.[168] One hundred years later in Terling the annual fuel bill was projected at 20s.[169] Wood was usually distributed in Poslingford only once a year, with each person receiving '2/4' load at a cost of 10s a person. Not enough to see them through the winter, the aged poor would have needed to supplement this supply privately. Cratfield, on the other hand, had inexpensive fuel supplied from the town lands. Only the cost of its cutting and distribution was borne by the parish.[170] On the occasions when the poor were given money in lieu of wood it was at an equivalent of 12s a load. We know too that five loads a year was considered enough to meet the needs of middling widows.[171] Therefore, given the reduced requirements of the aged poor, their overwhelming need to cut costs and a long history of hypothermia

[166] Appleby, 'Diet in Sixteenth Century England', pp. 108–9; Drummond and Wilbraham, *The Englishman's Food*, p. 49; and Harrison, *Description of England*, p. 264.

[167] Wrightson and Levine, *Poverty and Piety*, p. 40.

[168] Archer, *Pursuit of Stability*, p. 194.

[169] Wrightson and Levine, *Poverty and Piety*, p. 40.

[170] Cratfield's town lands – Rose Larkes and Sallow Pightells – supplied both wood and timber. When these properties were leased to Thomas Broadbank, a clause was inserted restricting the amount of wood he could have to six loads, leaving the remainder for the use of the town. Cratfield TB, SROI, FC62/E1/3 (1650).

[171] L. A. Botelho, '"The Old Woman's Wish": Widows by the Family Fire? Widows' Old Age Provision in Rural England, 1500–1700', *Journal of Family History* 7 (2002), pp. 59–78.

in old age, approximately 20s a year may be considered an average expenditure on this item.[172]

Clothing was the least important item in the poor's budget and the 'most awkward element' in their historical reconstruction.[173] The difficulty centres on the frequency with which clothing was replaced.[174] The parish records suggest it was seldom. Hannah White was uncharacteristic. She spent much of her life heavily subsidized by the parish, including the receipt of clothing in most years.[175] While a complete set of new garments yearly was unlikely for the poor, some items would need replacing or mending on a regular basis. Yet such expenses were outside the usual brief of the overseers.[176]

Cost-cutting strategies existed, such as the active second-hand trade and pawning which flourished in all communities. An often overlooked aspect of savings would be the repair, rather than the replacement, of clothing.[177] Mary Durant of Poslingford provides just one example of the parish paying for the 'mending' of her clothes. Clothes were also handed down from one generation to the next, and from gentry to poor.[178] The cost of clothing adult women changed little in the early modern period. Archer suggests that clothes were replaced annually in the 1590s at a cost of 14s a new suit.[179] Wrightson and Levine calculated 15s yearly expenditure for a gown, linen, stockings and shoes in the 1690s.[180] Poslingford's overseers monitored expenditure closely, itemizing amounts up to 15s to fit out female paupers with shoes, cap, neckcloth, bodice, shift and 'one linsey-wooley apron'.[181] However, 13s a person, such as that spent 'for cloathing of Hannah White' in 1695, was generally considered sufficient for the poor.[182] Second-hand clothing, repair, or simply doing without

[172] See also Barker-Read, 'Treatment', p. 92.

[173] See also M. Spufford's *The Great Reclothing of Rural England: Petty Chapman and his Wares in the Seventeenth Century* (London, 1984).

[174] The Tonbridge workhouse in Barker-Read's study replaced their inmates' clothing every three years. Barker-Read, 'Treatment', pp. 96–7.

[175] Hannah White received clothing in 1672, 1682, 1684, 1689, 1693, 1694, 1695, 1696, 1698, 1699 and 1700. Poslingford OSA, SROB, FL615/7/1.

[176] Poslingford OSA, SROB, FL615/7/1 (1675). Norwich in the 1570s, however, viewed clothing as an important aspect in the prevention of illness, and thus made it an item of 'considerable expenditure' in their accounts. Pelling, 'Healing the Sick Poor', p. 118.

[177] For an example of mending, see the mending of 'chapman's boys'' clothes. Poslingford OS, SROB, FL615/7/1 (1682).

[178] Wrightson and Levine, *Poverty and Piety*, pp. 38–9; Barker-Read, 'Treatment', p. 98.

[179] Archer, *Pursuit of Stability*, p. 193.

[180] Other examples of the cost and frequency of new clothes in London include a bequest providing 'a frieze gown, shirt and shoes for twelve men' each year at a cost of 13s a person in the 1570s, rising to 14s in the 1590s. Archer, *Pursuit of Stability*, p. 193; Wrightson and Levine, *Poverty and Piety*, p. 40.

[181] Cratfield OSA, SROB, FC62/A2/1 (1682, 1684, 1698).

[182] Poslingford OSA, SROB, FL615/7/1 (1695). For one of many similar examples, see 'to buy clothes for Sarah Smith, 13s 2d'. Poslingford OSA, SROB, FL615/7/1 (1693).

could further lessen the burden on annual budgets. Ten shillings a year might therefore be considered adequate.[183]

A typical annual budget for the aged poor in late seventeenth-century Suffolk might look like this:

Diet	60s
Rent	20s
Fuel	20s
Clothing	10s
Total 110s or £5 10s	

Desperate times breed desperate measures, and the poor could easily be forced to decrease their spending well below the levels suggested here. If a further 25 per cent were cut to create a 'saver budget', the total would be 82s 6d a year. These figures are much lower than Gregory King's estimates of the 'charge of the poor per head' living in institutions. He estimated that costs in London ranged between £11 and £16; in market towns and other cities, £10; and those in 'the rest of the kingdom', £8 10s.[184] Sadly, most poor relief schemes would not be able to match these projected expenses.

Earlier (Table 4.4) we noted that Cratfield spent £2 7s 9d annually on each old age pensioner, and Poslingford considerably less.[185] Even in the more generous Cratfield, with its odd jobs, additional cash payments, and relatively frequent help with rent and fuel, there was still a shortfall of £3 2s 3d between income and estimated annual costs. Clearly, organized relief alone was not sufficient to meet all the needs of Cratfield's aged poor. The situation in Poslingford is difficult to determine due to the distinctive practice of using third-party overseers. Still, I doubt that the £1 7s 8d spent annually on each aged pensioner was enough to offset the cost of an additional household member. It certainly did not come close to the level required for self-sufficiency: the shortfall between pension and projected self-sufficiency was £4 2s 4d.[186]

The gap between necessity and pension was bridged in a number of ways. First, the elderly's own labours, the spinning and nursing of the women, the message carrying and employments of the men, helped offset what the parish

---

[183] However, Lemire's work on second-hand and stolen clothing suggests that even the poorest were actively in pursuit of fashion. It also illustrates the wide range of alternatives to new clothing, including theft, hand-me-downs, gifts and reworking old clothes into new items. A cost-sensitive elderly woman had many options. Lemire, 'Theft', pp. 255–76.

[184] G. King, *Observations and Conclusions Natural and Political upon the State and Condition of England* (1696), repr. in G. Chalmers, *An Estimate of the Comparative Strength of Great Britain; and of the Losses of Trade, from every War since the Revolution . . . to which is now annexed, Gregory King's Celebrated State of England* (London, 1804), p. 73.

[185] See p. 138.

[186] Poslingford's projected shortfall was £4 2s 4d.

did not provide. Furthermore, the aged living in those remaining areas with an active manorial system may have benefited from the paternal oversight of its lord.[187] Nevertheless, more assistance was often needed. The give-and-take of mutual aid undoubtedly helped ease the burdens of the aged poor.[188] Small gifts, food, loans and all manner of support throughout a lifetime of shared friendship and close contact unquestionably resulted in tangible assistance for an elderly neighbour. Eventually, friends nursed the aged in times of sickness, and occasionally took the impotent elderly into their own homes.[189] The give-and-take of community living, the build-up of what some call 'social capital', made neighbourhood ties an essential aspect of old age survival.[190]

The elderly poor engaged in creative cost-cutting and incoming-generating schemes. We have already seen how the aged formed complex households made up of a variety of age combinations, thus 'cushioning . . . life-cycle risks'.[191] They also took in lodgers for extra income;[192] those with a little cash might loan it for profit;[193] or conversely they might seek a loan themselves. Likewise,

---

[187] Smith, 'Some Issues', pp. 82–3. For those old age provisions arranged in the manorial courts see Clark, 'Quest', pp. 189–90; Razi, 'Myth', p. 27; R. M. Smith, 'The Manorial Court and the Elderly Tenant in Late Medieval England' in *Life, Death and the Elderly*, pp. 1–38.

[188] See Jutte, *Poverty and Deviance*, for a discussion of 'the importance of social networks', pp. 83–99. Pelling's example from Norwich is typical: 'a lame but able woman in her fifties, did not work but had alms of 1d a week, distilled aqua vitae and "lived off her friends"'. Pelling, 'Healing the Sick Poor', p. 120. See also Beier, 'Social Problems', p. 68; Laslett, 'Family, Kinship and Collectivity', pp. 153–77, and his 'The Significance of the Past in the Study of Ageing', *Ageing and Society* 4 (1984), p. 385; Smith, 'Some Issues', pp. 77–9; Wales, 'Poverty', pp. 384, 386.

[189] For examples in Cratfield, see p. 345. See also the case of Margaret Moore of Ipswich in 1589. J. Webb, ed., *Poor Relief in Elizabethan Ipswich* (Suffolk Records Society, Vol. 9, 1966), p. 29, also quoted in Jutte, *Poverty and Deviance*, p. 95.

[190] On social capital, see P. Bourdieu, 'Cultural Reproduction and Social Reproduction' in R. Brown, ed., *Knowledge, Education and Cultural Change* (London, 1973), pp. 71–112; P. Bourdieu, 'The Forms of Capital' in J. G. Richardson, ed., *Handbook of Theory and Research for the Sociology of Education* (New York, 1986), pp. 241–58; van Leeuwen, 'Logic', pp. 603–4; Jutte, *Poverty and Deviance*, p. 85. The breakdown of such ties, according to Keith Thomas, could lead to accusations of witchcraft. K. Thomas, *Religion and the Decline of Magic* (New York, 1971), pp. 553–5, 557–9. Thomas also suggests that the *threat* of witchcraft was sometimes used to secure 'charity' from neighbours. Geoffrey Scarfe maintains that such arrangements were formed by accident rather than by design. G. Scarfe, *Witchcraft and Magic in Sixteenth and Seventeenth Century Europe* (Basingstoke, 1987), p. 42. See also MacDonald, *Mystical Bedlam*, pp. 107–8.

[191] Jutte, *Poverty and Deviance*, p. 87.

[192] Beier, 'Social Problems', p. 61.

[193] Cressy, 'Kinship and Kin Interaction', pp. 51–2; Evans, 'Holy Ghost Gild', p. 37; B. A. Holderness, 'Widows in Pre-Industrial Society: An Essay upon their Economic Function' in *Land, Kinship and Life-Cycle*, pp. 435–42. Pawnbroking also generated income for the aged. J. Boulton, *Neighbourhood and Society: A London Suburb in the Seventeenth Century* (Cambridge, 1987), p. 88; Holderness, 'Widows in Pre-Industrial Society', p. 439.

the guilds of pre-Reformation England loaned money to the robust and gave alms to the frail.[194] Agricultural labourers may well have received a price reduction when purchasing grains, or may have paid for it with the promise of future work.[195] Help-ales, as described by Judith Bennett, were still another form of early modern self-help.[196]

Other techniques employed by the aged poor to supplement parish provisions used 'the trifles of nature': collecting wood from 'heaths and hedgerows', feeding poultry with the neighbours' scraps or brewery waste, and collecting nuts and berries. Old women with knowledge of medicine collected plants to sell to local healers.[197] Begging, too, was often a tolerated option.[198] There was always the pawnshop where one could exchange personal items such as clothes for a quick, if small, infusion of cash: 'My wife she sold her Petticoat, and pawn'd her weeding ring/To Relieve me in my misery, in any kind of thing.'[199] Creativity born of despair would somehow fill the gap between pension and expenses. As Peter Laslett explains, such mixed methods could see a person well into old age: 'the old and the very old . . . could earn, beg, scrounge, or even pilfer little bits until very late in life'.[200] In the 1637 Hertfordshire corn crisis:

> the necessities of labouring men, and of poor people, by reason of the dearth of corn and want of work is so extreme . . . that having pawned and sold their goods, many of them do not only break hedges and spoil woods and wander abroad for relief, but also they steal sheep in the night . . . and pilfer for provision of victuals.[201]

Kin could also assist an aged family member, though as we have seen, adult children would have supplemented their parents' upkeep, and would have rarely assumed its entirety. Still, families could contribute towards their elderly parents in significant ways by giving aid in kind: chopping wood, gardening, mending houses, or sharing a pot of soup. Neighbours could often share this

---

[194] B. R. McRee, 'Charity and Gild Solidarity in Late Medieval England', *Journal of British Studies* 32 (1993), pp. 205, 211, 214, 216; Smith, 'Some Issues', p. 82.

[195] Walter, 'Social Economy of Dearth', pp. 100–1.

[196] J. D. Bennett, 'Conviviality and Charity in Medieval and Early Modern England', *Past and Present* 134 (1992), pp. 19–41.

[197] Barker-Read, 'Treatment', pp. 263–73.

[198] Laslett, 'Family, Kinship and Collectivity', p. 164; Pelling, 'Healing the Sick Poor', p. 119; Wales, 'Poverty', pp. 359–60.

[199] While in this example he is sick from drinking too much, it still demonstrates the recourse many needy families took to the pawnshop. *The Pleasant Conceites of Old Hobson the Merry London* (London, 1607).

[200] Laslett, 'Family, Kinship and Collectivity', p. 164.

[201] Slack, *Poverty and Policy*, pp. 101–2.

role with kin, or assume it in entirety in the absence of relatives. A helpful neighbour might be well advised to exercise tact, especially if there were adult children nearby, as some families could be sensitive about outside help. Ralph Josselin, the Essex vicar and diarist, was rebuked by one such adult son who forbad Josselin to help his ageing mother in the future. According to Josselin, 'he sent mee word I had business of my own, I should not trouble my selfe with his mother'.[202] Josselin may well have offered his assistance in an overtly critical manner, but the impulse to help the aged poor, even those without a blood tie, was unquestionable.

Unfortunately, there is no exact formula for a successful economy of makeshifts. Some of the aged poor's survival techniques have been described above, and many more remain undiscovered. What we do know is that supplements to the pension were available in rural communities, and more importantly, they were vital for survival. 'The frailty of the family economy of the poor', warns Olwen Hufton, 'cannot be over stressed.'[203] We have not yet discovered their full range of alternative incomes, their effectiveness, or the particulars of their use. We do know, however, that whatever form they took, such creative measures would have to contribute nearly half of the aged poor's annual budget.

Conclusion

Early modern England, indeed like much of the Continent, was preoccupied with discriminatory poor relief and obsessed with directing aid into the hands of the most needy: 'work for those that will labour, punishment for those that will not, and bread for those who cannot'.[204] This prevailing cultural ethos may have worked to the advantage of the elderly, as quintessential members of the aged poor. Their failing physical strength and the poverty which resulted from it were not their fault, not a product of any moral failing, nor the end result of idleness. Consequently, they approached the parish vestry from the moral high ground and with a solid negotiating platform. Yet, as the elderly themselves well knew, there were no guarantees of relief. In villages such as Poslingford, with high levels of poverty and relatively little wealth available for relief, the chances of not collecting a pension in old age were real. Poslingford was not an isolated case: Harbury, Warwickshire, for example, had to deny relief in 1648 to an elderly couple who had been living and working in the parish for over forty years.[205]

---

202 A. Macfarlane, ed., *The Diary of Ralph Josselin, 1616–1683* (London, 1976), p. 614.
203 Hufton, 'Begging, Vagrancy, Vagabondage and the Law', p. 107.
204 Dunning, *Plaine and Easie Method*, A3.
205 Hindle, *Birthpangs*, p. 12.

With the increase of poverty, and the inclusion of the labouring poor as part of the worthy poor, parishes were finding themselves with increasing poor relief obligations and the need to curb expenditure. Hard decisions needed to be made, a criterion for selection decided upon. Religious affinity often served as the deciding factor in any number of early modern England's decisions, from a place in an almshouse to the choice of Cambridge college. Therefore, in villages with more poverty than assistance, a shared religious understanding between vestry and petitioner could well be the deciding factor in collecting a pension. This was, I believe, the situation in Poslingford, a seat of an active puritan community. The village hosted large numbers of poor, both indigenous and itinerant. It could not feed, house or clothe them all. Given the nature of early modern religiosity and the demands of the poor, a shared spiritual identity may have been the only meaningful way to select pensioners from among the poor.

Even with a weekly stipend, the aged poor's battle for survival was still not over. The parish pension was not intended to supply the recipient with total support; it was not an early modern retirement scheme. Its goal, as the overseers were reminded in 1601, was to supplement the efforts of the aged poor. 'It is called relief,' wrote the author of *An Ease for Overseers*, 'because it is . . . an ease or lightening of the burden.'[206] As we have seen in the lives of Poslingford's and Cratfield's elderly pensioners, poor relief, including all of the extras one might collect in addition to the pension, was simply not enough to live on.

The lives of these aged individuals also reveal the limitations of our current understanding of early modern poor relief. The pension was undoubtedly a crucial component of survival, but it was not the only aspect of relief at play in the world of the poor. The historiographical overemphasis on the pension has obscured a fascinating mixture of mechanisms that worked together to ensure the aged poor's survival: work, informal and organized charity, miscellaneous relief, and the proximity to family. The relief of the aged was, in fact, the end result of the joint efforts of family, community, civil institutions, and the elderly themselves. The exact configuration of that joint project ultimately rested on a number of unpredictable variables, intangible cultural norms and local economic conditions.

[206] *An Ease for Overseers*, p. 22.

5

Conclusion

The aged poor of rural, early modern England were not uniformly assigned to the fringes of the physical community and to the extremities of its affection, as were the solitary woodsmen and terrifying witches that inhabit so many fairy-tales. The indigent elderly were very much part of the village's mental world, as well as within its physical bounds. They delivered messages, as well as babies. They nursed the sick, washed the dead, swept the church, and sometimes collected poor relief. They remained an active part of the daily give-and-take, the social exchange of village life.

Just as the elderly were an integrated component of rural living, so too was England part of Europe. England and the Continent faced the same problems of population pressure, unstable economies and the budding of capitalistic exchange that characterized much of the sixteenth and seventeenth centuries. They also shared a common intellectual climate that included civic humanism, religious reform (distinct, that is, from the Reformation) and the centralizing state. It was not, therefore, surprising to find similar solutions to similar problems across western Europe. However, just as humanism was adapted to suit the particulars of each region, such as a preoccupation with religious questions in the North, so too did these humanistically inspired thinkers adapt the tenets of the New Learning (as it was called in England) to solve the problems of poverty as manifested there. In England, poor relief was clearly cut from the same cloth as the rest of Europe, but the manner in which it was tailored resulted in a distinctive and in some areas unique form. Specifically, English poor relief was a national effort, theoretically uniform, and supported through a specific and designated poor rate. Each individual had a home parish which was legally obligated to support her or him in times of need. By the close of the sixteenth century, England had taken its first steps towards a national welfare system.

While standardized by statute, the particulars of each community's poor relief were shaped directly and significantly by its local environment. As we have seen above, whether a village was rich or poor affected greatly what they could do towards relieving poverty, as well as the manner in which they did it. In wealthy Cratfield, on the one hand, a fairly wide range of problems were addressed through the efforts of the village, and, in the cases of the very poor, this relief was at significantly high levels. In this community, a weekly stipend was combined with gifts of clothing, food, rent and cash, plus parish-provided odd jobs. Private charitable endowments only added to the already rich mix. Poslingford, on the other hand, was limited by the very poverty it sought to alleviate. A life spent in poverty is and was hard on the body, and the grinding poverty of Poslingford resulted consistently in earlier deaths than of their opposite numbers in Cratfield. While many in Poslingford were in need, only a desperate few were aided, leaving the majority to carry on by their own devices, at best collecting a small sum annually from carefully regulated private charity. For aged individuals lucky enough to be recognized by their overseers and singled out for aid, this assistance typically came at the loss of their personal independence. Those aged paupers were moved into the homes of other poor families, who, acting as third-party overseers, were paid by the parish to provide for their daily needs; while still others resided in the town house under the watchful eye of the entire village. Cratfield and Poslingford each adapted the statutes to match their needs, and in doing so created very different versions of the same statutory requirement to provide for their poor.

The defining aspects of the local context were not confined to the material and the economic, but extended as well into the nebulous realm of spirituality and religious affinity. This is not to say that puritanism was equated with parsimonious relief and a solid conviction that punishment and firm example could change the ways of the weak and the idle. In our case studies, both villages tended towards the hotter forms of Protestantism but still produced remarkably different poor relief schemes. Yet religion did have its role in the formation of local relief. A shared religious life (or at least the outward appearance of one) could well be the winnowing device used to separate those awarded regular relief and those left to limp by with infrequent and inadequate aid. In other words, in a community on the edge of economic collapse, such as Poslingford, overwhelmed with needy inhabitants, and unquestionably unable to help all who needed it, there had to be a selection mechanism. In a world deeply saturated with religion, who better to single out for aid than those who shared one's views? The religious leaning of Poslingford's chief inhabitants did not produce its rather draconian poor relief scheme – that was a product of the area's economic collapse and must be laid at the feet of the decimated cloth trade – but religion appears to have been the overseer's selection tool.

Whether in a prosperous parish or a particularly poor one, each potential pensioner had first to navigate the local micro-climate of the politicized parish. Often this involved a complex calculus of negotiation between elderly pauper and overseer. While the particulars of such exchanges remain obscure in Cratfield and Poslingford, we can draw upon other known negotiations and from the outcomes themselves to suggest that the successful applicant typically would have made much of at least the outward signs of their religiosity; they would have emphasized their local reputation if it was good, or downplayed it if it was bad; they would have recounted their years of previous service in and for the community; while at the same time reminding these officials of the religious and cultural dictums of honouring one's elders and providing for worthy souls who were no longer able to provide for themselves. Finally, a knowledge of the law itself could be called upon as initially unsuccessful applicants petitioned Justices for a reversal of a local decision. There was not yet a cultural expectation that the aged would receive assistance by right – there was no right to relief – yet there seems to be an expectation that aid would be available for those who could navigate the complex currents of local politics.

Once within the purview of the overseers, the assistance directed to the aged poor was individualized, reflecting that person's particular needs at that particular time. Firewood could supplement a pension. Food, help with rent or a loan could also be combined to ensure that the needs of that individual were addressed. This custom-cut approach would change over time, perhaps as late as the close of the eighteenth century, with aid becoming standardized and pre-packaged. However, during the early modern period, poor relief remained a national scheme, administered under localized circumstances, and the scale was such that it was tailored to the individual recipient.

The pressing question, therefore, is whether or not this proto-welfare system was successful. The answer is both No and Yes. The parish pension cannot be considered adequate by modern standards and compared to the modern welfare state. It did not provide complete support for the aged poor, not even when all recorded contributions of miscellaneous relief, such as food, clothing, rent and fuel, and all disbursements from private charities are taken into consideration. Yet the pension was successful according to its own guidelines which indicated assistance and not total maintenance. The statutes were based on the European-wide axiom that if one did not work, one did not eat. The English Poor Law provided help to those who were poor through no fault of their own and who concomitantly laboured as best they could towards their own upkeep. This last point has been largely overlooked by historians of the Poor Law, yet it appears to have been a key ingredient in the survival of the poor themselves.

Furthermore, the Elizabethan Poor Law was successful in real terms; it appears to have fundamentally improved both the quality and length of life of its recipients – at least in Poslingford and Cratfield. The qualitative aspect of a stipend is obvious: better food and better accommodation, if not warmer housing. The greatest testament to the success of the early Poor Law, at least in Cratfield and Poslingford, was the extended length of life it afforded the majority of the poor. The aged, marginally poor, who neither paid the rate nor received a pension, or who collected only miscellaneous relief at intervals, had the shortest collective life spans of the poor. These women and men worked hard to live, pulling together all possible resources in order to maintain their financial independence, in order to avoid the shame of 'going on the parish'. These efforts took years off their lives. In Poslingford, the marginally poor typically died at age 63 and in Cratfield at 69. The success of the English Poor Law can be measured – at least in these communities – by the positive effect that the weekly pension had on the life spans of its recipients. In Cratfield, the average age of a pensioner's death was 72 and in Poslingford it was 65. These figures are unquestionably drawn from too small a sample to draw too large a conclusion, but they are suggestive of the crucial role the Elizabethan

Poor Law may have played in the lives of the aged poor. It was as if the dependability of a fixed weekly sum relieved just enough of the burden of self-help to push these elderly into the material circumstances that promoted longevity. If success can be measured in terms of years on earth, the Elizabethan Poor Laws were clearly effective, at least through the opening years of the eighteenth century.

The value of a parish pension in old age cannot be denied; yet women and men experienced poverty in significantly different ways. Perhaps the most startling difference was that men seemed to need to be married in order to remain independent and not that women needed the protection and support of a male. Once elderly men were widowed they were frequently unable to manage alone. They quickly declined financially, entering the ranks of the pensioned poor. In fact, most elderly pensioners were single individuals. In Poslingford, with its limited poor relief to draw upon in times of need, the poorer members of the community tended to keep one daughter unmarried. In all likelihood, it was she who provided for her father in his old age, as is still the case in many families. While economic benefit was certainly derived from the ability of wives to live into old age, the value of companionship should not be underestimated. The loss of a life companion undoubtedly compounded the widower's economic problems and for many it appears to have been an impossible combination to overcome.

Judging from such experiences, more women were able to make the transition from middle age to old age than were men, although they did not fare as well thereafter. Typical women's work, such as spinning, sewing, victualling and nursing, tended to be poorly paid, which is why women on their own tended to be poor. Yet these were jobs which women did at all stages of life, from childhood through to death. Small as the income might be, it was steady. Her employment pattern was not broken as she grew older, while men often suffered a disturbing disruption to their work life, since the traditional jobs they once did with pride and ease were now too strenuous. Old men had to seek other employments, of which there were relatively few. These disruptions were difficult, both emotionally and economically; and doubly so if they occurred near the death of a spouse. Widows were known to 'cluster' in single households and grandchildren or other young children were also known to live with the elderly – both for company and for aid. Yet, women simply carried on. They did not have to find new forms of work; they did not have to redefine their role in the community; they did not have to experience the insecurity born of change. Instead, their business networks had been developed years earlier, and, if their reputation was good, they might continue to be employed past the point of peak efficiency as a form of dignified charity. This steady income, it appears, is what made the difference between marginal poverty and outright penury for the aged couple, and its loss was what prompted the widower's fall into serious indigence.

The nature of women's work had mixed results for the women themselves, arguably able to both shorten and lengthen their life spans in relation to the men of their community. In areas such as Poslingford, with its utter dependancy upon the cloth trade, female spinners would find work in all but the most dire circumstances. Age would have barely affected their ability to spin, given, as we saw above, blind and lame spinners in Norwich. The relatively steady income, coupled with parish relief, seems to have given aged women the competitive edge. Aged female pensioners in Poslingford tended to live a full six years longer than their male counterparts, dying only in their sixty-eighth year. Men, whose utility in the cloth trade was much more dependent upon their physical strength, their ability to operate the loom and to weave with the same speed as younger men, presumably worked less as they aged. In a world where the local economy was based on hand-spinning for the cloth trade, women may have been uniquely suited for self-help, if not always for self-sufficiency. Ironically, by the seventeenth century, it may have been the poorest women, in the poorest regions, who, among poor women, possessed the skills to best survive old age.

In non-cloth areas, with reduced by-employment for elderly women, aged females seem to have fared less well. This was certainly true in Cratfield. Old and poor women had relatively short life spans and were significantly outlived by men. Among Cratfield's marginally poor, the cost of staying off weekly poor relief was high in terms of years off a woman's life. Aged women who neither paid the rate nor collected relief typically died at age 64, while men carried on to the average age of 79. Similarly, of those who collected only miscellaneous relief, the average age of death was 65 for women and 72 for men. This pattern holds true for Cratfield's pensioners, as well. Men tended to live until their mid-seventies, on average until age 74, while women died at around age 66. The difference for women may lie in the nature of their work. Unlike Poslingford with the relatively physically undemanding spinning, women in Cratfield worked in the dairying trade. Such employment demanded strength and stamina. Old women, arguably, could not compete with the dairying maid. The benefits of a weekly pension could not compensate for the lack of employment probably experienced by this particular group of elderly women.

While focused on the aged poor, this study raises several considerations about the nature of old age in early modern England and underlines the importance of context when interpreting the past. First, the commonly held notion that in the past the elderly were few and far between, and consequently the centres of respect and reverence, has been utterly shattered. There was no rarity value in being old. Poslingford and Cratfield supported significant elderly populations; namely approximately 14 per cent of Cratfield's inhabitants were over 50 years of age and about 7 per cent of Poslingford's reached that bench-mark. The elderly were a common element of village life.

Once old, individuals did not suddenly stop being strong and productive members of society; they were not immediately weak and feeble. Poor Law payments reflected this pattern of physical decline, with more money and aid being added only gradually over the course of years and sometimes decades.

And, all the while, the aged poor were expected to work in whatever manner they could. As recognized by contemporaries, old age was divided into stages from the young-old to the old-old, and each individual travelled that path at his or her own pace.

Finally, the aged poor lived not only within the context of their community, but within the context of their own lives. In order to understand an individual's old age, one must also understand his or her youth. What networks had they built in youth that they could call upon in old age? How many children did they have? And, how well had they prospered? Had they, like Henry Worlich, run afoul of the vicar or other local worthy to the detriment of their political advancement? The foundations of how one's old age would be experienced (both materially and emotionally) were often laid in youth and middle age – adding a certain poignancy to the adage: As you sow so shall you reap.

The calculus of old age provision was a complex one. In addition, it may be that the best way to break down its variables into understandable components – and still be able to keep track of them – may be at the level of the individual and within the context of his or her politicized world.

Bibliography

MANUSCRIPT SOURCES

Bodleian Library, Oxford

Gough MS: Suffolk 4.
Gough MS: Suffolk 5.
Sancroft MS 28: Archbishop Sancraft Notebooks.
Tanner MS 226.
Tanner MS 324: List of manors in Suffolk with their chief inhabitants, 1655.
Top. Suffolk MS 6: Collections for the County of Suffolk.

British Library, London

Add MS 5,524.
Add MS 5,836: Extraneous Parochial Antiquities, or An Account of Various
    Churches with the Funeral Monuments in them in Divers Counties of
    England, William Cole Collection, 1746.
Add MS 8,189: Jermyn's Suffolk Collections, Vol. 22.
Add MS 15,520: Church Notes for the County of Suffolk, 1635–1665.
Add MS 19,102: Davy's Suffolk Collection, Risbridge Vol. I.
Add MS 19,103: Davy's Suffolk Collection, Risbridge Vol. II.
Add MS 19,132: Miscellaneous manuscripts relating to the Golding family.
Add MS 19,161: Davy's Suffolk Collection, Vol. LXXXV, Part I.
Add MS 32,496: Three contemporary impressions of witches and their familiars
    (1621).
Add MS 38,492: Puritan Survey of Church's Ministry to Reveal Inadequacies
    of the Established Religion, 23 August 1582.
Harleian MS 595: Archbishop Whitgift's Return, 1603.
Royal MS 18.c.vi: William Marshall's Poor Relief Proposal, 1536.

Cambridge University Library

Ff.V.13: This book is an abstract of the large [*Valor Ecclesiasticus*].

Hengrave MS 20: Visitation of Suffolk with Church Notes by William Hervey Clarenceux, 1561.
Hengrave MS 29: Suffolk Notes, Vols. I–II.
Hengrave MS 39: Antiquitates Suffolciences.
Vanneck MSS: Records of Cratfield Manor.

Huntington Library, San Marino, CA

EL 34: The Right Honorable Richard Earle of Carbery his Advice to his Sonn, Golden Grove, 30 September 1651.
EL 2522: Orders to be appointed to be executed in the Citie of London for setting roges and ydle persons to woorke and for the releife of the poore (1597).
EL 8572: Undated proposal for dealing with poverty by providing more responsible vestrymen, c. 1649–86.
MS STG Manorial Box 5, folder 34: The Stowe Collection, Wooton Underwood, Buckinghamshire, Overseers Rates, 1756–57.

Gloucestershire Record Office, Gloucester

Gloucestershire Diocesan Records, Vol. 40.

Lambeth Palace Library, London

Comm. XIIa/15/520–22: Parliamentary Survey, 15 October 1650.

Public Record Office, Chancery Lane, London

PROB 11: Prerogative Court of Canterbury; Wills from Cratfield and Poslingford, Suffolk, 1500–1700.

Suffolk Record Office, Bury St Edmunds

Archdeaconry of Sudbury:
IC500/5/1–7: Archdeaconry of Sudbury Court Books, 1544–73, 1577–96, 1605–12, 1630–1652, 1664–78, 1678–98, 1697–1739.

Bury St Edmunds:
GB519/25: Cadge's Charity Account Book, Bury St Edmunds.
GB519/25: Charity Documents.

Clare:
FL501/11/164: Cadge's Charity.
FL501/11/15, 165–186: Charity Documents.
FL501/11/50: Deeds.
FL501/11/58, 137–164, 230: Goose Croft Bread Charity.

Little Waldingfield:
FL645/1/2: Town Book.
K1/1: Will.

Poslingford:
FL615/4/1: Parish Register.
FL615/7/1: Charity Documents.
FL615/7/1: Churchwardens' Accounts.
FL615/7/1: Constables' Accounts.
FL615/7/1: Overseers' Accounts.
FL615/7/1: Town Book.
Probate Inventories, 1500–1700.
Wills, 1500–1700.

Suffolk Record Office, Ipswich

Cratfield:
FC62/A2/1: Overseers' Accounts.
FC62/A3/1: Solemn Vow and Covenant, 1642.
FC62/A6/1–363: Churchwardens' Accounts.
FC62/D1/1–3: Parish Registers.
FC62/E1/1–2: Town Book.
FC62/G9/1–2: Settlement Certificates.
FC62/G10/1–4: Removal Orders.
Probate Inventories, 1500–1700.
Unpublished letter from Stanford, Broom and Stanford Auctioneers, Valuers
    and Estate Agents to the Trustees of Cratfield's Town Estate, dated 19 April
    1961.
Wills, 1500–1700.

Fressingfield:
FC90/L3/8: Deed.

Quarter Sessions.
B105/2/7–10.

PRINTED PRIMARY SOURCES

The Acts and Monuments of John Foxe, edited by G. Townsend. Vol. 5. London, 1846.

Allen, R., *A Treatise of Christian Beneficence*. London, 1600.

An Answer to the Forced Marriage, or the Old Mans Vindication. London, 1685(?).

Arthington, H., *Provisions for the Poor*. London, 1597.

Articles to be Enquired of by the Church-Wardens and Questmen in the Ordinary Visitation of the Right Worshipfull Mr Robert Pearson, Doctor of Divinitie, and Archdeacon of Suffolk, or his Officall, London, 1618.

Articles . . . of John Lord Bishop of Norwich. Cambridge, 1619.

Articles . . . of Master Doctor Pearson, Archdeacon of Suffolke. London, 1625.

Articles . . . of Richard, Lord Bishop of Norwich. Cambridge, 1633.

Articles . . . of Master Doctor Pearson Arch-Deacon of Suffolke. London, 1633.

Articles to be enquired of in the Metropoliticall Visitation of the Most Rev. Father William . . . Lord Arch-Bishop of Canterbury . . . and for the Diocese of Norwich. London, 1635.

Articles . . . of Master Doctor Pearson, Archdeacon of Suffolk. London, 1636.

Articles of . . . Matthew Bishop of Norwich. London, 1636.

Articles . . . of Richard Mountaigu Bishop of Norwich. This Book of Articles, being extremely negligently printed at London, (which impression I disavow) I was forced to review it and have it printed at Cambridge. Cambridge, 1638.

Articles of . . . Mr. Doctor Pearson, Archdeacon of Suffolke. London, 1638.

Articles of . . . Doctor Bostock, Arch-Deacon of Suffolk. London, 1640.

Articles of . . . Edward Lord Bishop of Norwich. London, 1662.

Articles Agreed upon by the Archbishop and Bishops. London, 1669.

Articles Agreed upon by the Archbishop and Bishops. London, 1686.

Articles Agreed upon by the Archbishop and Bishop. London, 1693.

B., J., *The Intriguing Widow: Or the Honest Wife*. London, 1705.

Bacon, F., *The Cure of Old Age and Preservation of Youth*. London, 1683.

Ball, J., *A Short Treatise Contayning All the Principall Grounds of Christian Religion* (9th edn). London, 1633.

Banbury Corporation Records: Tudor and Stuart. The Banbury Historical Society, Vol. 15. Oxford, 1977.

Baxter, R., *Compassionate Counsel to all Young-Men. Especially I. London Apprentices. II. Students of Divinity, Physick, and Law. III. The Sons of Magistrates and Rich Men*. London, 1681.

Bellers, F., *Abrahams Interment: Or The Good Old-Mans burial in a good Old Age Opened in a Sermon, At Bartholomews Exchange, July 24, 1655. At the Funerall of the Worshipfull John Lamotte Esq; Sometimes Alderman of the City of London*. London, 1656.

Betterton, T., *The Amorous Widow; or, the Wanton Wife*. London, 1706.

—— *The Counterfeit Bridegroom, Or, the Defeated Widow*. London, 1677.

Boxford Churchwardens' Accounts, 1530–1561, edited by P. Northeast, Suffolk Records Society, Vol. 23. Woodbridge, 1982.

Brooks, T., *Apples of God for Young Men and Women, and a Crown of Glory for Old Men and Women. Or, the Happiness of Being Good Betimes, and the Honour of Being an Old Disciple. . . . Also, the Young Mans Objections Answered and the Old Man's Doubtes Resolved* (4th edn). London, 1662.

Calamay Revised being a Revision of Edmund Calamy's Account of the Ministers and Others Rejected and Silenced, 1660–2, edited by A. G. Matthew. Repr. Oxford, 1988.

Calendar of State Papers, Domestic: 1634–5.

Calendar of State Papers, Domestic: 1639–40.

Calendar of State Papers, Domestic: 1640–1.

Carpenter, J., *The Plaine-Man's Spirituall Plough.* London, 1607.

Cecil, W., *Precepts. Or, Directions for the Well Ordering and Carriage of a Mans Life, through the Whole.* Bound with Sir Walter Raleigh's *Sir Walter Raleighs Instructions to his Sonne and to Posterity.* London, 1633.

Cornarus, L., *A Treatise of Temperance and Sobrietie: Written by Lud. Cornarus,* translated by F. Herbert. London, 1634.

Crowley, R., *The Select Works of Robert Crowley,* edited by J. M. Cowper, Early English Text Society. London, 1872.

Cuffe, H., *The Differences of the Ages of Man.* London, 1607.

Defoe, D., *Giving Alms No Charity and Employing the Poor. A Grievance to the Nation, Being an Essay upon this Great Question.* London, 1794.

—— *A Tour thro' the Whole Island of Great Britain.* London, 1968.

The Devil and the Strumpet, or the Old Bawd Tormented. London, 1700.

Dictionary of Herveys of All Classes, Callings, Counties and Spellings from 1040 to 1500, Vol. III, Suffolk Green Books, No. 20. Ipswich, 1927.

A Discourse Translated Out of Italian, That a Spare Diet is Better then a Splendid and Sumptuous. London, 1634.

Dives and Pauper edited by P. Barnum, Early English Text Society. London, 1976.

[Drayton, T.], *An Answer According to Truth that Trembles not, nor Quakes, Nor Quayleth, bound with Certain Counter Queries Propounded by James Parnel and his Associates the New and Former Sectaries.* London, n.d.

Dunning, R., *A Plaine and Easie Method: Shewing How the Office of the Poor may be Managed.* London, 1685.

The Dutiful Advice of a Loving Sonne to His Aged Father. London, 1626.

An Ease for Overseers of the Poore Abstracted From the Statutes. Cambridge, 1601.

Edwards, A. C., *English History from Essex Sources 1550–1750.* Chelmsford, 1952.

Erasmus, *Enchiridion Militis Christiani, whiche may be called in Englysshe, the Hansome Weapon of a Christen Knyght.* London, 1534.

Estey, G., *A Most Sweete and Comfortable Exposition, upon the Tenne Commaundements, and upon the 51 Psalme.* London, 1602.

Everitt, A., ed., *Suffolk and the Great Rebellion, 1640–1660,* Suffolk Records Society, Vol. III. Ipswich, 1960.

A Faithful Narrative of the Wonderful and Extraordinary Fits which Mr Tho.

Spatchet (Late of Dunwich and Cookly) was under by Witchcraft . . . The Whole Drawn up and Written by Samuel Petto, Minister of the Gospel at Sudbury in Suffolk, who was an Eye-Witness of a Great Part. London, 1693.

Farthing, W., The Old Mans Complaint. London, 1680.

The First and Best Part of Scoggin's Jest . . . by Andrew Boord. London, 1626.

Gardiner, R., England's Grievance Discovered. London, 1655.

A Glasse Wherein those Enormities and Foule Abuses may most Evidently bee Seen, which are the Destruction and Overthrow of Every Christian Common Wealth. Likewise the Onley Means Howe to Prevent such Dangers: By Imitating the Wholesome Advertisements Contained in thys Booke. Which Sometimes was the Jewell and Delight of the Right Honourable Lord, and Father to his Country, Francis, Earle of Bedford, Deceased. London, 1639.

Gough, R., The History of Myddle, edited by D. Hey. Harmondsworth, 1981.

Gouge, W., Of Domesticall Duties. London, 1622.

Griffith, M., Bethel: Or A Forme for Families. London, 1634.

Harrison, W., The Description of England, edited by G. Edelen, 1587 (2nd edn). Ithaca, NY, 1968.

—— 'Harrison on Changes in His Day, 1577–87'. Tudor Economic Documents, Vol. III. London, 1924.

Heath, R., 'On the Unusual Cold and Rainy Weather in the Summer, 1648'. In The New Oxford Book of Seventeenth Century Verse, edited by A. Fowler. Oxford, 1992.

Historical Manuscripts Commission. Salisbury MS, Hatfield House Part IX. London, 1902.

Historie of Life and Death, With Observations Naturall and Experimentall for the Prolonging of Life. London, 1638.

Hoby, M., Diary of Lady Margaret Hoby, 1599–1605, edited by D. M. Meads. London, 1930.

Holland, W., Cratfield: A Transcript of the Accounts of the Parish, from A.D. 1490 to A.D. 1642, with Notes, edited by J. J. Raven. London, 1895.

Hopkins, M., Discoverie of Witches. London, 1647.

Hughes, P. L. and Larkin, J. F., eds, Tudor Royal Proclamations, Vol I. New Haven, CT, 1964–69.

The Humble Petition of the Clothiers of Suffolk and Essex. London, 1641.

The Ingrateful Son, Or, An Example of God's Justice upon the Abusefull Disobedence of a Fake Hearted and Cruel Son to his Aged Father. London, 1672.

Josselin, R., The Diary of Ralph Josselin 1616–1683, edited by A. Macfarlane, British Academy, Records of Social and Economic History, n.s., iii. London, 1976.

King, G., Observations and Conclusions, Natural and Political, upon the State and Condition of England. London, 1694. Reprinted in G. Chalmers, An Estimate of the Comparative Strength of Great Britain; and of the Losses of Trade, from every War since the Revolution . . . to which is now annexed, Gregory King's Celebrated State of England. London, 1804.

Kirby, J., The Suffolk Traveller: or, a Journey through Suffolk. Ipswich, 1735.

Lenton, F., *The Young Gallents Whirligg*. London, 1629.

Lessius, L., *Hygiasticon: Or, the Right Course of Preserving Life and Health into Extreme Old Age*. London, 1634.

Letters and Papers, Foreign and Domestic of Henry VIII, Vol. XVI, 1898. Repr. London, 1965.

Lupton, D., *London and the Countrey Carbonadoed and Quartred into Severall Characters*. London, 1632.

MacCulloch, D., ed., *The Chorography of Suffolk*, Suffolk Records Society, Vol. 19. Ipswich, 1976.

Maimonides, M., *The Preservation of Youth*, translated by R. E. Lewis. Athens, GA, 1978.

Marshal, W., *The Forme and Maner of Subvention of Helping for Pore People*. In *Some Early Tracts on Poor Relief*, edited by F. R. Salter, pp. 36–76. London, 1926.

Metcalfe, W. C., ed., *The Visitations of Essex by Hawley, 1552; Hervey, 1558; Cooke, 1570; Raven, 1612 and Owen and Lilly, 1634*, Vol. I. London, 1878–79.

Montague, M. W., *Letters of the Right Honourable L. M. W. M.: Written during her Travels in Europe, Asia and Africa*, 3 Vols. London, 1763.

More, T., *Utopia*, translated by P. Turner, 1961. Repr. Harmondsworth, 1987.

A Most Certain, Strange and True Discovery of a Witch. London, 1643.

A Most Excellent New Ballad, of an Olde Man and his Wife Which in their Olde-Age and Misery . . . Disdained and Scornfully Sent Away Succourlesse and How the Vengeancc[sic] of God was Justly Shewed upon them for the Same. London, *c*.1600.

Mother Shiptons Prophesie: with and XX more, All most Terivle and Wonderful Strange Alterrations to Befall this Climate of England. London, 1685.

Nicholes, A., *A Discourse on Money and Wiving*. London, 1615.

Norden, J., *The Labyrinth of Mans Life. Or Vertues Delight and Envies Opposite*. London, 1614.

The Office of Christian Parents. Cambridge, 1616.

Old Meg of Herefordshire. London, 1609.

Old Mr Dod's Sayings, Composed in Verse for the Better Help of Memory, and the Delightfulness of Childrens Reading and Learning Them, Whereby they may the Better be Ingrafted in their Memories and Understanding. London, 1678.

The Old Mans Guide to Health and Longer Life: With Rules for Diet, Exercise and Physick; for Preserving a Good Constitution, and Preventing Disorders in a Bad One (2nd edn). London, 1765.

Parnell, J., *Goliahs Head Cut Off with His Own Sword*. London, 1655.

Passion and Discretion, in Youth, and Age. London, 1641.

Pasquils Jests with the Merriments of Mother Bunch. London, 1650(?).

Pepys Ballad Collection, Madgalene College, Cambridge:

    The Bashfull-Maidens No, No, No, Turn'd to I, I, I. Or, The Down-Right Wooing of Tom and Doll. London, 1680 (Pepys, III: 183).

    Brittains Truimph. London, 1685 (Pepys, II: 230).

[Campion, T.], A Friends Advice: In an Excellent Ditty, concerning the Variable Changes in this World. London, 1650–58 (Pepys, I: 55).

A Caveat for Young-Men. London, 1680–82 (Pepys, II: 36).

The Country Lass, Who Left her Spinning-Wheel for a More Pleasant Employment. London, 1690 (Pepys, III: 290).

England's New Bell-Men Ringing into All Peoples Ears, God's Dreadful Judgement to this Land and Kingdom. London, 1690 (Pepys, II: 61).

The Extravagant Youth, Or, An Emblem of Prodigality. London, 1684–85 (Pepys, II: 92).

Fancy, P., The Age and Life of Man. Here you ma [sic] See the Fraility that in Men, Till they have Run the Years Threescore and Ten. Tune of Jane Shore. London, 1675 (Pepys, II: 32).

The Father's Wholesome Admonition: Or, A Lumping Pennyworth of Good Counsel for Bad Husbands. London, 1685–91 (Pepys, II: 83).

The Golden Age: Or, An Age of Plaine-Dealing. London, 1698 (Pepys, I: 152).

Good Admonition Or To Al sorts of People this counsell I Sing, That in Each Ones Affaire, To Take Heed's a Faire Thing. London, n.d. (Pepys, I: 50).

A Goodfellowes Complaint Against Strong Beere, Or, Take Heed Goodfellowes for Heere You may See How it is Strong Beere that Hath Undone Me. London, 1630 (Pepys, I: 438).

The Good Shepherds Sorrow for the Death of his Beloved Sonne. London, n.d. (Pepys, I: 352).

Oh Gramercy Penny: Being a Lancashire Ditty, and Chiefly Penn'd, to Prove that a Penny is a Mans Best Friend. London, n.d. (Pepys, I: 218–19).

[Hill, T.], The Doleful Dance, and Song of Death; Intituled, Dance After my Pipe. London, 1655 (Pepys, II: 62).

The Lamentable Burning of the Citty of Corke (in the Province of Munster in Ireland) by Lightning. London, n.d. (Pepys, I: 69).

The Lamentable Ditty of Little Mousgrove, and the Lady Barnet. London, 1658 (Pepys, I: 365).

Mans Amazement: It being a True Relation of one Thomas Cox, a Hackney-Coach-Man, to Whom the Devil Appeared on Friday Night. . . . London, 1684 (Pepys, II: 175).

A Merry New Catch of All Trades. London, 1656 (Pepys, I: 164).

A Most Excellent Ballad, of an Old Man and his Wife, Who in their Great Want and Misery Sought to Children for Succour, by Whom they were Disdained, and Scornefully Sent Away Succourlesse, and Gods Vengeance Shewed upon them for the Same. London, 1658–64 (Pepys, I: 43).

A Most Notable and Worthy Example of an Ingratious Sonne. London, 1658–64 (Pepys, II: 180–1).

A Most Sorrowfull Song, Setting Forth the Miserable End of Banister, Who Betraied the Duke of Buckingham, his Lord and Master. London, n.d. (Pepys, I: 64).

A Mournful Caral: Or, An Elegy Lamenting the Tragical Ends of Two Unfortunate Faithful Lovers, Frankin and Cordelius, He being Slain, She Slew herself with her Dagger. London, 1680–2 (Pepys, II: 76).

A New Ballad Intituled, The Old Mans Complaint Against his Wretched Sonne. London, n.d. (Pepys, I: 137).

Pope, W., *Old Mans Wish.* London, 1684 (Pepys, IV: 370).

The Old Mans Advice to Batchellors, About the Choice of their Wives. London, n.d. (Pepys, IV: 104).

The Old Mans Sayings Concerning the Alteration of the Times. London, n.d. (Pepys, IV: 301).

The Old Miser Slighted. London, 1685–92 (Pepys, IV: 8).

The Old Woman's Resolution. London, 1688–92 (Pepys, III: 186).

Pitties Lamenation for the Cruelty of this Age. London, n.d. (Pepys, I: 162).

A Pleasant New Ballad of Tobias. London, 1655–58 (Pepys, I: 488–9).

The Poor Folks Complaint: Or, a Hint of the Hard Times. London, 1668 (Pepys, IV: 340).

The Poor Man's Complaint: Or, The Sorrowful Lamentation of Poor Plain-Dealing at this Time of Distress and Trouble. London, 1690–1700 (Pepys, IV: 300).

The Poor Man Put to a Pinch: Or, A Declaration of these Hard Times. London, n.d. (Pepys, IV: 299).

The Poor Peoples Complaint of the Unconscionable Brokers and Talley-Men. London, 1667–89 (Pepys, IV: 353).

Poor Robins Dream: Commonly Called Poor Charity. London, 1673(?) (Pepys, IV: 295).

The Protestants Great Misery in Ireland, Relating the Inhumane Cruelties that are Daily Committed There by the French and Irish Papists. London, 1691 (Pepys, II: 332).

The Rarest Ballad that Ever was Seen, Of the Blind Beggers Daughter of Bednal-Green. London, 1658–64 (Pepys, I: 490–1).

The Second Part of the Jewes Crueltie, Setting Forth the Mercifulnesse of the Judge Towardes the Marchant. London, n.d. (Pepys, I: 145).

The Shepheard and The King, and of Gillian The Shepherds Wife, with Her Churlish Answers: Being Full of Mirth and Merry Pastime. London, 1650(?) (Pepys, I: 76–7).

The Sorrowful Wife: Or, Love in a Tub. London, 1683–1700 (Pepys, IV: 116).

The Subtil Miss of London; or, The Ranting Hector Well Fitted by this Cunning Miss. London, n.d. (Pepys, III: 253).

A Third Touch of the Times. London, 1688 (Pepys, IV: 311).

Times Alteration: Or the Old Mans Rehearsall, What Brane [sic] Dayes he Knew, A great While Agone, When this Old Cap was New. London, 1641 (Pepys, I: 160).

The Western-Triumph: Or, The Royal Progress of Our Gracious King James the II, into the West of England. London, 1688 (Pepys, II: 246).

A *Worthy Example of a Vertuous Wife, Who Fed her Father with her Own Milk, Being Condemned to be Starved to Death*. London, 1658–64 (Pepys, I: 492).

The Young–Mans Repentance. London, 1685–88 (Pepys, II: 37).

The Pleasant Conceites of Old Hobson the Merry Londoner. London, 1607. In *Humour, Wit, and Satire of the Seventeenth Century*, edited by J. Ashton. New York, 1970.

Potts, T., *The Wonderfull Discoveries of Witches in the Countie of Lancaster*. London, 1613.

Quarles, F., *Hieroglyphikes of the Life of Man*. London, 1638.

Raine, A., ed., *York Civic Records Vol. VIII*, Yorkshire Archaeological Society Record Series, CVIV. York, 1953.

Raleigh, W., *Sir Walter Raleighs Instructions to his Sonne and to Posterity*. London, 1633.

Redstone, V. B., trans. and ed., *The Ship-Money Returns for the County of Suffolk, 1639–1640*, Suffolk Institute of Archaeology and Natural History. Ipswich, 1904.

Rowlands, S., *Doctor Merry Man*. London, 1616.

Ryece, R., *Suffolk in the XVIIth Century. The Breviary of Suffolk by Robert Reyce*, edited by Lord Francis Hervey. London, 1902.

S., P., *A New Song: Or, the Old Woman's Wish. To the Tune of the Old Man's Wish*. London, 1684.

Sanitatis, H., *The Noble Lyfe and Natures of Man, of Bestes, Serpentys, Fowles and Fisshes*, translated by L. Andrewe. Andwarpe, 1527.

Sheafe, T., *Vindiciae Senectutis, or, A Plea for Old-Age: Which is Senis Cujusdam Cygnea Cantio*. London, 1639.

Sherington, R., *Two Sermons Preached in St Mary's Church in Cambridge by Robert Sherington*, Thomson Tract E 285 (1). London, 1645.

Smith, J., *The Pourtract of Old Age. Wherein is Contained a Sacred Anatomy both of Soul, and Body, and a Perfect Account of the Infirmities of Age Incident to the Both*. London, 1666.

Sparke, M., *Truth Brought to Light and Discovered by Time*. London, 1651.

Spenser, E., *Faerie Queen*. London, 1590.

Spiritual Journey of a Young Man, towards the Land of Peace, to Live therein Essentially in God, who met in his Journey with Three Sorts of Disputes, Withsome Proverbs and Sentences, which the Old-Age spake to the Young Man, translated from Dutch. London, 1659.

Statutes of the Realm, 11 Vols, 1817. Repr. London, 1963.

Steele, R., *A Discourse Concerning Old-Age*. London, 1688.

Strype, J., *Lessons Moral and Christian for Youth and Old Age in Two Sermons Preach'd at Guildhall Chappel, London*. London, 1699.

Suffolk in 1524, Being the Return of a Subsidy Granted in 1523, Suffolk Green Books, No. 10. Woodbridge, 1910.

Suffolk in 1568, Being the Return for a Subsidy Granted in 1566, Suffolk Green Books, No. 12. Woodbridge, 1909.

Suffolk in 1674, Being the Hearth Tax Returns, Suffolk Green Books, No. 11, Vol. 13. Woodbridge, 1905.

Swinburne, H., *A Brief Treatise of Testaments and Last Wills*, London, 1590.

Tales and Quicke Answeres, Very Mery, and Pleasant to Rede. London, 1625?. In A Hundred Merry Tales and Other Jestbooks of the Fifteenth and Sixteenth Centuries, edited by P. M. Zall. Lincoln, NB, 1963.

Taylor, J., *A Bawd. A Vertuous Bawd, A Modest Bawd: As She Deserves Reproove, or Else Applaud*. London, 1635.

—— *The Old, Old, Very Old Man*. London, 1635.

Temple, W., 'Of Health and Long Life'. In *The Works of Sir William Temple*, 3 Vols. London, 1720.

Two East Anglian Diaries, 164–1729: Isaac Archer and William Coe, edited by M. Storey, Suffolk Records Society, Vol. 36. Woodbridge, 1994.

Valor Ecclesiasticus Hen. VIII, Vol. III. London, 1817.

Visitation Articles and Injunctions of the Period of the Reformation. Vol. III 1559–1575, Alcuin Club Collections, XVI. London, 1910.

Vives, J., *De Subventione Pauperum*. In *Some Early Tracts on Poor Relief*, edited by F. A. Salter, pp. 2–30. London, 1926.

Wager, W., *A Very Mery and Pythie Commodie called the Longer Thou Livest the More Foole Thou Art* (1569), The Tudor Facsimile Texts. New York, 1970.

Walker Revised being a Revision of John Walker's Suffering of the Clergy during the Grand Rebellion, 1642–60, edited by A. G. Matthews. Repr. Oxford, 1988.

Webb, J., ed., *Poor Relief in Elizabethan Ipswich*, Suffolk Records Society, Vol. 9. Ipswich, 1966.

Whiteman, A., ed., *The Compton Census of 1676: A Critical Edition*, British Academy, Records of Social and Economic History, n.s. 10. London, 1986.

Williams, J. F., ed., *Diocese of Norwich Bishop Redman's Visitation 1597. Presentments in the Archdeaconries of Norwich, Norfolk, and Suffolk*, Norfolk Record Society, Vol. 18. Norwich, 1946.

Willis, T., *Dr. Willis's Practice of Physick*. London, 1684.

Witches Apprehended, Examined and Executed. London, 1613.

Wit Restor'd in Severall Select Poems not Formerly Published. London, 1658.

The Wonderful Discoverie of Margaret and Philip Flower. London, 1619.

Zerbi, G., *Gerontocomia: On the Care of the Aged, and Maximianus, Elegies on Old Age and Love*, translated by L. R. Lind. Philadelphia, 1988.

SECONDARY SOURCES

Acheson, R. J., *Radical Puritans in England 1550–1660*, Seminar Studies in History. London, 1990.

Adman, P., Baskerville, S. W. and Beedham, K. F., 'Computer-Assisted Record Linkage: Or How Best to Optimize Links Without Generating Errors'. *History and Computing* 4 (1992): 2–19.

Alsop, J. D., 'Religious Preambles in Early Modern English Wills as Formulae'. *Journal of Ecclesiastical History* 40 (1989): 19–27.

Amundsen, D. W. and Dyers, C. J., 'The Age of Menarche in Medieval Europe'. *Human Biology* 45 (1973): 363–9.

Amussen, S. D., *An Ordered Society: Gender and Class in Early Modern England.* Oxford, 1988.

Anderson, M., 'Household Structure and the Industrial Revolution: Mid-Nineteenth-Century Preston in Comparative Perspective'. In *Household and Family in Past Times,* edited by P. Laslett and R. Wall, pp. 215–35. Cambridge, 1972.

Apfel, W. and Dunkley, P., 'English Rural Society and the New Poor Law: Bedfordshire, 1834–47'. *Social History* 10 (1985): 37 68.

Appleby, A. B., 'Diet in Sixteenth Century England: Sources, Problems, Possibilities'. In *Health, Medicine and Mortality in the Sixteenth Century,* edited by C. Webster, pp. 97–117. Cambridge, 1979.

Archer, I., *The Pursuit of Stability: Social Relations in Elizabethan London.* Cambridge, 1991.

Aries, P., *Centuries of Childhood.* New York, 1973.

Arkell, T., 'The Incidence of Poverty in England in the Later Seventeenth Century'. *Social History* 12 (1987): 23–48.

Aston, M., *England's Iconoclasts. Vol. I. Laws Against Images.* Oxford, 1988.

Attreed, L. C., 'Preparation for Death in Sixteenth Century Northern England'. *Sixteenth Century Journal* 13 (1982): 37–66.

Aydelotte, F., *Elizabethan Rogues and Vagabonds.* Oxford, 1913.

Barron, C. M., 'The Parish Fraternities of Medieval London'. In *The Church in Pre-Reformation Society,* edited by C. M. Barron and C. Harper-Bill, pp. 13–37. Woodbridge, 1985.

Barry, J. and Brooks, C., eds, *The Middling Sort of People. Culture, Society and Politics in England, 1550–1800.* London, 1994.

Beier, A. L., *Masterless Men: The Vagrancy Problem of England, 1560–1640.* London, 1987.

—— *The Problem of the Poor in Tudor and Early Stuart England.* London, 1983.

—— 'Poor Relief in Warwickshire, 1630–1660'. *Past and Present* 35 (1966): 77–100.

—— 'Social Problems in Elizabethan London'. *Journal of Interdisciplinary History* 9 (1978): 203–21.

—— 'The Social Problems of an Elizabethan Country Town: Warwick, 1580–90'. In *Country Towns in Pre-Industrial England,* edited by P. Clark, pp. 46–85. Leicester, 1981.

—— 'Vagrants and the Social Order in Elizabethan England'. *Past and Present* 64 (1974): 3–29.

Ben-Amos, I. K., *Adolescence and Youth in Early Modern England.* New Haven, CT, 1994.

—— 'Service and the Coming of Age of Young Men in Seventeenth-Century England'. *Continuity and Change* 3 (1988): 41–64.

—— 'Women Apprentices in the Trades and Crafts of Early Modern Bristol'. *Continuity and Change* 6 (1991): 227–52.

Bennett, J. M., *Ale, Beer, and Brewsters in England: Women's Work in a Changing World, 1300–1600*. Oxford, 1996.

—— 'Conviviality and Charity in Medieval and Early Modern England'. *Past and Present* 134 (1992): 19–41.

Bever, E., 'Old Age and Witchcraft in Early Modern Europe'. In *Old Age in Preindustrial Society*, edited by P. N. Stearns, pp. 151–77. New York, 1982.

Blackwood, B. G., 'The Cavalier and Roundhead Gentry of Suffolk'. *The Suffolk Review* 5 (1985): 2–10.

—— 'The Gentry of Suffolk during the Civil War'. In *An Historical Atlas of Suffolk*, edited by D. Dymond and E. Martin, pp. 84–5. Bury St Edmunds, 1988.

Blalock, H. M., *Social Statistics* (2nd edn). London, 1981.

Bonfield, L., 'Normative Rules and Property Transmission: Reflections on the Link Between Marriage and Inheritance in Early Modern England'. In *The World We Have Gained*, edited by L. Bonfield, R. M. Smith and K. Wrightson, pp. 155–76. Oxford, 1986.

Botelho, L. A., 'Accommodation for the Aged Poor of Cratfield in the Late Tudor and Early Stuart Period'. *Suffolk Review* n.s. 24 (1995): 19–31.

—— 'Aged and Impotent: Parish Relief of the Aged Poor in Early Modern Suffolk' in *Charity, Self-Interest and Welfare*, edited by M. Daunton, pp. 91–112. London, 1996.

—— *Churchwardens' Accounts of Cratfield, 1640–1660*, Suffolk Records Society, Vol. 42. Woodbridge, 1999.

—— 'Old Age and Menopause in Rural Women of Early Modern Suffolk'. In *Women and Ageing in British Society Since 1500*, edited by L. Botelho and P. Thane, pp. 43–65. London, 2001.

—— '"The Old Woman's Wish": Widows by the Family Fire? Widows' Old Age Provision in Rural England, 1500–1700', *Journal of Family History* 7 (2002): 59–78.

Boulton, J., 'Going on the Parish: The Parish Pension and its Meaning in the London Suburbs, 1640–1724'. In *Chronicling Poverty: The Voices and Strategies of the English Poor, 1640–1840*, edited by T. Hitchcock, P. King and P. Sharpe, pp. 26–33. Basingstoke, 1997.

—— *Neighbourhood and Society: A London Suburb in the Seventeenth Century.* Cambridge, 1987.

Bourdieu, P., 'Cultural Reproduction and Social Reproduction'. In *Knowledge, Education and Cultural Change*, edited by R. Brown, pp. 71–112. London, 1973.

—— 'The Forms of Capital'. In *Handbook of Theory and Research for the Sociology of Education*, edited by J. G. Richardson, pp. 241–58. New York, 1986.

Brigden, S., 'Youth and the English Reformation'. *Past and Present* 95 (1982): 37–67.

Brodsky, V., 'Widows in Late Elizabethan London: Remarriage, Economic Opportunity and Family Orientations'. In *The World We Have Gained*, edited by L. Bonfield, R. M. Smith and K. Wrightson, pp. 124–54. Oxford, 1986.

Bullough, V. and Campbell, C., 'Female Longevity and Diet in the Middle Ages'. *Speculum* 55 (1980): 317–25.

Burgess, C., 'Late Medieval Wills and Pious Convention: Testamentary Evidence Reconsidered'. In *Profit, Piety and the Professions in Later Medieval England*, edited by M. A. Hick, pp. 14–33. Gloucester, 1990.

Burgess, C. and Kumin, B., 'Penitential Bequests and Parish Regimes in Late Medieval England'. *Journal of Ecclesiastical History* 44 (1993): 610–746.

Burn, R. A., *Clare in Suffolk and the Twenty-Four Villages of its Rural District.* Clare, 1952.

Burstein, S. R., 'Care of the Aged in England from Mediaeval Times to the End of the Sixteenth Century'. *Bulletin of the History of Medicine* 22 (1948): 738–46.

—— 'The "Cure" of Old Age: Codes of Health'. *Geriatrics* 10 (1955): 328–32.

Carlson, E., 'The Origins, Function, and Status of the Office of Churchwarden, with Particular Reference to the Diocese of Ely'. In *The World of Rural Dissenters, 1520–1725*, edited by M. Spufford, pp. 164–207. Cambridge, 1995.

Chalmers, G., *An Estimate of the Comparative Strength of Great Britain; and of the Losses of Trade, from every War since the Revolution . . to which in now annexed, Gregory King's Celebrated State of England.* London, 1804.

Chambers, J., *Population, Economy and Society in Pre-Industrial England.* Oxford, 1872.

Chapman, A., 'Astrological Medicine'. In *Health, Medicine and Mortality in the Sixteenth Century*, edited by C. Webster, pp. 275–300. Cambridge, 1979.

Clark, E., 'The Quest for Security in Medieval England'. In *Aging and the Aged in Medieval Europe*, edited by M. M. Sheehan, pp. 189–200. Toronto, 1990.

—— 'Some Aspects of Social Security in Medieval England'. *Journal of Family History* 7 (1982): 307–22.

Clay, R. M., *Medieval Hospitals in England.* London, 1909.

Clive, H., *Beyond Living Memory. The Story of a Suffolk Village.* Privately printed, 1979.

Coffman, G. R., 'Old Age from Horace to Chaucer: Some Literary Affinities and Adventures of an Idea'. *Speculum* 9 (1934): 249–77.

Coleman, D. C., *Industry in Tudor and Stuart England*, Studies in Economic and Social History. Basingstoke, 1975.

Collinson, P., *The Elizabethan Puritan Movement.* Oxford, 1967.

Compact Oxford English Dictionary (2nd edn). London, 1989.

The Concise Dictionary of National Biography, Part I. Oxford, 1983.

Coppel, C., 'Wills and the Community in Tudor Grantham'. In *Probate Records and the Local Community*, edited by P. Riden, pp. 71–90. Gloucester, 1985.

Cornwall, J., 'English Population in the Early Sixteenth Century'. *Economic History Review*, 2nd ser. 24 (1970): 32–44.

—— *Wealth and Society in Early Sixteenth Century England*. London, 1988.

Cressy, D., *Bonfires and Bells: National Memory and the Protestant Calendar in Elizabethan and Stuart England*. London, 1989.

—— 'Kinship and Kin Interaction in Early Modern England'. *Past and Present* 113 (1986): 38–69.

—— *Literacy and the Social Order. Reading and Writing in Tudor and Stuart England*. Cambridge, 1980.

Cross, C., 'Wills as Evidence of Popular Piety in the Reformation Period: Leeds and Hull, 1540–1640'. In *The End of Strife*, edited by D. Loades, pp. 44–51. Edinburgh, 1984.

Davis, N. Z., 'Poor Relief, Humanism, and Heresy'. In her *Society and Culture in Early Modern France*, pp. 17–64. London, 1975.

—— 'The Reasons of Misrule: Youth Groups and Charivaris in Sixteenth-Century France'. *Past and Present* 50 (1971): 41–75.

Demaitre, L., 'The Care and Extension of Old Age in Medieval Medicine'. In *Aging and the Aged in Medieval Europe*, edited by M. M. Sheehan, pp. 3–22. Toronto, 1990.

Dictionary of Quotations, 2 Vols. London, n.d..

Dobson, M., *A Chronology of Epidemic Disease and Mortality in Southeast England, 1601–1800*, Historical Geography Research Series No. 19. London, 1987.

Drummond, J. C. and Wilbraham, A., *The Englishman's Food. A History of Five Centuries of Diet*. London, 1957.

Duffy, E., *The Stripping of the Altars: Traditional Religion in England 1400–1580*. New Haven, CT, 1992.

Dyer, C., 'Changes in the Size of Peasant Holdings in Some West Midland Villages, 1400–1500'. In *Land, Kinship and Life-Cycle*, edited by R. M. Smith et al., pp. 277–94. Cambridge, 1984.

—— *Standards of Living in the Later Middle Ages. Social Change in England c. 1200–1520*. Cambridge, 1989.

Dymond, D., 'The Woollen Cloth Industry'. In *An Historical Atlas of Suffolk*, edited by D. Dymond and E. Martin, pp. 112–13. Bury St Edmunds, 1988.

—— and Betterton, A., *Lavenham: 700 Years of Textile Making*. Woodbridge, 1982.

Erickson, A. L., *Women and Property in Early Modern England*. London, 1993.

Evandrou, M., Arber, S., Dale, A. and Gilbert, G. N., 'Who Cares for the Elderly? Family Care Provisions and Receipt of Statutory Service'. In *Dependency and Interdependency in Old Age*, edited by C. Phillipson, M. Bernard and P. Strange, pp. 150–66. London, 1986.

Evans, I. H., *Brewer's Dictionary of Phrase and Fable*. London, 1988.

Evans, N., 'The Holy Ghost Gild and the Beccles Town Land Feoffees in the Sixteenth and Seventeenth Centuries'. *Suffolk Institute of Archaeology and Natural History* 37 (1989): 31–44.

—— 'Inheritance, Women, Religion and Education in Early Modern Society as Revealed by Wills'. In *Probate Records and the Local Community*, edited by P. Riden, pp. 53–70. Gloucester, 1985.

Farnhill, K., 'A Late Medieval Parish Guild: The Guild of St. Thomas the Martyr in Cratfield, c. 1470–1542'. *Proceedings of the Suffolk Institute of Archaeology and Natural History* 38 (1995): 261–7.

—— 'Religious Policy and Parish "Conformity": Cratfield's Lands in the Sixteenth Century'. In *The Parish in English Life*, edited by K. L. French, G. G. Gibbs and B. Kumin, pp. 217–29. Manchester, 1997.

Fitch, S., *Sudbury Quakers 1655–1953*. Bury St Edmunds, n.d.

Fletcher, A., *Reform in the Provinces: The Government of Stuart England*. London, 1980.

Folts, J. D., 'Senescence and Renascence: Petrach's Thoughts on Growing Old'. *Journal of Medieval and Renaissance Studies* 10 (1980): 207–37.

Forbes, T. R., 'By What Disease or Casualty: The Changing Face of Death in London'. In *Health, Medicine and Mortality in the Sixteenth Century*, edited by C. Webster, pp. 117–40. Cambridge, 1979.

Ford, J. and Sinclair, R., *Sixty Years On. Women Talk About Old Age*. London, 1987.

Foster, A., 'Churchwardens' Accounts of Early Modern England and Wales: Some Problems to Note, but Much to be Gained'. In *The Parish in English Life*, edited by K. L. French, G. G. Gibbs and B. Kumin, pp. 74–93. Manchester, 1997.

Fowler, D. H., Fowler, L. J. and Lamdin, L., 'Themes of Old Age in Preindustrial Western Literature'. In *Old Age in Preindustrial Society*, edited by P. Stearns, pp. 20–42. New York and London, 1982.

French, K., 'Parochial Fund-Raising in Late Medieval Somerset'. In *The Parish in English Life*, edited by K. L. French, G. G. Gibbs and B. Kumin, pp. 118–23. Manchester, 1997.

Geremek, B., *Poverty: A History*. Oxford, 1997.

Gillis, J. R., *Youth and History. Tradition and Change in European Age Relations, 1770–Present*. New York, 1974.

Gittings, C., *Death, Burial and the Individual in Early Modern England*. London, 1984.

Glass, K. and Dymond, D., 'Protestant Nonconformity'. In *Historical Atlas of Suffolk*, edited by D. Dymond and E. Martin, pp. 90–1. Bury St Edmunds, 1988.

Gordon, C., 'Familial Support for the Elderly in the Past: The Case of London's Working Class in the Early 1930s'. *Ageing and Society* 8 (1988): 287–320.

Green, I., 'The Persecution of "Scandalous" and "Maligant" Parish Clergy During the English Civil War'. *English Historical Review* 94 (1979): 507–31.

Grell, O. P. and Cunningham, A., eds, *Health Care and Poor Relief in Protestant Europe 1500–1700*. London, 1997.

Gruman, G. J., A *History of Ideas about the Prolongation of Life: The Evolution of Prolongevity Hypotheses to 1800*. Philadelphia, PA, 1966.

Hadwin, F., 'Deflating Philanthropy'. *Economic History Review*, 2nd ser. 31 (1978): 105–20.

Hall, J., *Dictionary of Subjects and Symbolism in Art*. London, 1974.

Hampson, E. M., *The Treatment of Poverty in Cambridgeshire, 1601–1834*. Cambridge, 1934.

Hanawalt, B., *Growing Up in Medieval London. The Experience of Childhood in History*. Oxford, 1993.

Hareven, T. K., 'The Last Stage: Historical Adulthood and Old Age'. In *Aging, Death, and the Completion of Being*, edited by D. van Tassel, pp. 165–89. Philadelphia, PA, 1979.

Harper, R., 'A Note on Corrodies in the Fourteenth Century'. *Albion* 15 (1983): 95–101.

Harvey, B., *Living and Dying in England 1200–1540. The Monastic Experience*. Oxford, 1993.

Heal, F., 'The Idea of Hospitality in Early Modern England'. *Past and Present* 102 (1984): 66–93.

Herlan, R. W., 'Poor Relief in London during the English Revolution'. *Journal of British Studies* 18 (1979): 30–51.

—— 'Relief of the Poor in Bristol from Late Elizabethan Times until the Restoration Era'. *Proceedings of the American Philosophical Society* 126 (1982): 212–28.

Hervey, M. W., *Annals of a Suffolk Village being Historical Notes on the Parish of Horringer*. Cambridge, 1930.

Hill, B., *The First English Feminist: Reflections Upon Marriage and Other Writings*. New York, 1986.

Hill, C., 'The Secularization of the Parish'. In *Society and Puritanism in Pre-Revolutionary England*, edited by C. Hill, pp. 420–42. London, 1966.

—— *Society and Puritanism in Pre-Revolutionary England*. London, 1966.

Hilton, H., *The English Peasantry in the Later Middle Ages*. Oxford, 1975.

Hindle, S., *The Birthpangs of Welfare: Poor Relief and Parish Governance in Seventeenth-Century Warwickshire*. Dugdale Society Occasional Papers No. 42, 2000.

—— 'Dearth, Fasting and Alms: The Campaign for General Hospitality in Late Elizabethan England'. *Past and Present* 172 (2001): 44–86.

—— 'Exclusion Crisis: Poverty, Migration and Parochial Responsibility in English Rural Communities, c. 1560–1660'. *Rural History* 7 (1996): 125–49.

—— 'Exhortation and Entitlement: Negotiating Inequality in English Rural Communities, 1550–1650'. In *Negotiating Power in Early Modern Society: Order, Hierarchy and Subordination in Early Modern Britain and Ireland*, edited by M. Braddick and J. Walter, pp. 102–22. Cambridge, 2001.

—— 'Power, Poor Relief, and Social Relations in Holland Fen, c. 1600–1800'. *The Historical Journal* 41 (1998): 67–96.

—— *The State and Social Change in Early Modern England c. 1550–1700*. Basingstoke, 2000.

Hitchcock, T., King, P. and Sharpe, P., 'Introduction: Chronicling Poverty – The Voices and Strategies of the English Poor, 1640–1840'. In *Chronicling Poverty: The Voices and Strategies of the English Poor, 1640–1840*, edited by T. Hitchcock, P. King and P. Sharpe, pp. 1–18. Basingstoke, 1997.

Hoak, D., 'Witch-Hunting and Women in the Art of the Renaissance'. *History Today* (1981): 22–6.

Holderness, B. A., 'Widows in Pre-Industrial Society: An Essay upon their Economic Function'. In *Land, Kinship and Life-Cycle*, edited by R. M. Smith *et al.*, pp. 423–42. Cambridge, 1984.

Houlbrooke, R., *The English Family 1450–1700*. London, 1984.

—— *Church Courts and People*. Oxford, 1979.

Houston, S. J., *James I*, Seminar Studies in History. London, 1973.

Howell, C., 'Peasant Inheritance Customs in the Midlands, 1280–1700'. In *Family and Inheritance: Rural Society in Western Europe 1200–1800*, edited by J. Goody, J. Thirsk and E. P. Thompson, pp. 112–55. Cambridge, 1976.

Hufton, O., 'Begging, Vagrancy, Vagabondage and the Law: An Aspect of the Problem of Poverty in Eighteenth-Century France'. *European Studies Review* 2 (1972): 97–124.

—— *The Poor of Eighteenth-Century France, 1750–1789*. Oxford, 1974.

Hussey, S., '"An Inheritance of Fear": Old Women in the Twentieth-Century Country Side'. In *Women and Ageing in British Society Since 1500*, edited by L. Botelho and P. Thane, pp. 186–206. London, 2001.

Hutton, R., *The Rise and Fall of Merry England. The Ritual Year 1400–1700*. Oxford, 1994.

Ingram, M., 'Religion, Communities and Moral Discipline in Late Sixteenth- and Early Seventeenth-Century England: Case Studies'. In *Religion and Society in Early Modern Europe, 1500–1800*, edited by K. von Greyerz, pp. 177–93. London, 1984.

Innes, J., 'Prisons for the Poor: English Bridewells, 1555–1800'. In *Labour, Law, and Crime. An Historical Perspective*, edited by F. Snyder and D. Hay, pp. 42–122. London, 1987.

Jarvis, H., 'Poslingford Church'. *Proceedings of the Suffolk Institute of Archaeology and Natural History* 8 (1894): 241–56.

Johnson, P., 'Historical Readings of Old Age and Ageing'. In *Old Age from Antiquity to Post-Modernity*, edited by P. Johnson and P. Thane, pp. 1–18. London, 1998.

Jones, G. S., *History of the Law of Charity, 1532–1827*. Cambridge, 1969.

Jones, J. W., 'Observations on the Origin of the Divisions of Man's Life into Stages'. *Archaeologia* 35 (1853): 167–89.

Jordan, W. K., *Edward IV: The Threshold of Power*. London, 1970.

—— *Philanthropy in England 1480–1640: A Study of the Changing Pattern of English Social Aspirations*. Westport, CN, 1978.

Jutte, R., 'Aging and Body Image in the Sixteenth Century: Herman Weinsberg's (1518–97) Perception of the Aging Body'. *European History Quarterly* 18 (1988): 259–90.

—— *Poverty and Deviance in Early Modern Europe*. Cambridge, 1994.

Kent, J. R., *The English Village Constable*. Oxford, 1986.

Kerridge, E., *The Agricultural Revolution*. London, 1967.

Kidd, A. J., 'Historians or Polemicists? How the Webbs Wrote their History of the English Poor Law'. *Economic History Review*, 2nd ser. 40 (1987): 400–17.

Klassen, S., 'Old and Cared For: Places of Residence for Elderly Women in Eighteenth-Century Toulouse'. *Journal of Family History* 24 (1999): 35–52.

—— 'Social Lives of Elderly Women in Eighteenth-Century Toulouse'. In *Power and Poverty: Old Age in the Pre-Industrial Past*, edited by S. R. Ottaway, L. A. Botelho and K. Kittredge, pp. 49–66. Westport, CT, 2002.

Kumin, B., *The Shaping of a Community: The Rise and Reformation of the English Parish, c. 1400–1560*. Aldershot, 1996.

Kussmaul, A., *Servants in Husbandry in Early Modern England*. Cambridge, 1981.

Labarge, M. W., 'Three Medieval Widows and Second Careers'. In *Aging and the Aged in Medieval Europe*, edited by M. M. Sheehan, pp. 159–72. Toronto, 1990.

Lake, P., 'The Laudian Style: Order, Uniformity and the Pursuit of the Beauty of Holiness in the 1630s'. In *The Early Stuart Church, 1603–1642*, edited by K. Fincham, pp. 161–85. Basingstoke, 1993.

Larner, C., 'Witch Beliefs and Witch-Hunting in England and Scotland'. *History Today* (1981): 32–6.

Laslett, P., 'Family, Kinship and Collectivity as Systems of Support in Pre-Industrial Europe: A Consideration of the "Nuclear-Hardship" Hypothesis'. *Continuity and Change* 3 (1988): 153–76.

—— 'Mean Household Size in England since the Sixteenth Century'. In *Household and Family in Past Time*, edited by P. Laslett and R. Wall, pp. 125–58. Cambridge, 1972.

—— 'The Significance of the Past in the Study of Ageing'. *Ageing and Society* 4 (1984): 379–89.

—— 'Size and Structure of the Household in England Over Three Centuries'. *Population Studies* 23 (1969): 199–223.

—— 'The Study of Social Structure from Listings of Inhabitants'. In *An Introduction to English Historical Demography*, edited by E. A. Wrigley, pp. 160–208. London, 1966.

—— *The World We Have Lost. England Before the Industrial Age* (2nd edn). London, 1971.

Laurence, A., *Women in England 1500–1760: A Social History*. New York, 1994.

Lees, L. H. *The Solidarities of Strangers. The English Poor Laws and the People, 1700–1948*. Cambridge, 1998.

—— 'The Survival of the Unfit: Welfare Policies and Family Maintenance in Nineteenth-Century London'. In *The Uses of Charity: The Poor on Relief in the Nineteenth-Century Metroplis*, edited by P. Mandler, pp. 68–91. Philadelphia, PA, 1990.

Lemire, B., 'Consumerism in Preindustrial and Early Industrial England: The Trade in Secondhand Clothes'. *Journal of British Studies* 27 (1988): 1–24.

—— *Dress, Culture and Commerce: The English Clothing Trade before the Factory 1660–1800*. Basingstoke, 1997.

—— 'The Theft of Clothes and Popular Consumerism in Early Modern England'. *Journal of Social History* 24 (1990): 245–76.

Leonard, E. M., *The Early History of English Poor Relief*. London, 1900.

Lis, C. and Soly, H., *Poverty and Capitalism in Early Modern Europe*. Bristol, 1982.

Litzenberger, C., 'Local Responses to Changes in Religious Policy Based on Evidence from Gloucestershire Wills (1541–1580)'. *Continuity and Change* 8 (1993): 417–39.

Locke, P. E., *Report on the Town House, Cratfield, Suffolk. Prepared for the Society for the Protection of Ancient Buildings*. London, 1960.

MacCulloch, D., 'Catholic and Puritan in Elizabethan Suffolk'. *Archive for Reformation History* 72 (1981): 232–87.

—— *The Later Reformation in England 1547–1603*. Basingstoke, 1990.

—— *Suffolk and the Tudors. Politics and Religion in an English County 1500–1600*. Oxford, 1986.

MacDonald, M., *Mystical Bedlam: Madness, Anxiety and Healing in Seventeenth Century England*. Cambridge, 1981.

Macfarlane, A., *Marriage and Love in England: Modes of Reproduction 1300–1840*. Oxford, 1986.

—— *Reconstructing Historical Communities*. Cambridge, 1977.

McIntosh, M. K., *A Community Transformed. The Manor and Liberty of Havering, 1500–1620*. Cambridge, 1991.

—— 'Local Responses to the Poor in Late Medieval and Tudor England'. *Continuity and Change* 3 (1988): 209–45.

—— 'Networks of Care in Elizabethan English Towns: The Example of Hadleigh, Suffolk'. In *The Locus of Care: Families, Communities, Institutions, and the Provision of Welfare Since Antiquity*, edited by P. Horden and R. M. Smith, pp. 13–14. London, 1998.

—— 'Servants and the Household Unit in an Elizabethan English Community'. *Journal of Family History* 9 (1984): 3–24.

McManners, J., *Death and the Enlightenment. Changing Attitudes to Death among Christians and Unbelievers in Eighteenth-Century France*. Oxford, 1981.

McRee, B. R., 'Charity and Gild Solidarity in Late Medieval England'. *Journal of British Studies* 32 (1993): 195–225.

Marsh, C., 'In the Name of God? Will-Making and Faith in Early Modern England'. In *The Records of the Nation*, edited by G. H. Martin and P. Spufford, pp. 215–49. Woodbridge, 1990.

Mayhew, G., 'Life-Cycle Service and the Family Unit in Early Modern Rye'. *Continuity and Change* 6 (1991): 201–26.

Mencher, S., *Poor Law to Poverty Program*. Pittsburgh, PA, 1967.

Midelfort, H. C. E., 'Heartland of the Witchcraze: Central and Northern Europe', *History Today* (1981): 27–31.

Mill, A. D., *A Dictionary of English Place-Names*. Oxford, 1991.

Milward, R., *A Glossary of Household, Farming and Trade Terms from Probate Inventories* (3rd edn). Derbyshire Record Society, Occasional Paper No. 1. Chesterfield, 1989.

Minois, G., *History of Old Age: From Antiquity to the Renaissance*, translated by S. H. Tenison. Oxford, 1989.

Morris, R. J., 'Nominal Record Linkage: Into the 1990s'. *History and Computing* 4 (1992): iii–vi.

Newman Brown, W., 'The Receipt of Poor Relief and Family Situation: Aldenham, Hertfordshire, 1630–90'. In *Land, Kinship and Life-Cycle*, edited by R. M. Smith *et al.*, pp. 405–22. Cambridge, 1984.

Nichols, A. E., 'Broken Up or Restored Away: Iconoclasm in a Suffolk Parish'. In *Iconoclasm vs. Art and Drama*, edited by C. Davidson and A. E. Nichols, pp. 164–96, Early Drama, Art, and Music Monograph, No. 11. London, 1989.

Nitecki, A. K., 'The Convention of the Old Man's Lament in *The Pardoner's Tale*'. *Chaucer Review* 16 (1981–2): 76–84.

Ottaway, S. R., *'The Decline of Life': Old Age in Eighteenth-Century England*. Cambridge, 2004.

—— 'The Old Woman's Home in Eighteenth-Century England'. In *Women and Ageing in British Society Since 1500*, edited by L. Botelho and P. Thane, pp. 111–38. London, 2001.

—— 'Providing for the Elderly in Eighteenth-Century England'. *Continuity and Change* 13 (1998): 391–418.

Outhwaite, R. B., *Inflation in Tudor and Early Stuart England* (2nd edn). Basingstoke, 1982.

—— ed., *Marriage and Society. Studies in the Social History of Marriage*. New York, 1982.

Oxley, G. W., *Poor Relief in England and Wales, 1601–1834*. London, 1974.

Palliser, D. M., 'Introduction: The Parish in Perspective'. In *Parish, Church and People: Local Studies of Lay Religion 1350–1700*, edited by S. J. Wright, pp. 5–28. London, 1988.

—— 'Popular Reactions to the Reformation During the Years of Uncertainty 1520–70'. In *The English Reformation Revised*, edited by C. Haigh, pp. 94–113. Cambridge, 1988.

Patten, J., 'Changing Occupational Structure in the East Anglian Countryside'. In *Change in the Countryside: Essays on Rural England, 1500–1900*, edited by H. S. A. Fox and R. A. Butlin, pp. 103–21, Institute of British Geographers Special Publication, No. 10. London, 1979.

—— 'The Hearth Taxes, 1662–1689'. *Local Population Studies* 7 (1971): 14–27.

—— 'Village and Town: An Occupational Study'. *The Agricultural History Review* 20 (1972): 1–16.

Pearl, V., 'Change and Stability in Seventeenth Century London'. *The London Journal* 51 (1970): 3–34.

—— 'Puritans and Poor Relief: The London Workhouse, 1649–1660'. In *Puritans and Revolutionaries: Essays in Seventeenth Century History Presented to Christopher Hill*, pp. 206–32. Oxford, 1978.

—— 'Social Policy in Early Modern London'. In *History and Imagination. Essays in Honour of H. R. Trevor-Roper*, edited by H. Lloyd-Jones, V. Pearl and B. Worden, pp. 115–31. London, 1981.

Pelling, M., *The Common Lot: Sickness, Medical Occupations and the Urban Poor in Early Modern England*. London, 1998.

—— 'Healing the Sick Poor: Social Policy and Disability in Norwich, 1550–1640'. *Medical History* 29 (1985): 115–37.

—— 'Illness Among the Poor in an Early Modern English Town: The Norwich Census of 1570'. *Continuity and Change* 3 (1988): 273–90.

—— 'Old Age, Poverty, and Disability in Early Modern Norwich: Work, Remarriage and Other Expedients'. In *Life, Death and the Elderly: Historical Perspectives*, edited by M. Pelling and R. M. Smith, pp. 74–101. London, 1991.

—— 'Old People and Poverty in Early Modern Towns'. *Bulletin of the Society for the History of Medicine* 34 (1984): 42–7.

—— 'Who Most Needs to Marry? Ageing and Inequality among Women and Men in Early Modern Norwich'. In *Women and Ageing in British Society Since 1500*, edited by L. Botelho and P. Thane, pp. 21–42. London, 2001.

—— and Smith, R. M., 'Introduction'. In *Life, Death and the Elderly: Historical Perspectives*, edited by M. Pelling and R. M. Smith, pp. 1–38. London, 1991.

Pevsner, N., *Buildings of England: North-East Norfolk and Norwich*. London, 1962.

Phillips, J., *The Reformation of Images: Destruction of Art in England, 1535–1660*. Berkeley, CA, 1973.

Phythian-Adams, C., *Desolation of a City. Coventry and the Urban Crisis of the Late Middle Ages*. Cambridge, 1979.

Pinchbeck, I. and Hewitt, M., *Children in English Society*. London, 1969.

Pollock, L., *Forgotten Children: Parent–Child Relations 1500–1900*. Cambridge, 1983.

Post, J. B., 'Ages of Menarche and Menopause: Some Medieval Authorities'. *Population Studies* 25 (1971): 83–7.

Pound, J., *Poverty and Vagrancy in Tudor England*. London, 1971.

Preston, P., *A Dictionary of Pictorial Subjects from Classical Literature*. New York, 1983.

Pullan, B., 'Catholics and the Poor in Early Modern Europe'. *Transactions of the Royal Historical Society*, 5th ser. 26 (1976): 15–34.

Quintrell, B. W., 'Lancashire Ills. The King's Will and the Troubling of Bishop Bridgeman'. *Transactions of the Historical Society of Lancashire and Cheshire* 132 (1982): 67–102.

Raftis, J. A., *Tenure and Mobility: Studies in the Social History of the Medieval English Village*. Toronto, 1964.

Ransom, R. L. and Sutch, R., 'The Impact of Ageing on the Employments of Men in American Working-Class Communities at the End of the Nineteenth Century'. In *Aging in the Past: Demography, Society and Old Age*, edited by D. I. Kertzer and P. Laslett, pp. 303–27. Berkeley, CA, 1995.

Rappaport, S., 'Review of I. Archer's *In Pursuit of Stability*'. *History and Computing* 4 (1992): 149–50.

—— *Worlds Within Worlds: Structure of Life in Sixteenth Century London*. Cambridge, 1989.

Razi, Z., 'The Myth of the Immutable English Family'. *Past and Present* 140 (1993): 3–44.

Redstone, V. B., 'Chapels, Chantries, and Gilds in Suffolk'. *Suffolk Institute of Archaeology and Natural History* 12 (1906): 1–88.

Ribton-Turner, C. J., *A History of Vagrants and Vagrancy*. London, 1887.

Robin, J., 'The Role of Offspring in the Care of the Elderly: A Comparison Over Time, 1851–1881'. *Ageing and Society* 4 (1984): 505–15.

Rowlands, A., 'The Conditions of Life for the Masses'. In *Early Modern Europe: An Oxford History*, edited by E. Cameron, pp. 31–62. Oxford, 1999.

Rubin, M., *Charity and Community in Medieval Cambridge*. Cambridge, 1987.

Ruston, R., 'The Poor Law, the Parish and the Community in North-East England, 1600–1800'. *Northern History* 25 (1989): 135–52.

Scarfe, G., *Witchcraft and Magic in Sixteen and Seventeenth Century Europe*. Basingstoke, 1987.

Scarfe, N., 'Medieval and Later Markets'. In *An Historical Atlas of Suffolk*, edited by D. Dymond and E. Martin, pp. 64–6. Bury St Edmunds, 1988.

—— *The Suffolk Landscape*. London, 1972.

Schofield, R., 'Estimates of Population Size: Hearth Tax'. *Local Population Studies* 1 (1968): 30–4.

Sears, E. L., *The Ages of Man. Medieval Interpretations of the Life Cycle*. Princeton, NJ, 1986.

Shahar, S., *Growing Old in the Middle Ages*, translated by Y. Lotan. London, 1997.

—— 'Who Were Old in the Middle Ages?' *Social History of Medicine* 6 (1993): 313–42.

Sharpe, P., '"The Bowels of Compation": A Labouring Family and the Law, c. 1790–1834'. In *Chronicling Poverty: The Voices and Strategies of the English Poor, 1640–1840*, edited by T. Hitchcock, P. King and P. Sharpe, pp. 87–109. Basingstoke, 1997.

—— 'Poor Children as Apprentices in Colyton, 1598–1830'. *Continuity and Change* 6 (1991): 253–70.

Slack, P., *The English Poor Law, 1531–1782*, Studies in Economic and Social History. Basingstoke, 1990.

—— *From Reformation to Improvement: Public Welfare in Early Modern England*. Oxford, 1999.

—— 'Hospitals, Workhouses and the Relief of the Poor in Early Modern London'. In *Health Care and Poor Relief in Protestant Europe, 1500–1700*, edited by O. P. Grell and A. Cunningham, pp. 235–51. London, 1997.

—— *The Impact of Plague in Tudor and Stuart England*. Oxford, 1985.

—— *Poverty and Policy in Tudor and Stuart England*. London, 1988.

—— 'Poverty and Politics in Salisbury, 1597–1666'. In *Crisis and Order in English Towns, 1500–1700*, edited by P. Clark and P. Slack, pp. 164–203. London, 1972.

—— 'Poverty and Social Regulation in Elizabethan England'. In *The Reign of Elizabeth I*, edited by C. Haigh, pp. 221–42. Basingstoke, 1984.

—— 'Social Policy and the Constraints of Government 1547–58'. In *The Mid-Tudor Polity c. 1540–1560*, edited by R. Tittler and J. Loach. Totowa, NJ, 1980.

—— 'Vagrants and Vagrancy in England, 1598–1664'. *Economic History Review*, 2nd ser. 27 (1974): 360–79.

Smith, J. E., 'The Computer Simulation of Kin Sets and Kin Counts'. In *Family Demography, Methods and their Applications*, edited by J. Bongaarts, T. Birch and K. J. Wachter, pp. 249–66. Oxford, 1987.

—— 'Widowhood and Ageing in Traditional English Society'. *Ageing and Society* 4 (1984): 429–49.

Smith, R. M., 'Ageing and Well-Being in Early Modern England: Pension Trends and Gender Preferences Under the English Old Poor Law, c. 1650–1800'. In *Old Age from Antiquity to Post-Modernity*, edited by P. Johnson and P. Thane, pp. 64–95. London, 1998.

—— 'The Manorial Court and the Elderly Tenant in Late Medieval England'. In *Life, Death and the Elderly: Historical Perspectives*, edited by M. Pelling and R. M. Smith, pp. 39–61. London, 1991.

—— '"Modernization" and the Corporate Village Community in England: Some Sceptical Reflections'. In *Explorations in Historical Geography*, edited by A. H. R. Baker and D. Gregory, pp. 140–79. Cambridge, 1984.

—— 'Some Issues Concerning Families and their Property in Rural England 1250–1800'. In *Land, Kinship and Life-Cycle*, edited by R. M. Smith *et al.*, pp. 1–86. Cambridge, 1984.

—— 'The Structured Dependency of the Elderly as a Recent Development: Some Sceptical Historical Thoughts', *Ageing and Society* 4 (1984): 409–28.

—— 'The Structured Dependency of the Elderly: A Twentieth-Century Creation?' *Bulletin of the Society for the Social History of Medicine* 34 (1984): 35–41.

Snell, K., 'Parish Registration and the Study of Labour Mobility'. *Local Population Studies* 33 (1984): 29–43.

Sokoll, T., 'The Household Position of Elderly Widows in Poverty. Evidence from Two English Communities in the Late Eighteenth and Early Nineteenth Century'. In *Poor Women and Children in the European Past*, edited by J. Henderson and R. Wall, pp. 207–24. London, 1995.

—— 'Old Age in Poverty: The Record of Essex Pauper Letters, 1782–1834'.

In *Chronicling Poverty: The Voices and Strategies of the English Poor, 1640–1840*, edited by T. Hitchcock, P. King and P. Sharpe, pp. 127–54. Basingstoke, 1997.

—— 'The Pauper Households Small and Simple? The Evidence from Listings of Inhabitants and Pauper Lists of Early Modern England Reassessed'. *Ethnologia Europaea* 17 (1987): 25–42.

Souden, D., 'Movers and Stayers in Family Reconstitution Populations'. *Local Populations Studies* 33 (1984): 11–28.

Spufford, M., *Contrasting Communities: English Villagers in the Sixteenth and Seventeenth Centuries* (1974). Repr. Cambridge, 1987.

—— *The Great Reclothing of Rural England: Petty Chapman and his Wares in the Seventeenth Century*. London, 1984.

—— 'Peasant Inheritance Customs and Land Distribution in Cambridgeshire from the Sixteenth to the Eighteenth Centuries'. In *Family and Inheritance: Rural Society in Western Europe 1200–1800*, edited by J. Goody, J. Thirsk and E. P. Thompson, pp. 156–76. Cambridge, 1976.

—— 'Puritanism and Social Control'. In *Order and Disorder in Early Modern England*, edited by A. Fletcher and J. Stevenson, pp. 41–57. Cambridge, 1987.

—— 'The Scribes of Villagers' Wills in the Sixteenth and Seventeenth Centuries and their Influence'. *Local Population Studies* 7 (1971): 28–43.

—— *Small Books and Pleasant Histories. Popular Fiction and its Readership in Seventeenth-Century England*. London, 1981.

Spurr, J., *The Restoration Church of England, 1646–1689*. New Haven, CT, 1991.

Standen, E. A., 'The Twelve Ages of Man'. *Metropolitan Museum of Arts Bulletin* 12 (1954): 241–48.

—— 'The Twelve Ages of Man. A Further Study of a Set of Early Sixteenth Century Flemish Tapestries'. *Metropolitan Museum Journal* 2 (1969): 127–68.

Steadman, J. M., 'Old Age and *Contemptus Mundi* in *The Pardoner's Tale*'. *Medium Ævum* 33 (1964): 121–30.

Stephens, W. B., *Sources for English Local History*. Cambridge, 1973.

Stone, L., *The Family, Sex, and Marriage in England 1500–1800*. New York, 1977.

Strype, J., *The Life and Acts of Matthew Parker*, Vol. I. Oxford, 1821.

Thane, P., 'The Cultural History of Old Age'. *Australian Cultural History* 14 (1995): 23–39.

—— 'The Family Lives of Old People'. In *Old Age from Antiquity to Post-Modernity*, edited by P. Johnson and P. Thane, pp. 180–210. London, 1998.

—— 'Old People and their Families in the English Past'. In *Charity, Self-Interest and Welfare in the English Past*, edited by M. Daunton, pp. 113–38. New York, 1996.

Thirsk, J., *The Agrarian History of England and Wales. Vol. IV: 1500–1640*. Cambridge, 1967.

Thomas, J. H., *Town Government in the Sixteenth Century*, Reprints in Economic Classics (1933). Repr. New York, 1969.

Thomas, K., *Age and Authority in Early Modern England*, Proceedings of the British Academy, Vol. LXII. London, 1976.

—— *Religion and the Decline of Magic*. New York, 1971.

Thompson, E. P., 'The Moral Economy of the English Crowd in the Eighteenth-Century'. *Past and Present* 50 (1971): 76–136.

Thomson, D., 'The Decline of Social Welfare: Falling Sate Support for the Elderly since Early Victorian Times'. *Ageing and Society* 4 (1984): 451–82.

—— '"I am not my father's keeper": Families and the Elderly in Nineteenth-Century England'. *Law and History Review* 2 (1984): 265–86.

—— 'Welfare of the Elderly in the Past: A Family or Community Responsibility?' In *Life, Death and the Elderly*, edited by M. Pelling and R. M. Smith, pp. 194–221. London, 1991.

Thornton, G. A., *A History of Clare Suffolk*. Cambridge, 1928.

—— *A Short History of Clare Suffolk*. London, 1963.

Tierney, B., *Medieval Poor Law: A Sketch of Canonical Theory and its Application in England*. Berkeley, CA, 1959.

Tillotson, J. H., 'Pensions, Corrodies, and Religious Houses: An Aspect of the Relations of Crown and Church in Early Fourteenth-Century England'. *Journal of Religious History* 8 (1974): 127–43.

Tillyard, E. M. W., *The Elizabethan World Picture* (1943). Repr. London, 1972.

Tittler, R., *Architecture and Power. The Town Hall and the English Urban Community, c. 1500–1640*. Oxford, 1991.

Todd, H., and Dymond, D., 'Population Densities, 1377 and 1524'. In *An Historical Atlas of Suffolk*, edited by D. Dymond and E. Martin, pp. 64–7. Bury St Edmunds, 1988.

Todd, M., *Christian Humanism and the Puritan Social Order*. Cambridge, 1987.

Trexler, R., 'Widow's Asylum of the Renaissance: The Orbatello of Florence'. In *Old Age in Preindustrial Society*, edited by P. N. Stearns, pp. 119–45. London, 1982.

Trotter, E., *Seventeenth Century Life in the Country Parish, with Special Reference to Local Government*. London, 1968.

Underdown, D., *Fire From Heaven: Life in an English Town in the Seventeenth Century*. London, 1993.

Unwin, G., 'The History of the Cloth Industry in Suffolk'. In *Studies in Economic History: The Collected Papers of George Unwin*, edited by R. H. Tawney, pp. 262–301. London, 1927.

van Leeuwen, M. H. D., 'Logic of Charity: Poor Relief in Preindustrial Europe'. *Journal of Interdisciplinary History* 24 (1994): 580–613.

Vann, R. T., 'Wills and the Family in an English Town: Banbury, 1550–1800'. *Journal of Family History* 4 (1979): 356–67.

Venn, J. and Venn, J. A., compilers, *Alumni Cantabrigienses*, Part I. Cambridge, 1922.

Wales, T., 'Poverty, Poor Relief and the Life-Cycle: Some Evidence from Seventeenth-Century Norfolk'. In *Land, Kinship and Life-Cycle*, edited by R. M. Smith *et al.*, pp. 351–404. Cambridge, 1984.

Wall, B., *Sudbury through the Ages*. Ipswich, n.d.

Wall, R., 'Elderly Persons and Members of their Households in England and Wales from Pre-Industrial Times to the Present'. In *Aging in the Past: Demography, Society and Old Age*, edited by D. I. Kertzer and P. Laslett, pp. 81–106. Berkeley, CA, 1995.

—— 'Leaving Home and the Process of Household Formation in Pre-Industrial England'. *Continuity and Change* 2 (1987): 77–101.

—— 'Mean Household Size in England from Printed Sources'. In *Household and Family in Past Times*, edited by P. Laslett and R. M. Smith, pp. 163–203. Cambridge, 1972.

—— 'The Residence Patterns of Elderly English Women in Comparative Perspective'. In *Women and Ageing in British Society since 1500*, edited by L. Botelho and P. Thane, pp. 139–65. London, 2001.

—— 'Some Implications of the Earnings, Income and Expenditure Patterns of Married Women in Populations in the Past'. In *Poor Women and Children in the European Past*, edited by J. Henderson and R. Wall, pp. 312–55. London, 1994.

Walsham, A., *Church Papists. Catholicism, Conformity and Confessional Polemic in Early Modern England*. Woodbridge, 1994.

Walter, J., 'The Social Economy of Dearth in Early Modern England'. In *Famine, Disease, and the Social Order in Early Modern Society*, edited by J. Walter and R. Schofield, pp. 75–128. Cambridge, 1989.

—— and Schofield, R., 'Famine, Disease, and Crisis Mortality in Early Modern Society'. In *Famine, Disease and the Social Order in Early Modern Society*, edited by J. Walter and R. Schofield, pp. 11–74. Cambridge, 1989.

Wandel, L. P., *Always Among Us. Images of the Poor in Zwingli's Zurich*. Cambridge, 1990.

Warren, F. B., 'A Pre-Reformation Village Gild'. *Suffolk Institute of Archaeology and Natural History* 11 (1903): 81–109.

Watt, T., *Cheap Print and Popular Piety, 1550–1640*. Cambridge, 1991.

Wear, A., 'Making Sense of Health and the Environment in Early Modern England'. In *Medicine in Society: Historical Essays*, edited by A. Wear, pp. 141–7. Cambridge, 1992.

West Suffolk Illustrated, compiled by H. R. Barker. Bury St Edmunds, 1907.

Westlake, H. E., 'The Origin, Purposes and Development of Parish Gilds in England'. *Suffolk Institute of Archaeology and Natural History* 17 (1921): 163–74.

—— *The Parish Gilds of Medieval England*. London, 1919.

Whaley, J., ed., *Mirrors of Mortality. Studies in the Social History of Death*. London, 1981.

Willen, D., 'Women in the Public Sphere in Early Modern England: The Case of the Urban Working Poor'. *Sixteenth Century Journal* 19 (1988): 559–76.

Williamson, T., 'Ancient Landscapes'. In *An Historical Atlas of Suffolk*, edited by D. Dymond and E. Martin, pp. 40–1. Bury St Edmunds, 1988.

—— 'Parish Boundaries and Early Fields: Continuity and Discontinuity'. *Journal of Historical Geography* 12 (1986): 241–8.

—— 'Sites in the Landscape: Approaches to the Post-Roman Settlement of South Eastern England'. *Archaeological Review from Cambridge* 4 (1985): 51–64.

Woolf, S. J., *The Poor in Western Europe in the Eighteenth and Nineteenth Centuries*. London, 1986.

Wrightson, K., 'Alehouses, Order and Reformation in Rural England, 1590–1660'. In *Popular Culture and Class Conflict 1590–1914: Explorations in the History of Labour and Leisure*, edited by E. and S. Yeo, pp. 1–27. Brighton, 1981.

—— *English Society 1590–1680* (1982). Repr. London, 1986.

—— 'Kinship in an English Village: Terling, Essex 1500–1700'. In *Land, Kinship and Life-Cycle*, edited by R. M. Smith *et al.*, pp. 313–32. Cambridge, 1984.

—— 'The Social Order of Early Modern England: Three Approaches'. In *The World We have Gained. Histories of Population and Social Structure*, edited by L. Bonfield, R. M. Smith and K. Wrightson, pp. 177–202. Oxford, 1986.

—— '"Sorts of People" in Tudor and Stuart England'. In *The Middling Sort of People*, edited by J. Barry and C. Brooks, pp. 28–51. Basingstoke, 1994.

—— 'Two Concepts of Order: Justices, Constable and Jurymen in Seventeenth-Century England'. In *An Ungovernable People*, edited by J. Brewer and J. Styles, pp. 21–46. London, 1980.

—— and Levine, D., 'Death in Whickham'. In *Famine, Disease and the Social Order in Early Modern Society*, edited by J. Walter and R. Schofield, pp. 129–66. Cambridge, 1989.

—— and Levine, D., *Poverty and Piety in an English Village: Terling, 1525–1700* (2nd edn). Oxford, 1995.

Wrigley, E. A., 'Family Reconstitution'. In *An Introduction to English Historical Demography*, edited by E. A. Wrigley, pp. 46–159. London, 1966.

—— and Schofield, R., *The Population History of England, 1541–1871. A Reconstruction* (1981). Repr. Cambridge, 1993.

Young, A., *General View of the Agriculture of the County of Suffolk*. London, 1794.

UNPUBLISHED THESES AND PAPERS

Adair, R., 'Age at Death and Mortality in Whitchurch 1771–1802'. Unpublished paper, 1994.

—— 'Pensioners Under the Poor Law in Early Modern England'. Unpublished paper, 1992.

—— 'Pensioners in Clerkenwell: Some Comparative Data'. Unpublished paper, 1994.

—— 'Pensioners in Terling: Some Preliminary Results'. Unpublished paper, 1994.

Barker-Read, M., 'The Treatment of the Aged Poor in Five Selected West Kent Parishes from Settlement to Speenhamland (1662–1797)'. Open University Ph.D., 1988.

Ben-Amos, I. K., 'Apprenticeship, the Family, and Urban Society in Early Modern England'. Stanford University Ph.D., 1985.

Botelho, L. A., 'Provisions for the Elderly in Two Early Modern Suffolk Communities'. Cambridge University Ph.D., 1996.

Dobson, M. J., 'Population, Disease and Mortality in Southeast England'. Oxford University D.Phil., 1982.

Elford, K., 'Remarriage and Old Age in Pre-Industrial England'. Unpublished paper presented at the Cambridge Group for the Study of History of Population and Social Structure, Cambridge, n.d.

French, H., 'Chief Inhabitants and their Areas of Influence. Local Ruling Groups in Essex and Suffolk Parishes, 1630–1720'. Cambridge University Ph.D., 1993.

Griffiths, P., 'Some Aspects of the Social History of Youth in Early Modern England with Particular Reference to the Period c. 1560–140'. Cambridge University Ph.D., 1992.

Hussey, S., '"An Inheritance of Fear": The Elderly in Essex between the Wars'. Unpublished paper presented at 'Studying the Elderly in Essex and Suffolk', Day School, Local History Centre, University of Essex, March 1995.

Jarvis [Davey], C., 'Reconstructing Local Population History: The Hatfield and Bobbington Districts of Essex, 1500–1880'. Cambridge University Ph.D., 1990.

Kugler, A., 'Prescription, Culture, and Shaping Identity: Lady Sarah Cowper (1644–1720)'. University of Michigan, Ann Arbor Ph.D., 1994.

Kumin, B., 'The Late Medieval English Parish, c.1400–1560'. Cambridge University Ph.D., 1992.

Litzenberger, C. J., 'Responses of the Laity to Changes in Official Religious Policy in Gloucestershire (1541–1580)'. Cambridge University Ph.D., 1993.

McIntosh, M. K., 'Aid for the Worthy, Punishment for Idlers: Elizabethan Responses to the Poor in Hadleigh, Suffolk'. Unpublished paper presented at the Seminar on the History of Poverty, Oxford, May, 1991.

Maltby, J. D., 'Approaches to the Study of Religious Conformity in Late Elizabethan and Early Stuart England: with Special Reference to Cheshire and the Diocese of Lincoln'. Cambridge University Ph.D., 1991.

Thomson, D., 'Provisions for the Elderly in England, 1830 to 1908'. Cambridge University Ph.D., 1980.

Wales, T., 'Coping with Poverty: The Poor and Authority in Seventeenth-Century England'. Unpublished paper presented at the Cambridge Group for the Study of Population and Social Structure, Cambridge, 1988.

Index